FURTHER WELLNESS ISSUES FOR HIGHER EDUCATION

This essential resource addresses a range of student wellness issues confronting professionals in college and university settings. Building on the editor's previous publication, *Wellness Issues for Higher Education*, this latest volume comprehensively covers key topics that not only contribute to students' success in college, but also help students maintain wellness after graduation. Taking a holistic perspective of wellness, coverage includes numerous issues including body image, time management, financial wellness, dependence and recovery issues, career planning and civic engagement. It also addresses ways of organizing campus efforts on wellness. Each topical chapter includes proactive wellness advice and prepares the reader to better understand the facts, issues, controversies, misconceptions and strategies for addressing the issue. This practical guide prepares higher education and student affairs professionals to understand the wellness and health issues contributing to their students' overall well-being both during and after college.

David S. Anderson is Professor Emeritus of Education and Human Development at George Mason University, USA.

Further Wellness Issues for Higher Education

How to Promote Student Health During and After College

Edited by David S. Anderson

Routledge
Taylor & Francis Group

NEW YORK AND LONDON

First published 2017
by Routledge
711 Third Avenue, New York, NY 10017

and by Routledge
2 Park Square, Milton Park, Abingdon, Oxon, OX14 4RN

Routledge is an imprint of the Taylor & Francis Group, an informa business

Library of Congress Cataloging-in-Publication Data
Names: Anderson, David S., 1949– editor.
Title: Further wellness issues for higher education : how to promote student
    health during and after college / edited by David S. Anderson.
Description: New York, NY : Routledge, 2017. | Includes bibliographical
    references and index.
Identifiers: LCCN 2016009092 | ISBN 9781138101012 (hardback) |
    ISBN 9781138101029 (pbk.) | ISBN 9781315657271 (ebook)
Subjects: LCSH: Health. | College students—Health and hygiene. | College
    students—Mental health. | Universities and colleges—Health promotion
    services.
Classification: LCC RA777.3 .F87 2017 | DDC 613—dc23
LC record available at https://lccn.loc.gov/2016009092

ISBN: 978-1-138-10101-2 (hbk)
ISBN: 978-1-138-10102-9 (pbk)
ISBN: 978-1-315-65727-1 (ebk)

Typeset in Minion
by Apex CoVantage, LLC

Visit the eResources website: www.routledge.com/9781138101029

Contents

Preface

The final words of the Preface of *Wellness Issues for Higher Education: A Guide for Student Affairs and Higher Education Professionals* said it all: "I think our opportunity, indeed our challenge, is best summed up by the campus motto inscribed at the entrance of Radford University's Hurlburt Student Center: 'Investing in Lifetimes'" (Anderson, 2016, p. xiii). That was the emphasis of that volume, which addressed 12 specific wellness issues. This complementary volume, *Further Wellness Issues for Higher Education: How to Promote Student Health During and After College*, builds upon the insights and suggestions offered there. As a companion resource, this volume continues with the "investing" issue and moves more directly into the "lifetimes" aspect of the motto identified earlier.

Further Wellness Issues for Higher Education also continues a major theme identified with the first volume: praxis. A major emphasis with these volumes is to combine theory and practice. Each identified topic incorporates empirical research that is grounded and current; it includes guiding theories and conceptual frameworks used by specialists in those areas. Beyond that, it builds upon this foundation to promote sound and reasonable applications; the recommendations and approaches are practical for those in various roles on or surrounding the campus, all of which are appropriate for campus life today.

The audience of these volumes involves anyone in a leadership role, or seeking to provide leadership, on the campuses. Leadership can be instituted by those in higher-level positions on the campus; it can also be done by individuals in more entry-level, grassroots or extended roles (such as community members, alumni or parents). Regardless of whether the position is one of the job, or due to self-designation, being more informed and empowered will provide the foundation for impact and helpful consequences.

The important element in this volume is that of applicability. The recommendations and ideas are current and appropriate. They are reasonable and achievable. Further, they are important for not just sustaining or "making do," but in fact enhancing students' lives during and following their years in college. Ways of organizing and orchestrating campus efforts are a major aspect of this volume, with the final chapter highlighting strategies for making a difference for our students.

Why This Resource?

This book is grounded in two broad concepts: One emphasizes the impact on the ultimate audience of colleges and universities—the student; the other highlights the professionals who work on, or in conjunction with, the college campus. For the former, the aim is one of maximizing the nature and quality of the entire educational experience; for the latter, the goal is one of becoming better prepared to assist, guide, encourage and motivate students to succeed and excel.

Examining the student first, the basic thought is that, if a person is healthy, there is a much greater likelihood that greater learning will ensue. Consider the differences in learning between students who slept well and those who didn't; between those who are thinking clearly and those who are hungover or still under the influence of drugs or alcohol; between those with excellent time management skills and those whose procrastination is disempowering; between those with clear goal direction for a career and those who are floundering; and between those who are preoccupied with relationship concerns about others or themselves, with those who are well balanced.

With the student as an audience, the other scenario is also helpful; those who learn better are more likely to be healthy. Those who have current, accurate knowledge about tobacco, coupled with healthy attitudes, are less likely to be using the substance that kills more Americans than any other drug. Those who have sound knowledge of time management, along with sound practices, are more likely to prepare course materials and study for exams in a thorough and results-oriented way. Those who have good knowledge on nutrition, food preparation and healthy eating will be more likely to maintain balance in their lives. Those who exercise and work out, and do so using current, safety-oriented strategies, are more likely to be invigorated, clear thinking and focused.

The synergism between health and learning is both ways. This permeates the foundation of this book and its predecessor, as it highlights and specifies the important role that wellness plays with the overall academic mission of the institution. It also highlights the public sense of engagement with students and their success, both for their current enrollment in the institution itself and also for their engagement in life after their college years.

Turning to the professional staff members and other concerned individuals, the aim is to best prepare them to deal with the students. Even if all students were fully self-directed and self-motivated, there are needs that students have regarding any of a number of wellness issues. Indeed, campuses and their surrounding communities have numerous specialized resources ready and willing to help students; these may be study skills seminars or fitness check-ups or self-guided assessments on relationships and on monitoring time management. None of us has perfect management of our wellness issues; we all have issues that challenge us or are occasionally (or regularly) out of balance. We all have needs and issues that can be better addressed. And the same is even more true of students at our colleges and universities; this is quite expected, as they are in developmental phases in their lives, with traditional-age students learning how to manage and self-direct on so many issues, and many for the first time doing these primarily on their own.

The important role of professional staff, including student affairs professionals, faculty members, administrators and others on the campus, cannot be overstated; they have a major role in helping shape the lives of students. Further, other interested individuals, such as parents, alumni and community members, can play an important role with students as they experience life on and off the campus.

Thus, it is important that these professionals and other caring adults be as equipped as possible to aid the students. It is important that they provide quality information for students and, ideally, at least "do no harm." These individuals will be well served to have the latest information on any of a number of wellness topics; providing the insights about current knowledge on these topics can be most helpful. Further, as these individuals become aware of best practices and current strategies, they can help incorporate these on the campus; they may inform and influence the decision-makers and the implementation processes on the campus so that the campus leaders are implementing what is identified as the most current and supported approaches.

Not only is this professional preparation important from a general, good-sense point of view, but it is documented that academic programs do not adequately prepare professionals seeking to work in the higher education setting. As cited in each volume's introductions, little substantive background on wellness issues can be found in graduate preparation programs. Further, and not surprisingly, faculty members on campus who teach and research on a wide range of topics—from chemistry to economics, from history to education—are not well versed with current knowledge on the current issues facing students or the most appropriate ways of addressing these issues, whether through consultation, referral or resource assistance. Thus, this approach with current and applied information on issues of key importance to students can only help to enhance students' college experience.

Overview of the Book's Style and Contents

As highlighted, this book is about praxis—the intersection of theory and practice. Each author was asked to review current literature and to provide the reader with an update about current knowledge, address misperceptions and myths and highlight controversies that may exist. Authors were asked to provide good documentation—thus, chapters typically have lots and lots of references. In addition to the suggestions and recommendations provided in the chapters, authors offer an annotated summary of resources available on the publisher's website affiliated with this book.

It's a challenging job to summarize a topic area into a relatively succinct chapter—but that's what this resource is designed to do. While each topic has many books, manuscripts, articles and resources, the aim here is to be succinct and applied.

Just as with the first volume, this one is organized into distinct areas of wellness. No one volume (unless it was much more extensive than this one) accommodates all wellness issues. Further, as highlighted in the Introduction, different wellness frameworks exist. The schema for this volume is around five major thematic areas of wellness: emotional, social, intellectual, physical and occupational. The overall aim is about helping students be more organized and planful in their lives—both for their college careers and for their lives following college.

Within the *Emotional Wellness* area, the topic of *body image* is included; the authors highlight ways of approaching healthy perspectives among numerous students and student groups. This topic complements the stress management, mental health and technology chapters found in the first volume. For the area of *Social Wellness*, two topics are included: One is *disability awareness*, providing a greater understanding of types of disability faced by students and ways of addressing this; the other topic, *sexual violence*, incorporates a clear perspective about this behavior among college students and how campus leaders can best address it. These topics complement the chapters on relationships, sexual decision-making, alcohol abuse and illicit drug abuse found in the first volume.

For *Intellectual Wellness*, two topics are included: The chapter on *time management* highlights the different perceptions of time, as well as procrastination, and ways campus personnel can better guide students for healthier self-management. The *financial wellness* chapter seeks to inform and empower campus personnel to engage in this often-difficult topic with students and provides suggestions about appropriate resources a campus may provide. These chapters build upon the writing and study skills chapter from the earlier volume.

Physical Wellness has three chapters in this volume. The chapter on *disordered eating* helps the reader understand this concept and provides ways of addressing this among students of concern. The *tobacco* chapter highlights strategies for individuals and campuses and builds upon current knowledge and evolving product development. The *dependence and recovery* chapter addresses an important issue and audience, focusing on harm reduction, social justice and campus strategies for a healthy environment. The chapters on sleep, nutrition and exercise in the first volume benefit from the new topics. The *Occupational Wellness* section consists of two chapters: *career wellness* and *civic engagement*. The former chapter includes issues that help best prepare students for a fulfilling life after college and highlights changes in this campus service. The latter chapter orchestrates campus efforts of engagement and well-being and identifies strategies around personal and social responsibility. This section is offered in lieu of the *Spiritual Wellness* section and its chapter on spiritual development found in the first volume.

In addition to the ten topics incorporated in the five thematic areas, this volume also includes a chapter that cuts across all the topics, from this volume and the previous one. It addresses ways of orchestrating strategies around campus wellness issues. While many volumes have been written about organizing projects, and countless others addressing administrative structures and strategies specifically for the higher education setting, this chapter focuses specifically on wellness and offers insights using three helpful constructs.

All in all, this volume provides complementary resources for campus personnel as they seek to promote a healthier and safer campus. This volume provides the grounding and resource assistance suitable to any of a variety of individuals on the campus. While not intended as a step-by-step guide, this book does make it much easier for campus personnel to become inspired and to inspire others to make a positive difference on campus.

Campus Applications

While the content is provided well in each of the chapters in this volume, it is helpful to call attention to the themes and orientation offered in the book's Introduction. In that chapter, readers are provided with the important role of institutions of higher education. Colleges and universities are structures designed to prepare students well for a lifetime of career success, as well as to be successful in various other aspects of their lives. The focus upon the mission of the institution, and upon the academic thrust of colleges and universities, is an important one for this topic. Wellness is not simply "being well" or "not being ill"; wellness and a wellness orientation are important for the maximum achievement of the academic goals of the institution. This is not to reduce in importance the non-academic activities at all; I would be particularly remiss if I suggested that, particularly with my background in student affairs. I offer this as a practical matter and one that will ultimately help promote, I believe, not only the wellness effort but the academic and related missions of our nation's institutions of higher education.

Campus personnel can apply the knowledge and motivation encompassed in this volume in any of a number of ways. First, it is helpful for the campus leadership to *conduct a campus review* regarding the extent to which the various services and topics are addressed on the campus. Whether through an environmental scan or campus audit, what is important is to conduct periodic reviews on these and other wellness topics, from any of a range of perspectives. One may be program and services availability, another may be actual implementation and effectiveness, a third may be utilization and still another may be perceptions among various audiences, primarily students. Second, it would be appropriate for campus leaders to *review the nature and extent of professionals' understanding* of these various issues. This includes, of course, student affairs practitioners; it should also include campus administrators, faculty members (particularly those in topics affiliated with specific topics), and others such as community members, parents and alumni. The query may be with their perceptions of needs, current knowledge, awareness of resources and services, and suggestions for improvement. Third, *in-service training and attention* to these issues with professionals on the campus would be appropriate. This will emerge from the assessment protocols, as well as with various "hot buttons" or key issues for the campus at this particular point in time. Fourth, *preparation programs for higher education and related fields* should be examined to determine the extent to which the campus is addressing these with its own graduate students. This would also be relevant to examine preparation programs in other fields of study, such as business and management, marketing, communication, public affairs, sociology, education and more. The requisite knowledge and skills with wellness issues are not the sole purview of those seeking positions in institutions of higher education; other fields of study would benefit from attention to these issues, both for the preparation of their soon-to-be graduates for their work, as well as for these individuals in their lives in the community and society at large.

In short, campus leaders have the opportunity, if not the imperative, to address wellness in any of a variety of ways. Thoughtful and creative attention to these topics, and more, can be helpful for promoting quality of life on the campus and, ultimately, in the communities served and lived in by the graduates of these institutions of higher education.

A Final Note

Wellness is a process. Wellness is a journey. The job is never done. Similarly, the role of higher education is not just to help students earn a degree. Our nation's colleges and universities have a social mandate to help make our society better. They exist to promote sound knowledge, critical thinking, improvement and preparation for an evolving tomorrow. Enhancing these various skills and attributes helps students succeed today and also helps them succeed tomorrow and the months and years following tomorrow.

The aim is broad and ambitious. But it is achievable. The results will be clear and will make each of us proud that, from an institutional and a personal point of view, we were part of a "Well U."

Reference

Anderson, D. (Ed.). (2016). *Wellness Issues for Higher Education: A Guide for Student Affairs and Higher Education Professionals.* New York: Routledge.

1
Introduction
Wellness for the Future
DAVID S. ANDERSON

Overview

Attending to the basic elements of physical, emotional, social and intellectual functioning is important for routine living. However, attending to these wellness issues in quality ways is vital if meaningful results are to be obtained. Finally, and of utmost importance for this book, attending to these wellness issues in grounded and appropriate ways is critical for college students and young adults both for their achievement during the college years and for preparation for life after college. This is due in part to the formative nature of college student development during this time of life for the traditional-age student, and for all students, college is a time of discovery, critical thinking, exploration, refinement and achievement.

If this sounds similar to Maslow's Hierarchy of Needs, it is (Maslow, 1943). With Maslow, the importance of physiological, safety and belonging are vital and foundational for the development of self-esteem and actualization. With wellness, similar factors are important for a student to be successful with academic work and, ultimately, preparation for a vocation and other aspects of life with family, community and culture.

The key point is that these issues are both hierarchical (as demonstrated with Maslow's incorporation of a hierarchy) and interconnected. Applying this schema to wellness issues, many wellness issues are "must do" (foundational) before other assets can be attended to, and others complement these processes to aid students with their advancement through the academy and, ultimately, graduation. In fact, none of the wellness issues are ever "done" or "completed"; each can continue to grow and improve, with synergistic enhancement among them.

Wellness Redefined

Wellness as a construct has been around for decades. Its presence complements a health promotion orientation and emphasizes much more than the absence of disease or malady. The concept of wellness is much more than being physically fit and emotionally stable; it is more than an individual factor. Wellness is based on a holistic approach, with numerous factors included and all being interconnected. Various definitions of and frameworks for wellness exist, thus causing some confusion among the vast majority of individuals whose work doesn't focus primarily on this issue. Some common elements surrounding wellness do exist and are helpful for providing an overall framework.

1

The National Wellness Institute, long-recognized as a leader with these issues, acknowledges that many different views of "wellness" exist and that it is applied in many different ways. It offers this definition: "Wellness is an active process through which people become aware of, and make choices toward, a more successful existence" (National Wellness Institute, 2016). The National Wellness Institute construct incorporates six dimensions: Emotional, Physical, Social, Intellectual, Occupational and Spiritual. Some other wellness definitions differentiate between Intellectual and Mental Wellness. Further, other approaches raise certain topics to a higher level, rather than have them as a subset of another topic; examples include Financial Wellness, Environmental Wellness or Medical Wellness.

The first volume of *Wellness Issues for Higher Education* (Anderson, 2016) incorporated five primary dimensions of wellness: Emotional, Physical, Social, Intellectual and Spiritual. These were not meant to be all inclusive, due primarily to space considerations. Similarly, this current volume includes five dimensions, overlapping largely with those found in the first volume. A single volume of this series is not all-inclusive yet is representative of various wellness components supporting the overall framework of the volume. For example, the first volume of *Wellness Issues* included topics linked to student success and graduate from college; this volume focuses on planning ahead with a focus on a healthy future.

The overall wellness model used depends on which chosen framework best meets the sponsor's framework. This author adapts the model of the National Wellness Institute, with the addition of an environmental dimension. This modification addresses the important element of humankind's interaction with and respect for the environment; it also attends to the acknowledgement that humans are natural beings and are thus part of the natural world.

Thus, the articulated seven dimensions of wellness include, from an overall perspective, the following:

- Emotional: An individual's self-concept as well as how problems and situations are addressed
- Physical: Overall health, exercise regimens, diet and nutrition, sleep, stress management and related aspects of living
- Intellectual: Problem solving, critical thinking, memory, creativity, organization, adaptability, expression, logic and related cognitive abilities
- Social: Interpersonal dynamics, relationship skills, communication, etiquette and culture
- Occupational: Career readiness, professionalism, work ethic, task/process balance and job-oriented skills
- Environmental: Respect for nature and the environment, including a healthy personal perspective about one's self as part of nature
- Spiritual: Values, goal direction and personal connections to the larger world setting

Regardless of the specific framework used, four important points remain: First, wellness is a construct that emphasizes a *variety of dimensions*, not just physical aspects or physical aspects coupled with emotional health. Second, wellness is *interconnected*; its issues are not discrete factors that operate independently but are all interdependent. Third, wellness is *positive oriented*; it is much more than the absence of something (such as poor health, low self-esteem, limited ability or problems with selected issues). Fourth, wellness is *growth oriented*; it is not status quo-based, as it represents continuous improvement and advancement.

Wellness is thus an interconnected, fluid and evolving approach for living life. Implicit is that it is self-directed and not imposed by external sources. Also implicit is that it is individualized; one person's wellness agenda and activities are not necessarily appropriate for another person's approaches. Further, the overall thrust of "wellness" is that it can be very ambitious; since it is self-directed and positive and oriented toward continuous improvement, it is reasonable to expect that no "endpoint" exists.

It is within this overall wellness context and understanding that campus-based efforts to promote wellness are based. The focus on students' achievements, in all aspects of their college life, is emphasized with wellness-based initiatives. Further, these qualities are helpful for students during their college careers and further aid them with a sound preparation for the remainder of their lives.

The Higher Education Context

Institutions of higher education are viewed as repositories of knowledge and sources of wisdom, with faculty, staff, administration and other campus leaders ostensibly promoting thoughtful processes and high-quality results. Further, accountability for quality services and programs is paramount among institutions of higher education. Parallel to this is the increasing attention to the return on investment, an important factor marking students' investment in the higher education experience. With costs of a degree in higher education increasing, and general public funding support decreasing, it is incumbent upon all members of the higher education community to identify ways in which they can contribute, individually and through their organizational context, to a quality educational experience for students.

Further, the value of a higher education degree is an important consideration. In their publication "A Stronger Nation through Higher Education," the Lumina Foundation cites a goal of having 60% of citizens of the United States holding high-quality degrees, certificates or other credentials of a post-secondary education by 2025 (Lumina Foundation, 2013). They cite that, by 2020, 65% of jobs in the United States will require a college degree. They note, "In 2011, the most recent year for which data are available, the percentage of Americans between the ages of 25 and 64 with a two- or four-year college degree was 38.7%" (Lumina Foundation, 2013, p. 2). They note that this was 37.9% in 2009 and has increased, although quite slowly, every year since then. Complementing this is data demonstrating the payoff resulting from higher education. The median salary for those with a high school diploma is $29,423 and is 71% higher with a bachelor's degree, where the median salary is $50,360 (Zaback, Carlson, & Crellin, 2012). This data substantiates the potential role of incorporating wellness issues into the academic fabric of the institution; attention to ways of more formally and systematically maximizing students' attainment of degrees are worthwhile investments for this payoff.

Three additional considerations are valid within the higher education context. First, the successful completion of all *academic requirements* is typically the only factor that constitutes the award of the degree. It is that specific degree or diploma that is of utmost importance, as this becomes a condition of future employment and is verified by a valid transcript. Second, the college experience itself, with its skills development, knowledge acquisition and varied accomplishments, is most helpful for *life-long skills, success and advancement*. Third, the fact that an individual is admitted for enrollment in the institution of higher education is an *acknowledgement of at least basic attributes* suitable for positive achievement. Thus, it is reasonable to expect that these institutions will provide the necessary resources and services that facilitate individual students' success.

How does this link to wellness issues? Simply put, colleges and universities should identify ways in which they can promote success among their students. It is well founded that any of a wide range of wellness issues can confound and hinder a student's successful experience and ultimate graduation from college. Consider the following:

- A student uses marijuana and does so increasingly
- A student continues using current study skills, even those that result in mediocre results on papers and exams
- A first-year student hasn't learned personal time management skills, since previously the schedule was determined by parents
- Sleep is difficult for students because of high noise levels in the residence hall
- The increasing costs of tuition and books cause some students to withdraw from enrollment
- Students' self-esteem is based on selection as an officer or leader in a club or organization, which seems limited to only a few individuals
- Maintaining a good relationship with others is challenging because of limited social skills
- Preoccupation with social media and gaming websites cause havoc with numerous parts of life
- The infamous "freshman 15" has become a reality, plus some more pounds with late night snacks

College professionals, whether in student affairs, administration, faculty, advising or other roles, can easily see how these factors can each confound students' success in college. Not only these items but numerous others can cause consternation among these professionals who, in fact, want to see the students succeed. Further, most of these issues intersect with one another. For example, poor time management results in procrastination, resulting in poor study skills. Or, excessive drug or alcohol use results in poor interpersonal relationships, lack of civic engagement and poor academic performance. Similarly, low self-esteem may link to body image or disordered eating and thus to mental health concerns.

Some factors are even more troublesome and are a cause for more immediate concern. Consider, for example, a student who expresses extreme doubts about whether life is worth living, a student who experiences a medical emergency due to consuming alcohol when taking a prescription drug and a student who reports an incident of sexual assault; each of these is much more urgent in nature and requires a swift and competent response.

The nexus of higher education and wellness issues is clear. Numerous wellness issues have a significant role to play with students' success in college. Some of these issues result in disciplinary action, and others result in poor academic performance. These issues also affect students' preparation for "life after college" or "the real world." These skills, including but not limited to time management, dependence and recovery, stress management, writing, relationships and career planning, all contribute to students' quality of performance and life. When these and other wellness topics are not well developed during the college years, students (those who soon become alumni) will be less prepared to meet the regular challenges of an employee, a family member, a community member and fellow citizen. Beyond that, these individuals will not be as well prepared to embrace the opportunities that surround them, whether intellectual, cultural, social, recreational or other.

This is not to suggest that, upon graduation from college, all the necessary skills and attitudes are present. As noted, wellness is a life-long activity and is never fully achieved. Those with excellent skills in a specific area (e.g., writing, exercise, tobacco, financial health) will undoubtedly have a stronger start to their lives after college. Yet all graduates can improve upon each of these areas in the months, years and decades following graduation and can benefit from a healthy foundation as well as a "jump start" from their collegiate years.

The important consideration for professionals working in higher education revolves around the extent to which they as individuals, as members of specific work groups (such as student affairs divisions, academic units or other departments) and as a member in the institution as a whole are contributing to helping the students succeed. The question for each individual is how well they are helping students maximize their college experience, both in preparation for graduation as well as with preparation for a fulfilling life. And, if the higher education professional believes that all students admitted should, ultimately, graduate, what steps are being made to ensure that this happens? As Luoluo Hong stated in the closing plenary at the NASPA Strategy Conference on Alcohol, Other Drugs and Violence Prevention and Mental Health, a paradigm shift may be called for: "If a student fails, we now say 'it's the student's fault'; how about, 'it's our fault, what didn't we do right? What could we have done better?'" (Hong, 2016). This changes the nature of the question and the dialogue surrounding wellness issues.

Edgar Schein (2013) stresses a larger societal context that is helpful.

The U.S. Culture is individualistic, competitive, optimistic, and pragmatic. . . . We are impatient and, with information technology's ability to do things faster, we are even more impatient. Most important of all, we value task accomplishment over relationship building and either are not aware of this cultural bias or, worse, don't care and don't want to be bothered with it.

(p. 55)

Within his inquiry, what is the relative context for college and university campuses, and how can colleges and their professional staff and faculty members be better suited to achieve the goals of promoting wellness issues among students?

This is not to suggest that the responsibility for success in college and following college is entirely the responsibility of those working in the college setting. Indeed, much of the responsibility falls upon the students themselves. What it does suggest is that college personnel, through their individual and collective actions and with the environment they help to establish and maintain, have a significant responsibility to identify factors that contribute to and detract from the success of their students. It does suggest that systems and protocols be set up to promote the healthiest and safest college environment and that significant attention be provided to enhancing students' utilization of resources. It also suggests that college and university personnel should intervene early when it is clear that something is going awry, whether for an individual, a group of individuals (e.g., a living group, an athletic team or a demographic group) or the institution as a whole. The important theme of accountability is maintained, so colleges do all they can to maximize students' success and best prepare them to be successful in a future setting that appears fraught with uncertainty.

A Sense of Hope

When thinking about ensuring that wellness issues among students are addressed adequately, an obvious question is not so much "Why?" but "Why now?" as well as "What is different today?" As noted in the Introduction of the first *Wellness Issues for Higher Education* (Anderson, 2016), students report numerous areas and issues that should be of concern to college and university personnel. The ongoing National College Health Assessment provides a most helpful resource that can help institutional leaders gauge the nature and scope of concerns found among students (American College Health Association, 2015). Whether it is stress, anxiety, relationship difficulties, sleep difficulties or depression, institutions can take stock of current student needs and strive to address them in as much a preventive manner as possible.

It is clear that some things are different among students today. Thus, approaches useful 5, 10 and 20 years ago, while not necessarily invalid today, would be insufficient for meeting the needs of currently enrolled students. Similarly, what will this be like in five and ten years and the decade after that? For example, Facebook is, as of 2016, only 14 years old. Smartphones began widespread adoption in the middle 2000s, with iPhones introduced in 2007. A review of student behavior demonstrates high use of digital devices and less human interaction and time to "take in one's surroundings."

What has become of students' coping skills and their resilience with a range of issues? To provide some perspective, consider the following, from among the 50 developed for the Beloit College "Mindset List" for 2019 (McBride, Nief, & Westerberg, 2015):

Students heading into their first year of college this year are mostly 18 and were born in 1997. Since they have lived on the planet:

- Google has always been there
- They have never licked a postage stamp
- They have grown up treating Wi-Fi as an entitlement
- Cell phones have become so ubiquitous in class that teachers don't know which students are using them to take notes and which ones are planning a party
- Their parents have gone from encouraging them to use the Internet to begging them to get off it
- If you say "around the turn of the century," they may well ask you, "Which one?"
- The therapeutic use of marijuana has always been legal in a growing number of American states

The current generation of traditional-age college students is coming to campus with a very different background and orientation than those who preceded it. Current students do appear less resilient, with fewer inherent skills for anticipating, for coping, for adjusting and for managing themselves. Continuing the declining emotional health of college freshmen, the Cooperative Institutional Research Program at UCLA offered the following data:

In 2014, students' self-rated emotional health dropped to 50.7% (rating themselves as "above average" or "highest 10%" compared to people their age), its lowest level ever and 2.3 percentage points lower than the entering cohort of 2013. Additionally, the proportion of students who "frequently" felt depressed rose to 9.5%.

(Eagan et al., 2015)

Is this is due to increased technology, greater involvement of parents (including the "helicopter parent") or overscheduling (often designed to increase their acceptance to higher-quality colleges and universities)? What role is played by increased stress due to a world with continuous conflict and security concerns? And what factor does the uncertain financial future play, based on wide fluctuations in the stock market, the unemployment rate and the increasing global interdependence among nations of varying levels of wealth? Certainly, the world is a different place for these students.

And the world of higher education is looking like a much different place for the foreseeable future. Total enrollment in degree-granting postsecondary institutions is skyrocketing; it was 10 million students in 1974 (National Center for Education Statistics, 2015). It took over a quarter of a century, the year 2000, for it to reach 15 million students and then just 9 more years (National Center for Education Statistics, 2015) to increase by another 5 million, to 20 million students. The projections currently go to 2023, when student estimates are at 23.8 million. Thus, while continued increases are projected, the level of growth is slowing down dramatically. The continued changes do continue with regard to the female/male ratio; in 1947, this had 29% female and grew to 45% in 1974. In 2009, it was 57.1% and is projected to grow to 58.8% in 2023. The part-time/full-time ratio is expected to be 39.1% in 2023 slightly higher than the 2012 rate of 38.3% and the 1974 rate of 37.7%; this rate peaked in 1992 at 43.7%.

The sense of hope is important for this work on wellness. While a subjective view, it appears that increased attention to wellness topics is permeating society. Some of this attention is focused on individual issues, and some emphasizes wellness overall. What is apparent is that science-based foundations, with good knowledge, is growing, thus providing a stronger foundation and rationale for the imperative placed upon individuals, groups and institutions as a whole within colleges and university.

Yet the question remains, "Is change feasible?" And, if so, what will facilitate or ease its accomplishment? Some issues, such as sexual violence as well as drug and alcohol abuse, provide some modest evidence of the feasibility of change. For example, recent attention with sexual violence is found with increased discussions and public awareness surrounding mandates and Title IX; with the documentation regarding the importance and priority given to this on college campuses, more presidents and chief executives on campus are actually talking about this issue, which will hopefully translate into action and then substantive results. Similarly, with the 2015 College Alcohol Survey, co-authored by this chapter author, a question was asked about top administrative support for the campus effort; on a five-point scale where 5 represented "very much," the mean score across the 178 responses was 3.75 (Anderson & Santos, 2015). On a related note, the data from this survey shows notable progress with the extent of alcohol's involvement with a range of campus problems (from student attrition to property damage and from emotional difficulty to physical injury); the level of alcohol's involvement has, for these, been reduced by an average of 10 percentage points over a 30-year period. While this may be viewed as slow progress, it does provide some affirmation that progress is possible.

What these brief elements suggest is that greater attention to and support of some of these issues, and perhaps even wellness as a whole, is occurring. The purpose of incorporating attention to some sense of hope is to provide this context for campus leaders. If the attention was only on documenting the increasing needs found among students, a sense of futility may accompany the urgency of the issue. However, coupled with some hope are the glimmers of the change in discourse and support found, to some degree, on some of these issues. This greater awareness can lead to increased understanding, which can further lead to enhanced support and, ultimately, action.

Applications on Campus

Translating wellness issues into action is where the proverbial "rubber means the road." With the concept of wellness specified, and the role that wellness promotion can play in the lives of students, the key question is how to ensure that this happens. College campuses, like the rest of society, do not have unlimited resources, so the important consideration is to have an understanding of ways to promote the wellness initiative in the higher education environment.

The answer may sound obvious; after all, it only makes sense to invest in students' futures and identify ways of promoting their success. However, the reality is such that wellness issues are not particularly well-funded or well-established in colleges and universities across the nation. The College Alcohol Survey provides insight about the resources, excluding personnel, allocated by campuses for wellness issues and substance abuse services; in 2012, these averaged $54,147 per campus, with 45% going for wellness issues other than substance abuse. On a per capita basis, this is $4.10 for each student (Anderson & Gadaleto, 2012).

A recent study asked student affairs professionals, for each of 20 wellness topics, how well prepared they felt for addressing wellness needs among students; for each topic, their preparation was exceeded by the needs, thus acknowledging their own professional deficiencies (Anderson, Rose, & Williams, 2016). They were also asked about the extent to which their graduate program of study addressed wellness issues in other courses; only 26% reported "very much" or "pretty much." And, when asked about the source of preparation for five clusters of wellness issues (psychological, interpersonal, substance abuse, physical and occupational), the self-study/self-taught approach was the most common when compared with graduate programs, professional staff training, specialized training, conferences and mentoring (with the exception of substance abuse, where specialized training was slightly higher).

To address wellness issues requires a larger commitment on campus. This approach is consistent with the recent calls by the U.S. Surgeon General, who stated that he wants to move the U.S. to a "prevention-based society." He stated his vision that "every institution, whether they're a hospital or a clinic, or a school, an employer or a faith-based organization, recognizes and embraces the role that it can play in improving health" (Bernstein, 2015). To accomplish this with colleges and universities, it will be vital that campus leaders incorporate wellness issues, especially those from a prevention point of view, into the overall academic mission of the institution. The first volume of *Wellness Issues* attempted this with its incorporation of topics and issues that were linked, directly or indirectly, to students' success in college. The aim was to reduce attrition from the institution, by promoting those factors (such as stress management, drug or alcohol issues, sleep and study skills) that are likely to infringe upon students' success. This volume of *Wellness Issues* incorporates wellness topics associated with students' planning and a successful future orientation. This is designed to help incorporate these wellness issues into the lifeblood of the institution.

What, then, can the campus leaders do to help ensure that wellness issues are addressed more thoroughly with the professional staff? The framing of the question is twofold. First, what is it that the campus leaders can do to promote wellness issues overall for the campus? Second, how can the professional staff be better prepared to address these issues with students?

For the first issue of promoting wellness, the key factor is that campus leaders must make this a priority. To do so, it is vital that wellness be incorporated into the context and culture of the institution. Wellness must be viewed, and implemented, in ways that link directly to the central mission of the institution. Institutions of higher education are, by definition, about the education of students. While coursework, research, community service and supportive activities are all vitally important to the health and future of colleges and universities, it is the education of students that is the central and foundational core of these institutions. Thus, central to the implementation and sustenance of wellness issues is to link them to the academic, teaching, instructional focus of the institution; it is imperative to link wellness issues to the academic mission of the institution. As noted earlier, that has been the intent with the selection of topics for these wellness issues volumes; this has been further elaborated upon in earlier sections of this Introduction chapter as well as in the Introduction to the first volume.

With the question of professional staff preparation, quality attention must be directed to staff members who are employed as well as those who are new to the campus. Whether through training sessions for current faculty and staff, mandated preparation programs for new staff and faculty, support for professional conferences or intensive professional development, support for coursework for job-related skills or directed study programs, campuses can ensure quality attention to skills and attitudes among its employees. With each of these areas, campuses can take action in multiple areas.

- *Gather local data on a continuous basis.* This includes the need among students, including subsets of students (e.g., first year, veterans, organizational affiliation), as well as among professionals. Use the data for planning and targeting resources.
- *Identify ways in which the needs are linked to the academic success and non-success of student.* It is this linkage that will have the greatest likelihood of obtaining buy-in and longer-term support, as these factors are essential to the core of all institutions of higher education.
- *Document results, including both outcome and process measures, for all initiatives undertaken.* Seek to establish the value of wellness initiatives, as these are currently not well institutionalized. Campus leaders should use the results to make improvements as well as to sustain current efforts. In short, they must gather quality data, as it is important that they build arguments based on evidence.
- *Engage systematically in action planning, using clearly defined objectives, timelines, personnel allocated, resources needed and other key factors.* Actively use this action plan and review its utility on a regular basis.

- *Identify resources, partners, allies and collaborators.* Wellness should not be accomplished as a stand-alone process; rather, it needs to be incorporated into the fabric of the institution. Natural resources include, among others, faculty with specialties in identified areas, student organizations with influence and natural affiliation needs, administrators who have a personal interest in an issue, alumni with expertise, community organizations with affiliated topics and students with research or volunteering interests.
- *Synergize and integrate the various strands of the prevention effort to maximize impact and promote consistent messages.* Rather than competing for resources, identify ways of promoting common bonds.
- *Just as wellness issues are linked to academic issues, also identify ways of linking the wellness issues with various standards and accreditation activities.* For example, the Council for the Advancement of Standards in Higher Education (CAS) has prepared common criteria and guidelines on 12 categories. Various academic and non-academic units also have standards appropriate for linking, and conversations with staff and faculty in these areas can be helpful.
- *Focus on action and results, as well as an engaging process.* Not only should the campus have quality plans grounded in current science and good practice, there should also be attention to processes that involve and engage students.
- *Be translational with the topics, outcomes and processes.* The sociologist Irving Horowitz, founding editor of the scientific journal *Transaction* (now named *Society*), stressed the application of social science to inform educated and thoughtful general readers. Similarly, higher education professionals, whether faculty, student affairs professionals, administrators or others can help stress the importance of addressing wellness issues. Their importance can be stressed for their own sake (e.g., health), as well as for their relative contribution to the academic mission of the institution.
- *Be political and navigate the political environment.* Every college and university is a political environment; this is a reality. The specific culture of each campus will vary, based on factors such as institutional history, setting, needs and leadership. The higher education professional seeking to promote wellness issues must learn how many of these factors and structures, both formal and informal, work on the campus. One of the best strategies to address this is having positive, quality working relationships with others across the campus.

These suggestions provide a general framework for campus wellness efforts. While they are in no way a guarantee of success, they do serve as a helpful foundation for greater substance and results associated with the aspirational goals associated with wellness. They help to promote and, ultimately, institutionalize these efforts.

Final Reflections

As a way of pulling together this Introduction to this volume of *Wellness Issues*, some final thoughts are helpful. This is important because numerous challenges exist that can thwart the most well-intended effort.

First, it is important for all college professionals to *start with themselves* and reflect upon their own wellness, including any personal issues and challenges that might exist. While no one is perfect, the acknowledgement that wellness is a life-long commitment to doing better and to achieving balance is an important one. The commitment to the journey of improvement is a most helpful starting place. As part of this, awareness of opportunities and challenges or obstacles is also important; this allows for greater planning with approaches for enhancing the wellness lifestyle.

Second, it is helpful to *retain a positive attitude*. The acknowledgement that promoting wellness can be hard work, and will never be done, can often be discouraging. The fact that so many people know the facts yet don't translate them for their own lives can be frustrating. The presence of good data and quality results, yet having limited positive support from campus administrators or students, can be demoralizing. Having a positive attitude is not naïve or basic but rather is an acknowledgement that what is being represented here is an uphill battle and a cultural change. While much in the culture verbally supports wellness, action and accountability are often missing. Thus, campus professionals need to be deliberate and persistent and do so with a "can-do" spirit.

Third, acknowledge the important role of *student success and student development*. These are central to the institution, to its mission and to its future. Involve the students and engage them. Listen to what is important to them, yet challenge their perspectives and encourage greater critical thinking. These are very much a part of what makes an institution of higher education what it is.

Fourth, and related to the previous point, take pride in the *important role that colleges and universities play in society*. As institutions of higher education, colleges and universities are designed to serve as repositories of knowledge and grounded knowledge. They are ostensibly centers of excellence and quality. They provide a strong foundation for society in its larger context and also provide extensive resources for the local community. The service provided by colleges and universities, as institutions overall and by individual faculty and staff members, is valuable for the culture.

Fifth, remember the basic principle: *"without health, what do you have?"* When someone is ill, temporarily immobilized or otherwise impaired, they are not performing well with any of a number of tasks or responsibilities. One issue can affect another, such as when one's workout regimen is compromised when sick, as is one's nutritional intake, and these affect intellectual performance and sociability. Thus, promoting health in all aspects of a person's life, from physical to emotional, is important. Certainly, imbalance occurs periodically with everyone, and some are more pronounced and others are of longer duration. But the aim is one of full health and in a balanced way.

Sixth, acknowledge that *wellness is never ending*. This is a life-long journey. As such it is all about maximizing potential and continuous improvement. Wellness is about doing better, and better, and better. When hearing students who are ecstatic about passing a class, a question may be about how well they really could have done, if some of the wellness barriers or challenges had been addressed. Similarly, when hearing of students who talk about their hangover or potentially dangerous encounters, the question is one of what was their potential and what could their accomplishments have been had they not been so involved.

Finally, the key question is one of identifying *what role will be played in addressing wellness within the context of the academy.* What activities or advocacy will be undertaken to promote the quality campus environment and culture that so many envision? What responsibility is appropriate, knowing that the vast majority of college professionals are not specialists in time management or stress reduction, in health promotion or substance dependence, in disability awareness or body image? Professionally trained specialists exist in each of these areas and so many more. But the rest of the higher education professionals, whether a chemistry professor or an academic dean, whether a first-year residence hall director or a vice president who is nearing retirement, each have an important role to play. It is certainly not necessary to know everything about these various topics; what is important is to have some basic knowledge and to know where the various areas of specialization exist on the campus or in the community. What is important is to have a sense of shared responsibility about helping create a more positive and wellness-oriented campus culture. What is important is to identify where individual roles exist and how to be helpful in moving things forward for the campus and for the individuals who comprise that campus community. It's important to take part, to be a cog in the wheel, and it's vital that individuals and groups not be a roadblock toward a more positive and healthy future.

Conclusion

This introduction to *Further Wellness Issues for Higher Education* provides the contextual framework for higher education professionals as they seek to understand wellness issues for their campus setting. While it may not be inherently obvious, the role of wellness issues is integral to the success of students in their academic career at the institution; further, these wellness issues, and their successful adoption, are vital for success in their lives following graduation. The context of wellness within the academic setting has been highlighted; the importance of linking these issues to the academic mission of the school is stressed.

Vital throughout this introduction, and with the chapters contained in this and the earlier volume, is the important role played by all higher education professionals. This includes the student affairs professional, whether she or he is embarking on their career or has already spent decades in service to students and their institutions. It includes the faculty member, new and tenured, from all disciplines. It includes academic advisors and athletics personnel; it includes those in counseling and health services, as well as those working in police or security roles. The focus is upon engaging them as well as the students toward more wellness-oriented decisions and thus stronger personal and academic outcomes. Ideally, this is done as a collective effort; while an individualistic approach would focus on the "I," a team approach focuses on the "we." Noteworthy is when the "I" found in "Illness" is replaced by "we," the word is transformed to "Wellness."

There may also need to be some redefinition of the challenge; that is, the challenge with promoting wellness issues may be based on the emphasis upon a change in individuals' health or wellness behavior; in fact, the health and wellness behaviors are elements that can help, or hinder, a student's accomplishment of the common goal for the institution—academic success. Reflecting back on Dr. Hong's question cited earlier in this Introduction—"If a student fails, . . . what didn't we do right? What could we have done better?"—the issue becomes a different one. Rather than focusing just on the wellness issue (and perhaps the "wellness issue du jour"), college and university personnel would be well served to focus upon students' academic achievement and upon how to help them better accomplish this. Rather than addressing discrete topics, the focus should be on a holistic view and ways that students can incorporate skills and strategies for their unique circumstances. And rather than focus only on "success" today, the focus should be expanded to also include preparation for a life full of accomplishments and joy, satisfaction and comfort.

The foundation is prepared here for pursing positive directions. The message is one of being a change agent, for future with increased health and wellness. The theme is one of offering challenges and critical thinking and of providing good research and service. The focus is one of living up to the standards espoused in the institutional mission statements, regarding character and curiosity, reasoning and ethics, knowledge and understanding and society and service. Through planned change initiatives, individuals and institutions can flourish.

References

American College Health Association. (2015). *National College Health Assessment*. Spring 2014 Reference Group Executive Summary. Hanover, MD. Retrieved from http://www.acha-ncha.org/reports_ACHA-NCHAII.html

Anderson, D. (Ed.). (2016). *Wellness Issues for Higher Education*. New York: Routledge.

Anderson, D., & Gadaleto, A. (2012). *The College Alcohol Survey: 1979–2012*. George Mason University, Fairfax, VA. Retrieved from https://caph.gmu.edu/resources/college/review

Anderson, D., Rose, T., & Williams, A. (2016). How multi-dimensional are we on wellness? A closer look. NASPA Alcohol and Other Drug Abuse Prevention, Mental Health and Violence Prevention Conference, Orlando, FL, January, 2016.

Anderson, D., & Santos, G.-M. (2015). *The College Alcohol Survey: 1979–2015*. George Mason University, Fairfax, VA. Retrieved from https://caph.gmu.edu/resources/college/review

Bernstein, L. (2015). Surgeon General Vivek Murthy wants to move U.S. health care toward a 'prevention-based society.' *The Washington Post*, April 23, 2015. Retrieved from https://www.washingtonpost.com/news/to-your-health/wp/2015/04/23/surgeon-general-vivek-murthy-wants-to-move-u-s-health-care-toward-a-prevention-based-society/

Eagan, K., Stolzenberg, E. B., Ramirez, J. J., Aragon, M. C., Suchard, R. S., & Hurtado, S. (2015). *The American Freshman: National Norms Fall 2014*. Higher Education Research Institute at UCLA. Retrieved from http://www.heri.ucla.edu/briefs/TheAmericanFreshman2014-Brief.pdf

Hong, Luoluo. (2016). From compliance to courage—Leading transformational change in integrative prevention. Plenary Session. NASPA Alcohol and Other Drug Abuse Prevention, Mental Health and Violence Prevention Conference, Orlando, FL, January, 2016.

Lumina Foundation. (2013). *Strategic Plan. A Stronger Nation through Higher Education*. Retrieved from https://www.luminafoundation.org/files/file/2013-lumina-strategic-plan.pdf

Maslow, A. H. (1943). A theory of human motivation. *Psychological Review, 50*(4), 370–396. Retrieved from psychclassics.yorku.ca

McBride, T., Nief, R., & Westerberg, C. (2015). *The Beloit College Mindset List*. Beloit, WI: Beloit College. Retrieved from https://www.beloit.edu/mindset/guides/

National Center for Education Statistics. (2015). *U.S. Department of Education, Institute of Education Sciences. Table 303.10 Total Fall Enrollment in Degree-Granting Postsecondary Institutions, by Attendance Status, Sex of Student, and Control of Institution: Selected Years, 1947 through 2023*. Retrieved from http://nces.ed.gov/programs/digest/d13/tables/dt13_303.10.asp

National Wellness Institute. (2016). Retrieved from http://www.nationalwellness.org/?page=AboutWellness

Schein, Edgar H. (2013). *Humble Inquiry: The Gentle Art of Asking Instead of Telling*. San Francisco: Berrett-Koehler Publishers, Inc.

Zaback, K, Carlson, A., & Crellin, M. (2012). *The Economic Benefits of Postsecondary Degrees: A State and National Level Analysis*. Boulder, CO: National Center for Higher Education Management Systems.

Part I
Emotional Wellness

2

Body Image

Supporting Healthy Behaviors on College Campuses

NICOLE TAYLOR AND MIMI NICHTER

Introduction

Studies of body image have been numerous over the past three decades with researchers investigating the meaning and lived experience of this concept in a variety of social contexts. Researchers typically define body image as how individuals see themselves when they look in the mirror or when they picture themselves in their mind's eye. Body image is not a singular construct but rather a complex and multidimensional phenomenon that includes perceptual, attitudinal, affective and cultural components (Striegel-Moore & Franko, 2002). As a result, research on body image has focused on a wide range of topics including weight concerns, feelings about one's body shape, body esteem, body schema, weight dissatisfaction and body image disorder, to name but a few (Cash & Pruzinsky, 2002).

While body image is an important construct across the lifespan, it holds particular salience for college students. Being in college, especially for those who live on campus, is a time marked by new freedoms, when one is away from one's family and the watchful eyes of parents. For many young people, this is a time to try on "new selves" and craft new identities. It is an opportunity to experiment with one's physical appearance, to try to change one's body shape and to make food choices that were not possible when one was living at home. On-campus buffets, food courts and vending machines abound with myriad healthy and unhealthy options. Living in a residence hall with roommates and being surrounded by other students on a daily basis provide increased opportunities for comparing one's self to others.

Some years back, psychologist Kim Chernin described a "tyranny of slenderness" that ruled over women in the United States (Chernin, 1981). Indeed, many researchers have discussed how, from an early age, girls learn that having a thin body is linked to attractiveness and femininity. This is reinforced regularly through advertised images in magazines and through television and movies that project an ultra-slender look as desirable and attractive. One's sense of how their body size and shape conforms to culturally idealized notions of beauty is central to an understanding of body image. If one's body shape does not meet the cultural ideal, it can result in dissatisfaction with self ("negative" body image) and may lead to watching what one eats, dieting, guilt around eating and engaging in exercise strategies to change one's body shape.

This chapter reviews and summarizes the relevant literature on body image across a number of domains, including gender, ethnicity, sexuality and physical dis/ability. Further discussed is research on weight gain through the college years, especially the "freshman 15," how college students talk about body image (e.g., "fat talk") and the effects of body focused discourse, as well as the impact of social media on body image among college students. The objective is to provide an overview of salient body image–related issues experienced by college students, to suggest future directions for research and to identify interventions that college practitioners—faculty, staff, student affairs professionals and administrators—can implement to support healthy body image in a diverse student population.

Overweight and Obesity on Campus: Brief Overview

Despite cultural preferences for bodies that are thin, lean and fat free, the reality of life on campus reveals a different yet co-existent picture. Young adults (18–35 year olds) are gaining weight faster than their parents, averaging an increase of 30 pounds during this phase of the life course. Between 2004 and 2010, the prevalence of overweight and obesity for females aged 20–39 increased from 52% to 56%, and for males, from 62% to 67% (Gordon-Larsen, The, & Adair, 2010). Note that overweight and obesity are calculated on a person's body mass index (BMI): A BMI of 25.0 to 29.9 is overweight; a BMI of 30.0 and higher is obese. While much of this weight gain may occur after the college years, it needs to be recognized that eating and exercise behaviors are being shaped during college. Recent survey results from the National College Health Assessment (NCHA) revealed that 23% of college students nationwide were overweight and another 13% were obese (American College Health Association, 2015). Longitudinal NCHA survey data from a large southwestern university showed that weight increases across the years of college were significant: 26% of first-year students were overweight, compared to 40% of fourth-year students (Trainer, Brewis, Williams, & Chavez, 2015). Notably, despite high overweight and obesity rates among college students, pressures to conform to a narrow body image ideal persist.

There are several practical and pressing concerns with regard to body image among college students. Negative body image, or feeling dissatisfaction with one's body, is a risk factor that may lead to low self-esteem. Overweight and obesity are associated with an elevated risk for several chronic diseases including heart disease, diabetes and some types of cancer. Thus, the high rates of overweight and obese college students should be of concern to college health professionals as well as other college personnel because overweight young adults may well be overweight or obese for the rest of their lives.

Gender Differences in Body Image

Body image studies have traditionally focused on girls and women. However, as pressures for boys and men to achieve a certain body type have increased in recent years, researchers have begun to explore how males feel about the way they look, how they talk with each other about body image, how they tease each other about their bodies and the types of behaviors they engage in to achieve the ideal look (e.g., Gill et al., 2005; Grogan & Richards, 2002; Kehler & Atkinson, 2010; Ryan & Morrison, 2009; Taylor, 2011, 2015). Studies of male body image have increased over the past decade, yet it is still a relatively new area of inquiry, and there is a need for ongoing research, particularly among college students.

Historically, studies have found higher rates of body dissatisfaction among college women than among college men, with some reporting that more than 80% of female college students are unhappy with the way their bodies look (Heatherton, Mahamedi, Striepe, Field, & Keel, 1997; Neighbors & Sobal, 2007; Vohs, Heatherton, & Herrin, 2001). In fact, the college years stand out as a heightened time of body dissatisfaction among women. One study found the percentage of women wanting to lose weight dropped from 82% during college to 68% after college. The trend was reversed for men, who reported an increase in body dissatisfaction after college (Heatherton et al., 1997). Researchers theorize that body dissatisfaction may be more intense among college women who reside on campus than for those who commute because living together in such close quarters invites body-related scrutiny, constant comparison and the spread of weight preoccupation (Greenhalgh, 2015; Martin, 2007).

Some recent research suggests that men are catching up with women in feeling unhappy about the way their bodies look (Dakanalis et al., 2015; Thompson & Cafri, 2007). Unlike women, who are typically concerned with their weight, men tend to be more concerned with body shape and musculature. One study that examined self-perceived and idealized physical attributes among heterosexual White college men found that up to 91% of those surveyed wanted to be more muscular (Jacobi & Cash, 1994).

For women, the relationship between BMI (body mass index) and negative body image tends to be linear; the higher a woman's BMI, the worse she feels about the way her body looks (Striegel-Moore & Franko, 2002). However, among men, the relationship between BMI and negative body image is more complex. For example, results of one study that surveyed a random sample of 188 college men found that underweight, overweight and obese men reported higher levels of body dissatisfaction and greater weight and shape concerns than normal weight men (Watkins, Christie, & Chally, 2008).

Although college men are fast approaching the high levels of body dissatisfaction that women have long experienced, some research suggests that men and women are not yet equal in this regard. For example, one study examining body dissatisfaction among college students during the first three semesters of college found that female students' overall appearance evaluation started out less positive than male students' and remained less positive three semesters later despite increases in how they felt about themselves during this time (Gillen & Lefkowitz, 2012). The authors suggest that, because women's bodies are more objectified by society than those of men, women are more self-critical of their bodies, which leads to greater dissatisfaction. This begins in early adolescence and may continue throughout emerging adulthood and beyond.

The work of anthropologist Susan Greenhalgh (2015), who conducted body image research with male and female college students, supports and provides further insight into the trend of increasingly widespread body dissatisfaction among college students. Greenhalgh argues that the current "war on fat" has resulted in heightened anxieties about excess weight that pervade popular and news media and everyday conversation, resulting in a generation of young adults that have become weight-obsessed. Greenhalgh found that college men and women were concerned with body image and were teased for being fat. However, men were less likely to internalize the criticism than women, probably because men tend to be judged based on their accomplishments whereas evaluation of women is typically appearance driven. Also, girls are socialized from a young age to rely heavily on external feedback in developing their sense of self (Nichter, 2000), which sets them up for greater body dissatisfaction in the college years and beyond.

In terms of weight management efforts among college students, one study based on survey data of approximately 38,000 randomly selected college students found that male and female students with inaccurate body weight perception were more likely to engage in unhealthy weight loss strategies than those with accurate body weight perception (Wharton, Adams, & Hampl, 2008). Although weight loss was important to participants in the study, only 38% reported following standard weight loss guidelines, which include a combination of diet and exercise. More women than men were engaged in weight loss efforts even though more men were overweight or obese. Indeed, across the life span, women are far more likely to engage in dieting than men (Nichter, 2000). Negative body image not only leads to low self-esteem and related mental health issues, but it also impacts food-related behaviors and could lead to unhealthy dieting practices. Thus, supporting healthy body image among college students is crucial as it contributes to their overall well-being.

Ethnic Differences

In terms of ethnic identity, research has historically suggested that body-image ideals among African-American and Latina girls and women may be more flexible than those of White women (Parker et al., 1995). African-American women were found to embrace multiple ideas about beauty that do not focus so heavily on aesthetics but rather on how one moves and the importance of "making what you got work for you." The cultural notion of "looking good" has to do with projecting one's self image and confidence (having "tude," or attitude) and was not based on one's weight (Nichter, 2000; Parker et al., 1995). For example, one study based on analysis of focus-group data found that African-American and Latina college-educated women challenged the mainstream beauty ideal of slenderness by embracing an ethic of self-acceptance and nurturance (Rubin, Fitts, & Becker, 2003).

More recent studies suggest that the slender ideal has begun to influence non-White girls and women who increasingly want to rid their bodies of excess fat and achieve a more toned physique (Bordo, 2013). The integration of a slender body ideal into non-White culture has led to mixed findings in studies of body image among ethnic minority college students. For example, one study examining body image dissatisfaction of racially salient appearance areas (e.g., hair, lips, eyes, lower body) among approximately 300 White, Black and Latina female college students found that White and Latina women reported more dissatisfaction with their facial features, lips, lower body and overall body than Black women (Warren, 2014). However, Black and Latina women who identified most strongly with their ethnic group reported lower levels of body dissatisfaction on most appearance areas.

Another study found that African-American college women were more concerned with overall appearance than their White counterparts but, at the same time, were less dissatisfied with their bodies (Gillen & Lefkowitz, 2012). The authors suggest that African-American women may seem to be more appearance oriented because in African-American culture, one's appearance serves a dual purpose: It expresses one's individual identity and at the same time confers an image onto one's family and community. In a context in which the beauty standards of the larger society are often the antithesis of African-American physical attributes (facial features, body shape, body size and hair), receiving positive feedback about one's appearance from community members may serve as a protective factor against body dissatisfaction (Nichter, 2000; Parker et al., 1995).

Research based on in-depth interviews with African-American women attending a primarily White college found that women expressed a range of racial identities and varying levels of self-esteem and body satisfaction (Hesse-Biber, Livingston, Ramirez, Barko, & Johnson, 2010). The authors of this study challenge previous research claims that African-American women are insulated from mainstream body image ideals and have more positive body image regardless of weight, arguing instead that ethnic identity emerges through social practice and can vary across contexts (e.g., school, home, church, community). Some of the women in this study identified with White or Black culture while others floated between the two or expressed a more complex self-identity. These findings underscore the need to recognize diverse body image ideologies within ethnic groups based on such factors as influence of college and home communities, one's peers and family members and socioeconomic status.

Along these lines, anthropologist Stephanie McClure found a range of body image satisfaction among adolescent African-American girls, reporting that their experience with fitness and physicality shaped the way they felt about and presented their bodies (2017). McClure emphasizes the importance of exploring the complex, nuanced ways in which body image can vary within ethnic minority groups. She cautions against viewing race as a monolithic, static explanatory category and promotes an approach to the study of body image within any group that draws on multiple methodologies to understand how individuals' experiences and identities intersect with the various social contexts in which they operate (McClure, 2012).

Individuals who identify with ethnic minority groups that have traditionally been more accepting of larger body sizes and/or focused less on aesthetics than the

White mainstream culture may struggle more with body image issues as they move from their family and local communities onto a college campus. Efforts to improve body image and health-related behaviors among college students must address the complex ways in which ethnic identity intersects with ideas about body image and other aspects of an individual's identity (e.g., gender, socioeconomic status). Future research should explore body image ideology among other ethnic minorities, including Asian-American students, a notably understudied population.

GLBT Communities

Body image research among gay, lesbian, bisexual and transgender (GLBT) communities has produced inconsistent findings. Some early studies on lesbian college students and body image found no differences between lesbians and heterosexual women (e.g., Striegel-Moore, Tucker, & Hsu, 1990) while others found lesbians to be more accepting of their bodies than heterosexual women (e.g., Herzog, Newman, Yeh, & Warshaw, 1992). Early studies on gay men and body image found gay men desired a thinner ideal and had more body dissatisfaction than heterosexual men (Herzog, Newman, & Warshaw, 1991; Silberstein, Mishkind, Striegel-Moore, Timko, & Rodin, 1989). Yet a more recent study comparing the results of a computerized body image test for 37 gay men and 49 heterosexual men found no difference in body image ideals or body image distortion (Hausmann, Mangweth, Walch, Rupp, & Pope, 2004).

Some research has sought to identify sociocultural factors that might buffer or protect lesbian and bisexual women from the desire to achieve mainstream body ideals. Findings suggest that lesbians who identify as more butch or androgynous by favoring comfortable over fashionable clothing, by dressing for themselves rather than others and by giving up traditional feminine beauty rituals are less preoccupied with body image concerns than heterosexual women (Cogan, 1999; Ludwig & Brownell, 1999). Other research suggests there is a disconnect between values lesbians want to embrace and their actual beliefs and behaviors, providing a glimpse into the complex intersection of body image, sexual orientation and gendered identity. For example, one study comparing lesbian and heterosexual women found that lesbians thought dieting was oppressive; yet approximately half of the lesbians reported having dieted recently. Lesbians were also more critical of feminine beauty norms than heterosexual women, but about half of the lesbians surveyed were dissatisfied with their weight and had low body esteem (Heffernan, 1999).

Qualitative research on GLBT body image can offer additional insights. One study focusing on college-age women explored body image among lesbian, bisexual and heterosexual women through in-depth interviews (Leavy & Hastings, 2010). Lesbian and bisexual women expressed greater satisfaction with their bodies when compared to heterosexual women. Among the reasons cited were their feelings of exclusion from dominant feminine culture coupled with feelings of inclusion in GLBT subcultures that provided space for cultivating alternative femininities and exploring a broader range of appearance norms. Bisexual women, however, felt more pressure to conform to dominant feminine beauty norms when dating men than when dating women, suggesting a need for further research on body image and dating issues.

A noteworthy critique of extant research on this topic is that it tends to focus solely on sexual orientation without taking into account other meaningful aspects of an individual's identity that may impact body image, such as age, gender, ethnicity and socioeconomic status. In reality, these multiple aspects of identity intersect in unanticipated and varied ways, depending on social context (e.g., home, community, church). Furthermore, much of the research on body image in GLBT communities uses a comparative framework that emphasizes difference between categories of people (e.g., gay, straight, bisexual) and assumes sameness within categories. GLBT subcultures need further examination to provide a better understanding of variability within GLBT communities. For example, "bears" (gay or bisexual men with heavyset bodies who reject normative masculine appearance ideals) may have more flexible ideas about attractiveness than others in the GLBT community (Morrison & McCutcheon, 2012).

Body image in GLBT communities is an understudied topic overall and especially among college students. In particular, very little research has been done with bisexual men and women, and transgender individuals are rarely, if ever, mentioned in the extant literature. Qualitative studies are needed to tease apart the complex and nuanced relationships between body image, sexual orientation and other aspects of identity that contribute to a person's overall sense of self. Researchers need to talk to gay, lesbian, bisexual and transgender college students to gain a deeper understanding of their body image-related perspectives and experiences as well as how their ideas about body image are influenced by campus culture and the degree to which they feel supported socially, emotionally and academically in their college environments.

The Physically Disabled

Studies of people with physical disabilities report a range of body image satisfaction within this population. In general, men and women with disabilities tend to internalize negative body image attitudes more so than their non-disabled counterparts (Nosek, Howland, Rintala, Young, & Chanpong, 2001; Romeo, Wanlass, & Arenas, 1993; Taleporos & McCabe, 2002; Taub, Fanflik, & McLorg, 2003). One study found that individuals with moderate and severe disabilities expressed greater body image dissatisfaction than those with mild or no disabilities (Taleporos & McCabe, 2005). Another study using in-depth individual interviews found that male and female participants felt increased acceptance of their bodies over time by focusing on their favorable physical attributes, embracing positive feedback and support from loved ones and coming to terms with their physical limitations (Taleporos & McCabe, 2002).

In terms of gender differences, disabled men reportedly express greater dissatisfaction with their lower bodies than women, specifically, loss of musculature in legs and abdominal weight gain (Dewis, 1989; Taleporos & McCabe, 2005). Further, men's body image satisfaction decreases more than women's with a greater need for assistance (Taleporos & McCabe, 2005). The authors suggest physical disability makes traditional masculine norms of strength, independence and muscularity less attainable, which negatively impacts body image among disabled men.

Research has found participation in sports and physical activity a mediating factor in body image anxiety among men and women with physical disabilities (Blinde & McCallister, 2007; Martin, 2009). Body image anxiety is concern about others devaluing one's body. Fear of being subjected to rude comments or staring may lead people with disabilities to try to hide their disability by covering up with loose-fitting clothing and/or avoiding exercising in public, for example. Studies such as those cited earlier suggest that engaging in physical activity may help people with disabilities see their bodies as a source of strength, thereby reducing body image anxiety. Another study found that among amputees, body image satisfaction increased for participants who were satisfied with the aesthetic and functional aspects of their prosthesis. For women, body image satisfaction was more closely tied to aesthetic aspects of the prosthesis than for men (Murray & Fox, 2002).

Overall, little is known about body image among disabled college students despite the fact that approximately 11% of undergraduate students nationwide report having a physical disability (U.S. Department of Education, 2015). Further, almost all of the current literature on this topic is based on survey research that reveals broad trends but offers little understanding of the everyday lived experience of disabled students. Ethnographic research on college students with physical disabilities could provide important insights into their experiences with the social, academic and physical environment of the campus. This information would, in turn, enable college administrators and practitioners to better support this group.

The Freshman 15

Many students are familiar with the widespread belief that incoming freshman gain about 15 pounds during their first year of college. The phenomenon is commonly referred to as the "freshman 15." In reality, studies cite weight increases among freshmen ranging from approximately 3.5 to 8 pounds with an average gain of about 4 pounds (Crombie, Ilich, Dutton, Panton, & Abood, 2009; Lloyd-Richardson, Bailey, Fava, & Wing, 2009; Vella-Zarb & Elgar, 2009). Very little research has been done examining weight fluctuation trends beyond that first year, though one study found weight gain continued into the sophomore year (Lloyd-Richardson et al., 2009), and others have found gains through the final year of college (Racette, Deusinger, Strube, Highstein, & Deusinger, 2008; Trainer et al., 2015). Weight gain among college students begins during the first semester, suggesting factors associated with the transition into college, such as access to junk food, staying up late and partying, play an important role (Gillen & Lefkowitz, 2011; Lloyd-Richardson et al., 2009).

Studies of gender differences in weight gain among college students have produced mixed results. For example, one study found men gained more weight than women during the first semester (Cluskey & Grobe, 2009), but other research has found no significant gender differences in weight gain during the freshman year (Hoffman, Policastro, Quick, & Lee, 2006; Holm-Denoma, Joiner, Vohs, & Heatherton, 2008). Race and ethnicity do not appear to be a factor in college weight gain; several studies have found no difference between White and ethnic minority students, including Latinos, African-Americans and Asians (Gillen & Lefkowitz, 2011; Hoffman et al., 2006).

Weight gain among college freshmen has been attributed to increased stress, changes in physical activity and eating habits, increased consumption of alcohol and living on campus (Economos, Hildebrandt, & Hyatt, 2008; Hoffman et al., 2006; Yoon, Kim, & Lee, 2014). Students in one qualitative study attributed freshman weight gain to availability of unhealthy food on campus and eating for reasons other than hunger, including boredom, stress while studying, alcohol consumption and socializing (Nelson, Kocos, Lytle, & Perry, 2009). Anthropologist Carole Counihan conducted qualitative research with college students and found that many associated food with love and comfort, prompting them to indulge in sweets and other junk foods to deal with emotional stress (Counihan, 1992). Another study found that weight gain was related to increased alcohol consumption among college men and increased workload in college women, highlighting the effects of stress and health-related behaviors on students (Economos et al., 2008). College women who lived on campus were found to consume more calories and mono-saturated fat and drink alcohol more frequently than those who lived off-campus, probably due to college meal plans offering calorie-dense, high-fat foods and increased opportunities to drink alcohol (Yoon et al., 2014). After a long night of drinking alcohol, students are hungry and indulge in foods that are readily available such as pizza or tacos, adding significantly to their caloric intake of the day.

Other reasons for weight gain among college students include negative experiences using campus recreation facilities, inclement weather, difficulty carving out time for exercise, lack of motivation and inadequate social support (Nelson et al., 2009). It is not uncommon for students who are overweight or obese to avoid going to a campus recreation center because of their discomfort with their body or fear of being seen in their exercise clothes. Many students report that the recreation center attracts only those who are already the most fit. One study drawing on in-depth interviews with 15 male and female college students revealed that 6 of the 7 who self-reported larger body size felt uncomfortable using the campus recreation center because they felt like they were being watched and judged by other students. In particular, they felt intimidated by the "male- and mirror-dominated weight room within the recreation center" (Trainer et al., 2015, p. 271). The authors of this study note that previous research suggests a fear of experiencing weight stigma discourages people from exercising. It is clear that making recreation centers feel like safe and welcoming spaces for students of all sizes is an imperative.

On the positive side, living on campus can confer benefits. For example, one study found that students living in residence halls walked more steps per day than their off-campus counterparts and were more likely to use the campus recreational facilities (Yoon et al., 2014). Residential facilities were further from the campus and classrooms than commuter parking lots, which encouraged more walking among those who lived on campus. Campus exercise facilities and intramural sports activities were also thought to be more accessible for residential students.

College preparedness might impact weight gain among college freshmen as well. One study, conducted among 390 college men and women in the Northeastern U.S. who identified as African American (32%), Latino (27%) and White (41%), found that those who received lower Scholastic Aptitude Test (SAT) scores were more likely to gain the "freshman 15" (Gillen & Lefkowitz, 2011). The authors suggest that students with lower SAT scores may be less academically prepared for college, which can lead to unhealthy eating behaviors related to stress. This study also found that students who gained weight during their first year in college were less involved in campus organizations. Students who participate in campus activities tend to feel a greater sense of community, which may reduce unhealthy eating associated with feelings of isolation (DeNeui, 2003; Gillen & Lefkowitz, 2011). It is clear that weight gain across the college years is connected to food consumption behaviors as well as body image. Additional qualitative research needs to be done exploring these intersections to help college practitioners more effectively support healthy body image-related choices and attitudes among students.

Fat Talk

"Fat talk," a term coined by anthropologist Mimi Nichter, refers to a social ritual, a way of being among female friends that involves making overt statements like "I'm so fat" to which the culturally appropriate response is "Oh no, you're not!" Fat talk is an expression of concern about one's weight but is also an attempt to solicit emotional support and reassurance from friends, demonstrate personal responsibility for one's body size and call attention to one's flaws before others do (Nichter, 2000). Fat talk has been framed as a dynamic and collaborative process in which weight and body image issues are negotiated between individuals (Arroyo & Harwood, 2012).

In recent years, psychologists have examined the frequency and effects of fat talk on women's body image and self-esteem. Research suggests fat talk as conversational banter is pervasive among college women and has become a norm on campus. Indeed, one study found that over 90% of respondents reported engaging in fat talk with their friends (Salk & Engeln-Maddox, 2011). What is particularly troubling is that students perceived engagement in fat talk as *more typical* than positive body image talk for average weight and overweight women (Barwick, Bazzini, Martz, Rocheleau, & Curtin, 2012).

Is fat talk "just" a form of everyday women's speech, or does it have a pernicious effect on women's sense of self? Some research has concluded that fat talk is a mechanism by which negative feelings about one's weight can become amplified into broader negative feelings about the self (Arroyo & Harwood, 2012). Indeed, survey research with college women conducted over a 2-week span found that fat talk predicted higher levels of depression and perceived socio-cultural pressures to be thin (Arroyo & Harwood, 2012). Further, several researchers have concluded that fat talk among college students is associated with body dissatisfaction and drive for thinness (Salk & Engeln-Maddox, 2011; Stice, Maxfield, & Wells, 2003). Although some studies suggest a correlation between fat talk and elevated eating pathology scores (Clarke, Murnen, & Smolak, 2010; Ousley, Cordero, & White, 2008), this relationship is complex and influenced by many factors, including social context and motivation (Salk & Engeln-Maddox, 2011; Warren, Holland, Billings, & Parker, 2012). For example, fat talk may be deployed more frequently if one's peers do it and if one wants to appear similar to their friends in terms of body image concerns. Additionally, complaining about one's body by saying "I'm so fat" can be used as a means to "level the playing field," making it clear that one does not feel better about their body than others (Nichter, 2000). In this way, fat talk engenders rapport and bonding in a social group.

Some research has shown that having a strong tendency to draw social comparisons with others directly predicts fat talk among college females (Corning & Gondoli, 2012). These researchers found that, as a woman's body image concerns increased, her likelihood of engaging in fat talk also increased. While this is perhaps unsurprising, these researchers found that even at low levels of body image concern, fat talk was robust. Sufficient studies with college students across the country have confirmed fat talk as a salient feature in the everyday life of college students.

Intervention Approaches: Fat Talk Free Week

In 2008, a national sorority, Delta Delta Delta (also known as Tri Delta) in collaboration with health researchers, designed and disseminated a social marketing campaign to increase awareness of fat talk and to challenge this normative discourse among women, as well as to change the focus among women from one's weight to positive health. To date, the program has been implemented in some colleges and universities around the country. During this 7-day campus program, information is provided to students to raise awareness of fat talk and its harmful effects and to promote positive body conversations as an alternative. Students are encouraged to sign an online pledge to end personal engagement with fat talk. There is also a media component entitled "Friends Don't Let Friends Fat Talk" that is displayed via posters, magnets and social media sites.

To the authors' knowledge, only one pilot evaluation has been conducted on this campaign (Garnett et al., 2014). Findings collected from a sample of 180 students on two college campuses revealed significant mean decreases in self fat talk, fat talk exposure among peers, comparison to others and body dissatisfaction following this campaign. Notably, at baseline over 50% of participants engaged in fat talk *almost always* or *often* compared to 34% who reported fat talk at follow-up. It should be noted, however, that although these initial results are promising, follow-up was conducted just two weeks after the program concluded. Follow-ups after 3 and 6 months would be valuable to determine effectiveness and to establish the half-life of this social marketing campaign.

Social Media and Body Image

The use of social media is pervasive among young adults with 95% of college students regularly using Facebook and 40% reporting that they check their site in excess of 6 times per day (Perrin, 2015). Facebook is particularly popular among young women, many of whom post "selfies" and images of their weekday and weekend activities, from mundane to risqué. With regard to body image, researchers have found a positive relationship between Facebook usage and body dissatisfaction, postulating that young adult women who are more active on social media have increased opportunity for comparisons with others, which in turn leads to dissatisfaction with self (Fardouly & Vartanian, 2015; Fardouly, Diedrichs, Vartanian, & Halliwell, 2015; Kimbrough, Guadagno, Muscanell, & Dill, 2013). For those college-aged women who engage in more appearance-related comparisons, spending time on Facebook was found to lead to a greater desire to change one's face, hair and skin-related features (Fardouly et al., 2015).

Facebook and other social media allow individuals to use filters and edit themselves to maximize satisfaction with their projected image before posting. The "edited self," be this in the form of Facebook posts or "selfies" on sites such as Tumblr, Snapchat or Instagram, is then posted and available to be evaluated and commented upon by others. Research among Australian teens has shown that, in pursuit of "likes," young people often display specific body parts, with females showing cleavage and males featuring six-pack abs (Albury, 2015).

Monitoring one's Facebook page for peer responses can be a frustrating and even traumatic experience for women in college. Not getting sufficient "likes" from a posted image of one's self can negatively affect self-esteem, leaving a young woman to question her attractiveness and overall self-worth. Indeed, experimental research has found that Facebook usage can put women in a more negative mood, perhaps because of increased comparison to others. While negative mood can also occur as a result of viewing the thin-body ideal shown in magazines, it has been suggested that comparing one's self to peers (as opposed to models) can provoke *more frustration* as a friend's body type may be seen as more attainable. While quantitative results on this topic have been mixed (Ridolfi et al., 2011), recent qualitative research among college women has found nuanced distinctions in social media viewing (Williamson, 2015). Specifically, "selfies" of friends were easier to dismiss ("Oh she doesn't really look like that—it's just a really good picture with good lighting"), whereas an attractive picture of a distant friend or classmate was harder to dismiss and led to heightened self-consciousness and a feeling of inferiority. In a similar vein, research among college students has found that the more friends people include on Facebook whom they do not know personally, the stronger the belief that others had better lives than themselves and that these others were "always happy" (Chou & Edge, 2012).

Some research has shown "fitspiration" images (often "selfies"), defined as images that are taken with the intention of showing off an especially fit or athletic body (particularly showcasing one's muscles), can foster dissatisfaction and frustration with one's body, especially among those whose body type does not match the portrayed ideal. While sometimes well-intended as a source of inspiration for others, these images have been criticized for perpetuating the notion that only one body type is healthy or that body shape should be the key factor in determining self-worth (Tiggemann & Zaccardo, 2015).

Facebook is the most popular use of media among young women and will probably remain so among college students for some time in the future (Tiggemann & Miller, 2010). Thus, it is important to recognize that young adults' digital practices of self-representation may impact body image. Future research is needed to provide a more thorough understanding of how social media is affecting college women and men in relation to body image. Media literacy interventions, which have highlighted the impact of traditional media on young women's body image, should be enhanced to address the idealized nature of the images and content uploaded to social media. College-aged women and men could benefit from education on the potential impact of social comparisons, "selfies" and surveillance of self and others on their own sense of self.

Conclusion

Research suggests that those who internalize mainstream body image ideals experience the greatest degree of body dissatisfaction (Fitzsimmons-Craft et al., 2012; Neighbors & Sobal, 2007). Body ideals are unachievable for the vast majority of young adults, especially in light of the realities of modern college life, which include junk food consumption, increasing anxieties and stress and behaviors associated with partying, such as drinking and smoking. Given the dissonance between idealized images and high rates of overweight and obesity on college campuses, it is not surprising that overweight college students experience the greatest degree of dissatisfaction with their weight and body shape when compared with other students (Neighbors & Sobal, 2007).

With overweight and obesity rates on the rise, college campuses are increasingly diverse in terms of body size and shape as well as other aspects of identity, including gender, sexuality, ethnicity and physical dis/ability. Additional research is needed to better understand how body image intersects with these different aspects of identity among college students. Programs that address body image concerns among particular populations, including ethnic minorities, GLBT students and students with disabilities are also increasingly important. Findings from body image research among college students presented in this chapter underscore the importance of recognizing diversity within and among groups.

Students embody multiple identities, which, together with their life experiences, shape their relationships with their bodies. Identity becomes even more complex at the college level as students experiment with different aspects of themselves. Thus, body image awareness and intervention strategies must both speak to a broad audience and communicate recognition of individual difference. Those who facilitate awareness and intervention strategies need to be trained to address diverse groups of students like the ones highlighted in this chapter. While all of the groups discussed, including men, women, ethnic minorities, LGBT students and individuals with disabilities, expressed body image concerns, their concerns manifested in different ways.

It is important that college professionals represent the diversity of the student population in intervention activities so that a variety of perspectives are voiced in efforts to promote healthy body image on campus. It is clear that a "one-size-fits-all" approach will not be effective in body image intervention programs. Involving students in the planning of such efforts is a useful strategy for developing programs that are user friendly and appeal to a wide range of students.

Professionals working on college campuses, whether in health services, counseling services, faculty, student affairs, administration or other roles, have an opportunity to frame messages about the importance of physical activity and healthy eating as a way to promote overall health and well-being rather than as a means for students to achieve body image goals. However, promotion of healthy lifestyle choices must also occur within a campus environment that nurtures healthy decision-making by offering mostly healthy foods and beverages and providing opportunities and facilities for students of all sizes to engage in physical activity without feeling scrutinized or criticized.

Media literacy classes that raise awareness about traditional and social media have been shown to be an effective strategy in improving body esteem among college students (Chambers & Alexander, 2007; Irving & Berel, 2001). Specifically, these studies suggest media literacy can result in increased skepticism about media images, reduced beliefs that images of models are real and greater satisfaction with the appearance of one's own body. Chambers and Alexander (2007) found that videos and imagery combined with traditional texts led to greater satisfaction with one's current body than articles alone. Although students who took the short-term media literacy class felt better about their bodies as a result, their body image ideals did not change. The authors concluded that, in order to achieve a change in body image ideology, the result of living in a media saturated environment that promotes a thin body ideal, more extensive media literacy programming would need to be provided.

Counter-messages that challenge dominant narratives are necessary to foster awareness of how powerful the media is in influencing our ideas about gendered body image and social norms, attitudes about fat people, food consumption choices and exercise practices. Media literacy efforts must emphasize health over beauty, encourage students to broaden their ideas about what it means to be attractive and address obesity stigma by showing how fat people are often negatively portrayed in movies and television and emphasizing the importance of treating people of all sizes with respect.

In addition to offering media literacy classes, expanding outreach by providing workshops to organized student groups on campus could be an effective way to reach a broader audience. Additionally, freshmen could be targeted for wellness workshops promoting strategies for healthy eating, regular physical activity and healthy ideas about body image via meetings in residence halls and during freshman orientation when they are captive audience members.

Research shows that even short-term, one-time media literacy classes can help students learn to think more critically about media images. However, changing body image ideology requires more extensive programming. Finding ways to integrate lessons from media literacy curricula into the day-to-day lives and conversations of young people could contribute to longer-term impacts, such as changing body image ideology. For example, training peer mentors who could lead residence hall discussions and encourage critical thinking about media images and initiate positive body image talk in daily conversation with friends could be an effective strategy for supporting healthy body image among college students. This strategy could also be an effective way to address body image issues among specific groups on campus (e.g., ethnic minorities, LGBT) as students from these different groups could be trained to talk about body image among their peers. It will also be important to evaluate activities and classes designed to promote healthy body image on campus in order to assess how well they are working and find ways to improve programming based on the feedback and needs of students.

References

Albury, K. (2015). Selfies, sexts and sneaky hats: Young people's understandings of gendered practices of self-representation. *International Journal of Communication, 9*, 12.

American College Health Association. (2015). *American College Health Association–National College Health Assessment II: Reference Group Executive Summary Spring 2015*. Hanover, MD: American College Health Association.

Arroyo, A., & Harwood, J. (2012). Exploring the causes and consequences of engaging in fat talk. *Journal of Applied Communication Research, 40*(2), 167–187.

Barwick, A., Bazzini, D. G., Martz, D. M., Rocheleau, C. A., & Curtin, L. A. (2012). Testing the norm to fat talk for women of varying size: What's weight got to do with it? *Body Image, 9*, 176–179.

Blinde, E. M., & McCallister, S. G. (2007). Women, disability, sport and physical fitness activity: The intersection of gender and disability dynamics. In J. O'Reilly, & S. K. Cahn (Eds.), *Women in Sports in the United States: A Documentary Reader* (pp. 131–138). Boston: Northeastern University Press.

Bordo, Susan. (2013). Not just "a White girl's thing": The changing face of food and body image problems. In C. Counihan, & P. Van Esterik (Eds.), *Food and Culture: A Reader* (3rd edition, pp. 265–275). New York: Routledge. Originally published in H. Malson and M. Burns, *Critical Feminist Approaches to Eating Dis/orders* (New York: Routledge, 2009).

Cash, T. F., & Pruzinsky, T. (Eds.). (2002). *Body Image: A Handbook of Theory, Research and Clinical Practice*. New York: The Guilford Press.

Chambers, K. L., & Alexander, S. M. (2007). Media literacy as an educational method for addressing college women's body image issues. *Education, 127*(4), 490.

Chernin, K. (1981). *The Obsession: Reflections on the Tyranny of Slenderness*. New York: Harper and Row.

Chou, H. T. G., & Edge, N. (2012). "They are happier and having better lives than I am": The impact of using Facebook on perceptions of others' lives. *Cyberpsychology, Behavior, and Social Networking, 15*(2), 117–121.

Clarke, P. M., Murnen, S. K., & Smolak, L. (2010). Development and psychometric evaluation of a quantitative measure of "fat talk." *Body Image, 7*(1), 1–7.

Cluskey, M., & Grobe, D. (2009). College weight gain and behavior transitions: Male and female differences. *Journal of the American Dietetic Association, 109*, 325–329.

Cogan, J. C. (1999). Lesbians walk the tightrope of beauty: Thin is in but femme is out. *Journal of Lesbian Studies, 3*, 77–89.

Corning, A. F., & Gondoli, D. M. (2012). Who is most likely to fat talk? A social comparison perspective. *Body Image, 9*(4), 528–531.

Counihan, C. (1992). Food rules in the United States: Individualism, control, and hierarchy. *Anthropological Quarterly, 65*(2), 55–66.

Crombie, A. P., Ilich, J. Z., Dutton, G. R., Panton, L. B., & Abood, D. A. (2009). The freshman weight gain phenomenon revisited. *Nutrition Reviews, 67*, 83–94.

Dakanalis, A., Zanetti, A. M., Riva, G., Colmegna, F., Volpato, C., Madeddu, F., & Clerici, M. (2015). Male body dissatisfaction and eating disorder symptomatology: Moderating variables among men. *Journal of Health Psychology, 20*(1), 80–90.

DeNeui, D.L.C. (2003). An investigation of first year college students' psychological sense of community on campus. *College Student Journal, 37*, 224–234.

Dewis, M. E. (1989). Spinal cord injured adolescents and young adults: The meaning of body changes. *Journal of Advanced Nursing, 14*, 389–396.

Economos, C. D., Hildebrandt, M. L., & Hyatt, R. R. (2008). College freshman stress and weight change: Differences by gender. *American Journal of Health Behavior, 32*(1), 16–25.

Fardouly, J., Diedrichs, P. C., Vartanian, L. R., & Halliwell, E. (2015). Social comparisons on social media: The impact of Facebook on young women's body image concerns and mood. *Body Image, 13*, 38–45.

Fardouly, J., & Vartanian, L. R. (2015). Negative comparisons about one's appearance mediate the relationship between Facebook usage and body image concerns. *Body Image, 12*, 82–88.

Fitzsimmons-Craft, E. E., Harney, M. B., Koehler, L. G., Danzi, L. E., Riddell, M. K., & Bardone-Cone, A. M. (2012). Explaining the relation between thin ideal internalization and body dissatisfaction among college women: The roles of social comparison and body surveillance. *Body Image, 9*, 43–49.

Garnett, B. R., Buelow, R., Franko, D. L., Becker, C., Rodgers, R. F., & Austin, S. B. (2014). The importance of campaign saliency as a predictor of attitude and behavior change: A pilot evaluation of social marketing campaign fat talk free week. *Health Communication, 29*(10), 984–995.

Gill, R., Henwood, K., & McLean, C. (2005). Body projects and the regulation of normative masculinity. *Body and Society, 11*(1), 37–62.

Gillen, M. M., & Lefkowitz, E. S. (2011). The "freshman 15": Trends and predictors in a sample of multiethnic men and women. *Eating Behaviors, 12*, 261–266.

Gillen, M. M., & Lefkowitz, E. S. (2012). Gender and racial/ethnic differences in body image development among college students. *Body Image, 9*, 126–130.

Gordon-Larsen, P., The, N. S., & Adair, L. S. (2010). Longitudinal trends in obesity in the United States from adolescence to the third decade of life. *Obesity, 18*(9), 1801–1804.

Greenhalgh, S. (2015). *Fat-Talk Nation: The Human Costs of American's War on Fat*. Ithaca: Cornell University Press.

Grogan, S., & Richards, H. (2002). Body image: Focus groups with boys and men. *Men and Masculinities, 4*(3), 219–232.

Hausmann, A., Mangweth, B., Walch, T., Rupp, C. I., & Pope, H. G. (2004). Body image dissatisfaction in gay versus heterosexual men: Is there really a difference? *The Journal of Clinical Psychiatry, 65*(11), 1555–1558.

Heatherton, T. F., Mahamedi, F., Striepe, M., Field, A. E., & Keel, P. K. (1997). A 10-year longitudinal study of body weight, dieting, and eating disorder symptoms. *Journal of Abnormal Psychology, 106*, 117–125.

Heffernan, K. (1999). Lesbians and the internalization of societal standards of weight and appearance. *Journal of Lesbian Studies, 3*, 121–127.

Herzog, D. B., Newman, K. L., & Warshaw, M. (1991). Body image dissatisfaction in homosexual and heterosexual males. *Journal of Nervous and Mental Disease, 179*, 356–359.

Herzog, D. B., Newman, K. L., Yeh, C. J., & Warshaw, M. (1992). Body image satisfaction in homosexual and heterosexual women. *International Journal of Eating Disorders, 11*, 391–396.

Hesse-Biber, S., Livingston, S., Ramirez, D., Barko, E. B., & Johnson, A. L. (2010). Racial identity and body image among black female college students attending predominantly white colleges. *Sex Roles, 63*, 697–711.

Hoffman, D. J., Policastro, P., Quick, V., & Lee, S. K. (2006). Changes in body weight and fat mass of men and women in the first year of college: A study of the "freshman 15." *Journal of American College Health, 55*, 41–45.

Holm-Denoma, J. M., Joiner, T. E., Vohs, K. D., & Heatherton, T. F. (2008). The "freshman fifteen" (the "freshman five" actually): Predictors and possible explanations. *Health Psychology, 27*, 53–59.

Irving, L. M., & Berel, S. R. (2001). Comparison of media literacy programs to strengthen college women's resistance to media images. *Psychology of Women Quarterly, 25*, 103.

Jacobi, L., & Cash, T. F. (1994). In pursuit of the perfect appearance: Discrepancies among self-ideal percepts of multiple physical attributes. *Journal of Applied Social Psychology, 24*(5), 379–396.

Kehler, M., & Atkinson, M. (Eds.). (2010). *Boys' Bodies: Speaking the Unspoken*. New York: Peter Lang Publishing.

Kimbrough, A. M., Guadagno, R. E., Muscanell, N. L., & Dill, J. (2013). Gender differences in mediated communication: Women connect more than do men. *Computers in Human Behavior, 29*(3), 896–900.

Leavy, P., & Hastings, L. (2010). Body image and sexual identity: An interview study with lesbian, bisexual, and heterosexual college-age women. *Electronic Journal of Human Sexuality, 13*. Retrieved from http://www.ejhs.org/volume13/bodyimage.htm

Lloyd-Richardson, E. E., Bailey, S., Fava, J. L., & Wing, R. (2009). A prospective study of weight gain during the college freshman and sophomore years. *Preventative Medicine, 48*, 256–261.

Ludwig, M. R., & Brownell, K. D. (1999). Lesbians, bisexual women, and body image: An investigation of gender roles and social group affiliation. *International Journal of Eating Disorders, 25*, 89–97.

Martin, C. E. (2007). *Perfect Girls, Starving Daughters: How the Quest for Perfections Is Harming Young Women*. New York: Penguin.

Martin, J. J. (2009). Social physique anxiety, body image, disability, and physical activity. In T. M. Robinson (Ed.), *Social Anxiety: Symptoms, Causes, and Techniques* (pp. 29–46). Hauppauge, NY: Nova Science Publishers.

McClure, S. (2012). Body image among African Americans. In T. Cash (Ed.), *Encyclopedia of Body Image and Human Appearance* (Volume I, pp. 89–94). London: Academic Press.

McClure, S. (2017). Symbolic body capital of an 'other' kind: African American females as a bracketed subunit in the calculus of female body valuation. In E. P. Anderson-Fye, & A. Brewis (Ed.), *Fat Planet: Obesity, Culture, and Symbolic Body Capital*. Santa Fe, NM: SAR Press; Albuquerque: University of New Mexico Press.

Morrison, T. G., & McCutcheon, J. M. (2012). Body image among gay, lesbian, and bisexual individuals. In T. Cash (Ed.), *Encyclopedia of Body Image and Human Appearance* (Volume I, pp. 103–107). London: Academic Press.

Murray, C. D., & Fox, J. (2002). Body image and prosthesis satisfaction in the lower limb amputee. *Disability and Rehabilitation, 24*, 925–931.

Neighbors, L. A., & Sobal, J. (2007). Prevalence and magnitude of body weight and shape dissatisfaction among university students. *Eating Behaviors, 8*(4), 429–439.

Nelson, M. C., Kocos, R., Lytle, L. A., & Perry, C. L. (2009). Understanding the perceived determinants of weight-related behaviors in late adolescence: A qualitative analysis among college youth. *Journal of Nutrition Education and Behavior, 41*, 287–292.

Nichter, Mimi. (2000). *Fat Talk: What Girls and Their Parents Say about Dieting*. Boston: Harvard University Press.

Nosek, M. A., Howland, C., Rintala, D. H., Young, M. E., & Chanpong, G. F. (2001). National study of women with physical disabilities. *Sexuality and Disability, 19*(1), 5–39.

Ousley, L., Cordero, E. D., & White, S. (2008). Fat talk among college students: How undergraduates communicate regarding food and body weight shape and appearance. *Eating Disorders: The Journal of Treatment & Prevention, 16*, 73–84.

Parker, S., Nichter, M., Nichter, M., Vuckovic, N., Sims, C., & Ritenbaugh, C. (1995). Body image and weight concerns among African American and White adolescent females: Differences that make a difference. *Human Organization, 54*(2), 103–114.

Perrin, Andrew. (2015). Social media usage: 2005–2015. *Pew Research Center*, October 8, 2015. Retrieved from http://www.pewinternet.org/2015/10/08/social-networking-usage-2005–2015/

Racette, S. B., Deusinger, S. S., Strube, M. J., Highstein, G. R., & Deusinger, R. H. (2008). Changes in weight and health behaviors from freshman through senior year of college. *Journal of Nutrition Education and Behavior, 40*, 39–42.

Ridolfi, D. R., Myers, T. A., Crowther, J. H., & Ciesla, J. A. (2011). Do appearance focused cognitive distortions moderate the relationship between social comparisons to peers and media images and body image disturbance? *Sex Roles, 65*(7–8), 491–505.

Romeo, A. J., Wanlass, R., & Arenas, S. (1993). A profile of psychosexual functioning in males following spinal cord injury. *Sexuality and Disability, 11*(4), 269–276.

Rubin, L., Fitts, M., & Becker, A. (2003). "Whatever feels good in my soul": Body ethics and aesthetics among African American and Latina women. *Culture, Medicine and Psychiatry, 27*, 49–75.

Ryan, T. A., & Morrison, T. G. (2009). Factors perceived to influence young Irish men's body image investment: A qualitative investigation. *International Journal of Men's Health, 8*(3), 213–234.

Salk, R. H., & Engeln-Maddox, R. (2011). If you're fat, then I'm humongous!: Frequency, content, and impact of fat talk among college women. *Psychology of Women Quarterly, 35*, 18–28.

Silberstein, L. R., Mishkind, M. E., Striegel-Moore, R. H., Timko, C., & Rodin, J. (1989). Men and their bodies: A comparison of homosexual and heterosexual men. *Psychosomatic Medicine, 51*, 337–346.

Stice, E., Maxfield, J., & Wells, T. (2003). Adverse effects of social pressure to be thin on young women: An experimental investigation of the effects of "fat talk." *International Journal of Eating Disorders, 34*, 108–117.

Striegel-Moore, R. H., & Franko, D. L. (2002). Body image issues among girls and women. In T. F. Cash, & T. Pruzinsky (Eds.), *Body Image: A Handbook of Theory, Research, and Clinical Practice* (pp. 183–191). New York: The Guilford Press.

Striegel-Moore, R. H., Tucker, N., & Hsu, J. (1990). Body image dissatisfaction and disordered eating in lesbian college students. *International Journal of Eating Disorders, 9*, 493–500.

Taleporos, G., & McCabe, M. P. (2002). Body image and physical disability-personal perspectives. *Social Science and Medicine, 54*, 971–980.

Taleporos, G., & McCabe, M. P. (2005). The relationship between the severity and duration of physical disability and body esteem. *Psychology and Health, 20*(5), 637–650.

Taub, D. E., Fanflik, P. L., & McLorg, P. A. (2003). Body image among women with physical disabilities: Internalization of norms and reactions to nonconformity. *Sociological Focus, 36*(2), 159–176.

Taylor, N. (2011). "Guys, she's humongous!" Gender and weight-based teasing in adolescence. *Journal of Adolescent Research, 26*(2), 178–199.

Taylor, N. (2015). *Schooled on Fat: What Teens Tell Us about Gender, Body Image, and Obesity*. New York and London: Routledge.

Thompson, J. K., & Cafri, G. (2007). *The Muscular Ideal: Psychological, Social and Medical Perspectives*. Washington, DC: American Psychological Association.

Tiggemann, M., & Miller, J. (2010). The Internet and adolescent girls' weight satisfaction and drive for thinness. *Sex Roles, 63*(1–2), 79–90.

Tiggemann, M., & Zaccardo, M. (2015). "Exercise to be fit, not skinny": The effect of fitspiration imagery on women's body image. *Body Image, 15*, 61–67.

Trainer, S., Brewis, A., Williams, D., & Chavez, J. R. (2015). Obese, fat, or "just big"? Young adult deployment of and reaction to weight terms. *Human Organization, 74*(3), 266–275.

U.S. Department of Education, National Center for Education Statistics. (2015). *Digest of Education Statistics, 2013 (NCES 2015–011), Table 311.10*. Retrieved from https://nces.ed.gov/fastfacts/display.asp?id=60

Vella-Zarb, R. A., & Elgar, F. J. (2009). The "freshman 5": A meta-analysis of weight gain the freshman year of college. *Journal of American College Health, 58*, 161–166.

Vohs, K. D., Heatherton, T. F., & Herrin, M. (2001). Disordered eating and the transition to college: A prospective study. *International Journal of Eating Disorders, 29*, 280–288.

Warren, C. S. (2014). Body area dissatisfaction in White, Black, and Latina female college students in the USA: An examination of racially salient appearance areas and ethnic identity. *Ethnic and Racial Studies, 37*(3), 537–556.

Warren, C. S., Holland, S., Billings, H., & Parker, A. (2012). The relationships between fat talk, body dissatisfaction, and drive for thinness: Perceived stress as a moderator. *Body Image, 9,* 358–364.

Watkins, J. A., Christie, C., & Chally, P. (2008). Relationship between body image and body mass index in college men. *Journal of American College Health, 57*(1), 95–99.

Wharton, C. M., Adams, T., & Hampl, J. S. (2008). Weight loss practices and body weight perceptions among US college students. *Journal of American College Health, 56*(5), 579–584.

Williamson, T. (2015). *Selfie Awareness: How Social Media Affects Body Image and Social Connectedness among Female Freshmen.* Honors Thesis, University of Arizona, School of Anthropology.

Yoon, A., Kim, K., & Lee, S. (2014). The effects of residence on the eating and exercise habits of college freshmen in US. *International Journal of Applied Sports Sciences, 26*(1), 1–10.

Part II
Social Wellness

3

Understanding Disability
The Psychological and Sociocultural Experience

M. DOLORES CIMINI

Introduction

During the past several decades, many doors to opportunity have been opened for individuals with disabilities in the areas of education and the world of work. In conjunction with such vast opportunities, an increasing number of students with physical, learning, cognitive and psychiatric disabilities are entering colleges and universities across the nation, making it critical for higher education professionals to have a solid understanding of the experience of disability and its impact within higher education settings.

To address this critical need, this chapter will provide higher education professionals with an overview of the research on disability, including a discussion of models of disability and the role of disability in the context of other identities a person may have. The chapter will outline nine core domains that student affairs professionals, faculty, staff and other professionals may examine to work most effectively with disabled students to support their success in college, graduate study and entry into the workforce.

What Is Disability?

Disability is a broad concept that encompasses a wide range of impairments, functional limitations and barriers to participation in community life (World Health Organization, 2001). Generally, disabilities are physical, mental and/ or sensory characteristics that affect a person's ability to engage in activities of daily life (U.S. Department of Health and Human Services, 2005). The Americans with Disabilities Act (ADA) Amendments Act of 2008 defines disability as a physical or mental impairment that substantially limits a major life activity, having a record of such impairment, or being regarded as having such impairment because of an actual or perceived physical or mental impairment. This definition is true even when the individual uses equipment designed to minimize the disability. Based on this definition, for example, a person with a hearing impairment that interferes with most social interactions would be considered as having a disability even if the use of a communication device such as a hearing aid or sign language interpreter significantly improves his or her ability to engage in conversations.

Models of Disability

The two oldest models of disability include the moral model and the biomedical model. The *moral model* views disability as an embodiment of evil, a punishment for a family member's or ancestor's transgression, a divine gift, fate or a test of faith and opportunity to overcome a challenge (Groce, 2005; Mackelprang & Salsgiver, 1999; Olkin, 1999b). Without realizing it, professionals or disabled individuals themselves may be affected by these deep-seated historical constructs in a way that influences their relationship. The *biomedical model* of disability views an individual's pathological condition or impairment as a medical problem that deviates from the norm (Gill, Kewman, & Brannon, 2003). Here, the focus is on the person's deficits and the elimination of the pathology or restoration of functional capacity. Holding this view may lead a professional or disabled individual to solely focus on the hope for a cure and to ignore how to move on with the tasks of life and adapt to challenges related to the disability.

Unlike these disability paradigms, the *social model* of disability conceptualizes disability as a product of the ongoing interaction between individuals and their environments (DePoy & Gilson, 2004; Gill et al., 2003; Hahn, 1999; LoBianco & Sheppard-Jones, 2007; Longmore, 1995; NIDRR, 1999; Smart, 2001; Smart & Smart, 2007). This model focuses on the dynamic interactions of the disabled person's individual characteristics (e.g., conditions, functional status, personal and social qualities) with the natural, built, cultural and social environments (NIDRR, 1999).

The social model helps us understand how environments may impede or facilitate individual functioning by erecting or removing barriers to full participation (Linton, 1998) while emphasizing social and functional accommodations. Within the social model, potential solutions to address barriers may include using universal design to create accessibility for everyone, allowing disabled individuals to make their own decisions, educating the public about disability issues and attitudes and enforcing laws to ensure equal access and protection (Olkin, 1999b; Smart, 2001). In this model, a higher education professional can facilitate a student's positive disability identity and self-advocacy skills or consult with others to ensure that the student has adequate accommodations, opportunities for participation in both academic and co-curricular activities and a voice in decision making.

The *functional model* of disability views disability as a social consequence of functional capacities and limitations (Chan, Gelman, Ditchman, Kim, & Chiu, 2009; Nagi, 1965; Smart, 2001). It assumes that the relationship between functioning and disability is best understood in the context of social and educational/occupational demands. For example, blindness may lead to a career-altering disability in an airline pilot but not in a teacher, psychologist or social worker. In this model, higher education professionals can facilitate a student's functional improvement and the development of strategies that compensate for limitations, given educational and other life demands and the support system that is in place for the student.

The World Health Organization's International Classification of Functioning, Disability, and Health (ICF) model of disability integrates the medical, social and functional dimensions and provides a positive, enablement-focused rather than disability-oriented framework. It views disability as restriction in participation in life activities and as an interactive construct (Peterson, 2005, 2001; WHO, 2001). The ICF assesses domains such as body function and structure, activity and participation, and personal and environmental factors such as access to transportation. In the ICF, functional limitations of impairment become disabling in the context of broader physical, social and attitudinal factors (Chan et al., 2009; Peterson, 2005; Schultz, Stowell, Feuerstein, & Gatchel, 2007).

Disability Awareness in the Context of Human Diversity

People with disabilities, like all people, have influences in their lives that contribute to their development, such as their culture, religion, family of origin, community, education, friends, significant others and co-workers. Such common influences may shape a person's unique disability experience. For instance, different parents of children with disabilities may convey very different messages about what it means to have a disability. One child may be protected from risk, while another is expected to tackle challenges. Similarly, a person with a disability who lives in a community that is inclusive of people with disabilities will likely have a more positive self-image than a person without such opportunities. Moreover, each person with a disability has a unique disability identity. A person with an apparent impairment may not necessarily identify as having a disability. Many deaf individuals believe they have a language barrier, not a disability. Other people with disabilities may see themselves as members of a disability community and culture that shares common experiences (e.g., Linton, 1998; Longmore, 1995).

The language that we use to describe disability can pose a challenge, especially because no one wants to offend another person or to appear to be insensitive. Disability culture advocates and disability studies scholars have challenged the rationale for and implications of exclusive person-first language use ("persons with disabilities"), promoting use of identity-first language (e.g., "disabled people"). One reasonable possibility is to use person-first and identity-first language interchangeably when talking about disability (Dunn & Andrews, 2015).

In summary, it is clear that there is rich theory and research available to help us understand the disability experience and its intersection with our multiple identities and the society in which we live. The next section describes how we can integrate this knowledge into practice as higher education professionals.

Working Effectively with Students with Disabilities in Higher Education Settings: Nine Key Strategies

No matter where we sit within the vast array of professions within higher education, it is critical for us to understand and be able to effectively respond to the needs and challenges presented by our students with disabilities. Individuals with disabilities are perhaps one of the most marginalized groups in American society, and national data indicate that the more advanced the higher education level, the fewer students with disabilities we see enrolled in these more advanced programs.

After people with disabilities complete their education, we can also expect that about 75% will be unemployed or underemployed.

Keeping this in mind, higher education professionals are in a unique role to help open doors to opportunity for students with disabilities by providing them with accepting, supportive and life-changing environments that help them thrive. Helping disabled students negotiate new environments and make necessary and appropriate accommodations and adaptations and empowering them to advocate for what they need and deserve through support and mentoring are all ways that professionals within colleges and universities can help reduce barriers in higher education and help students with disabilities succeed and excel as they prepare for work and life after college and graduate school.

There are a number of steps that higher education professionals can take to expand their knowledge about students with disabilities and make efforts toward inclusion and celebration of the diversity they contribute to the collegiate environment. The following nine domains can assist in our understanding of the disability experience.

1. Learn about Disability and Examine Your Own Attitudes Toward It

Research suggests that higher education professionals, as well as service providers across a variety of professions, often lack sufficient knowledge of disability issues and have limited experience in working with disabled people (Leigh, Powers, Vash, & Nettles, 2004; Strike, Skovholt, & Hummel, 2004). With little understanding of the disability experience, a professional may feel anxious, repulsed, fearful and vulnerable when working with a student who has disabilities (Olkin, 1999a).

Lack of experience may lead to unsubstantiated assumptions about students with disabilities. One such assumption is the "spread" effect in which a professional might assume that any person with a disability must have certain related characteristics (Livneh, 1982; Olkin, 1999b; Wright, 1983). For example, a professional might believe that a double amputee or who is blind or deaf has no interest in sex. A professional may also misattribute a psychological characteristic to having a disability, such as assuming that a person's shyness is attributable to having a sensory or motor loss without considering other explanations. Sometimes as well, professionals may engage in diagnostic overshadowing; this means over-emphasizing or mistakenly focusing on a person's disability while ignoring important aspects of one's life, such as life events, capabilities and strengths and other issues related to the person's presenting problems (Jopp & Keys, 2001; Kemp & Mallinckrodt, 1996; Mason, 2007; Reiss, Levitan, & Szyszko, 1982; White, Nichols, Cook, & Spengler, 1995). Conversely, professionals may under-emphasize disability-related concerns or even assume individuals use their disabilities as an excuse. Additionally, lack of familiarity with disability may influence how a professional perceives and works with the emotions that people with disabilities express. Disabled individuals often experience microaggressions and macroaggressions, including lack of accommodations, personal slights, insensitive behavior and discrimination. They may express feelings of sadness, anger and frustration about their disability experiences. A professional may perceive such expressions as a sign that a person has not adjusted to a disability, rather than as an emotional response to painful experiences (Olkin, 1999a; Vash & Crewe, 2004).

Self-examination and familiarity with disability-related issues are two ways to minimize biases, faulty assumptions and negative emotional reactions (Blotzer & Ruth, 1995; Olkin, 1999b: Vash & Crewe, 2004: Wilson, 2003). The following are practical suggestions for professionals to accomplish these two tasks:

a) Examine preconceptions, beliefs and emotional reactions towards persons with disabilities
b) Consider how disability-related and other life experiences, separately or together, might be related to the individual's current problems
c) Assess the person's strengths and weaknesses and incorporate them into interventions
d) Emphasize the person's possibilities rather than limitations in social, vocational and educational endeavors
e) Integrate disability-related case material and topics into professional discussions, study groups and seminars
f) Identify and contact professionals in the community who can provide consultation and/or supervision when needed
g) Become familiar with disability resources in one's institution or community; examples of resources might include a disability services office within a college or university, local centers for independent living, state assistive technology projects and advocacy groups

2. Know the Basics about Disability Laws

The goal of laws that protect the rights of disabled individuals is to ensure their freedom to participate fully in all aspects of society (Crawford, Jackson, & Godbey, 1991; Pullin, 2002). Three primary federal laws focus on disabled individuals: Sections 503 and 504 of the Rehabilitation Act of 1973, the Americans with Disabilities Act of 1990 and the Individuals with Disabilities Education Act (IDEA) (amended in 1997 and 2004).

Sections 503 and 504 of the Rehabilitation Act of 1973 (Public Law 93–122) prohibit disability-based discrimination by federally funded institutions, including colleges and universities.

The *Americans with Disabilities Act (ADA)* and the *ADA Amendments Act of 2008* provide comprehensive civil rights protection to disabled individuals. Title I prohibits discrimination in employment on the basis of a disability for qualified individuals who, with or without a reasonable accommodation, are able to perform the essential functions of an academic program or job. Institutions of higher education and employers are expected to provide reasonable accommodations for people with disabilities (Americans with Disabilities Act, 1990; Bruyère & O'Keeffe, 1994). The ADA's Title II prohibits excluding a qualified individual with a disability, by reason of such disability, from participating in or securing the benefits of services, programs or activities of a public entity (42 U.S.C § 12131 et seq.). This title includes all aspects of school programs, facilities and services, including college and university services. Title III promotes accessibility for "places of public accommodations" (42 U.S.C § 12181–12189 et seq.), and the Americans with Disabilities Act Accessibility Guidelines specify the standards such entities must meet. Title IV covers telephone and television access for people with hearing and speech disabilities. It requires telecommunication companies to provide interstate and intrastate relay service 24 hours a day, 7 days a week to individuals who use telecommunication devices for the deaf (47 U.S.C. § 201 et seq.). Title V includes miscellaneous provisions, such as the recovery of legal fees for successful proceedings pursuant to the act. It also prohibits coercing, threatening or retaliating against people with disabilities or those attempting to aid people with disabilities in asserting their rights under the ADA (42 U.S.C 12201 et seq.).

The *Individuals with Disabilities Education Act (IDEA)*, enacted in 1975 (Public Law 94–142) and amended in 1997 and 2004, mandates that each student suspected of having a disability be assessed in all relevant areas, which may include health, vision, hearing, social, emotional, general intelligence, academic status, adaptive behavior, communication and motor skills. If a student is determined to be eligible for special education services, a team identifies his or her strengths and needs, writes an individual education plan (IEP), develops specially designed instruction and establishes benchmarks to measure the student's academic and behavioral progress (National Council on Disability, 1996). Decisions are based on specific educational needs and performance on multiple measures. While IDEA does not apply directly to students enrolled in colleges and universities, some disabled college students may enter college with IEPs as documentation for accommodations.

These federal laws are enforced by the Department of Justice, which relies on the reports and complaints of disabled individuals in order to take action. The intersection of laws and institutional policies needs to be considered. In some cases, state laws may provide more protection than federal laws for citizens with disabilities.

3. Provide a Barrier-Free Physical and Communication Environment

To facilitate service delivery to students with disabilities, it is critical for higher education professionals to offer accessible environments. As an alternative, a student affairs professional, faculty member or other staff member may deliver services in a mutually convenient accessible location or refer the student to an appropriate professional with similar or greater qualifications whose workspace is more easily accessible. Accessibility includes the following:

- Accessible transportation services in order to get to a service delivery location on or off campus. An office location with nearby accessible public transportation enhances access to services for students with disabilities. However, at times, public transportation may entail effort, time and cost. It is also helpful to be aware of other accessible transportation options, such as wheelchair-accessible van services.

- Physical accessibility of a building in which services are delivered allows a student with a disability to enter and move about. Parking lots need designated parking; pathways to buildings need curb cuts; external and internal doorways should be wide enough for wheelchair access; doors need automatic openers or easily manipulated handles; bathrooms should be accessible; ramps and elevators should be available as needed; lighting should be adequate for people who rely on vision for orientation or communication, and there should be barrier-free access to safety exits (ADA Accessibility Guidelines, 2005; McClain, 2000; Olkin, 1999b).

- Communication access also accommodates various disabilities. Students with communication disabilities may require quiet environments and appropriate use of specific methods or technology to facilitate service delivery. Privacy concerns must be addressed, and communication choice respected. Students with speech disabilities may communicate with alternative or augmentative communication such as speech boards, speech synthesizers or computers. Students with hearing loss and/or speech disabilities may call or be called via telephone relay services, Internet relay services and video relay services. Each service uses operators sworn to confidentiality to facilitate communication (Federal Communications Commission, 2006). Other students may prefer to use cell phone text messaging and secure electronic mail or secure videophone or teletype equipment. Sign language interpreters or computers may be used for interpersonal communication during sessions. Students with cognitive disabilities or linguistic needs may require simplified, easy-to-understand documents, such as office paperwork (Wehmeyer, Smith, & Palmer, 2004). Students with visual disabilities may need documents in large print, as text files on disk or CD or in Braille (Lighthouse International, 2006; Olkin, 1999b).

4. Use Disability-Affirmative Language and Respectful Behavior

Whether we are aware of it or not, language may reveal our attitudes toward people with disabilities (Hauser, Maxwell-McCaw, Leigh, & Gutman, 2000). Excessively positive language (e.g., "heroic," "despite his disability" or references to "overcoming disability") or excessively negative language (e.g., "afflicted with," "suffering from" or "confined to a wheelchair") regarding people with disabilities focuses on stereotypes, rather than individuals (Katz, Hass, & Bailey, 1988). People-first language (e.g., "a woman with multiple sclerosis" or "a student who is depressed") is typically used to maximize focus on the person (APA, 2010). However, other individuals prefer disability identity-first language (Dunn & Andrews, 2015; National Federation of the Blind, 1993; Sinclair, 2007). It is important to avoid stereotypical or derogatory phrases that imply deficiency or inadequacy such as "deaf mute" since a deaf person is perfectly capable of intelligent communication (Gill et al., 2003; Khubchandani, 2001; Olkin, 2002).

Even though we assume that communication is mostly verbal (i.e., spoken, signed and written language), approximately 70–80% of communication is nonverbal, including facial and body language, personal mannerisms and style (Mehrabian, 1968a, 1968b). As such, it is a powerful tool for shaping the context of the student-professional dialogue. A professional who responds appropriately validates the student and minimizes possible bias and misperception about the student's disability (Khubchandani, 2001; Kosciulek, 1999; Olkin, 1999b). Examples of appropriate responses include sustaining eye contact with a student who uses a sign language interpreter to communicate, rather than shifting to the interpreter. You may also ask if a student who has a disability needs assistance with a task, but do not volunteer to help without permission. Rather, ask for specific instructions on how to be most helpful.

The way that a student with a disability speaks or moves his or her body may result in misunderstandings (Leigh & Brice, 2003; Wright, 1989). Facial expressions may be involuntary or can have multiple meanings, reflecting, not only possible underlying psychological issues, but often responses to issues such as chronic pain or memory problems. Sign language users rely on facial expressions to convey many nuances of meaning. Body language may reflect disability-related needs, such as frequently changing position in a wheelchair to prevent pressure sores or adjusting position in response to lighting or temperature changes. Verbal and non-verbal messages may conflict (Wright, 1987), and a professional can easily misinterpret the amount or type of presented emotion and undervalue or ignore a student's input.

Higher education professionals can enhance and accommodate their students' communication by acknowledging that it may take extra time to communicate effectively with a student who has a disability (Leigh & Brice, 2003). Sensitive higher education professionals will adjust their listening to the student's rate of speech. A student with a visual disability may need specific descriptions to enhance awareness of the immediate environment. It helps to articulate words clearly and pause between statements for students who have language processing disabilities. A professional can first say the name of a student with an attention disorder, make eye contact with the student and then proceed with verbal communication. Some students may use visual communication systems, speech synthesizers, other specialized approaches or sign language interpreters (Olkin, 1999b). The best way to facilitate effective service delivery is to ask the student about communication preferences and to consult experts for additional information, if needed. Such steps are critical to ensure accurate representation of the student in determining assessment outcomes and therapy procedures.

5. Understand the Roles of Individual, Social and Contextual Factors in the Lives of Persons with Disabilities

The presence of a disability reveals little about a person (Dunn & Dougherty, 2005; Olkin, 1999b). In addition to their own disability experiences and those experiences that they share with other people who have disabilities, disabled individuals have unique life histories. Becoming acquainted with the experience of living with a disability increases empathy and understanding and thus enhances the quality of service delivery.

Daily barriers are a common disability experience. A person who uses a wheelchair may need a friend to verify that a restaurant has an accessible bathroom before deciding to eat there. A student with a visual impairment must make arrangements to obtain an alternative format (e.g., large print, electronic version) of a textbook or secure the services of a reader. A person with a brain injury may need to use special mnemonic devices or procedures to complete errands or juggle course schedules and appointments. Such added challenges can be frustrating, exhausting and time consuming.

Disabled individuals are often more socially isolated than people without disabilities (Livneh & Antonak, 1997; Nosek, Howland, Rintala, Young, & Chanpong, 2001). They experience discrimination and stigmatization, which may contribute to feeling ostracized and different. Limited contact with other people who have disabilities in their families, at school or on the job exacerbates this experience of being different from others.

The dimensions of an individual's disability may influence personal experiences. For example, individuals with visible disabilities may feel marginalized. The stares and questions of others often make them feel as if they are on display (Olkin, 1999b). Individuals with invisible disabilities (e.g., learning disabilities, psychiatric disabilities, chronic pain) may have difficulty convincing others that they have a disability (Smart, 2001; Taylor & Epstein, 1999). Other aspects of disability that may affect a person's disability experience include functional capacities; energy levels; pain; age of onset; manner of onset (e.g., military trauma) and whether the disability is static, episodic or progressive.

The intersection between multiple identities impacts any person's experience and social opportunities. To work effectively with students who have disabilities, it is important for higher education professionals to consider how a student's disability-related issues interact with his or her other cultural and social identities and experiences. In the United States, African American, American Indian and Latina/o adults are more likely to have a disability than their non-Latina/o White and Asian/Pacific Islander counterparts (U.S. Census Bureau, 2000). Higher rates of disability in people of color are related to several factors, including disproportionately high levels of poverty and unemployment and disproportionately low levels of formal education and access to health care (e.g., Flack et al., 1995).

Different cultural, religious and underrepresented groups may attribute different causes and meanings to disability. Some believe disability is a gift or challenge while others see it as punishment or fate. Disability-related concepts such as independent living and autonomy may vary or not apply to different groups (Bryan, 2007; Lomay & Hinkebein, 2006; Uswatte & Elliott, 1997).

Women with disabilities report experiencing significant levels of depression and low self-esteem (Hughes, Nosek, & Robinson-Whelen, 2007; Niemeier, 2008; Nosek, Howland et al., 2001), both of which are associated with social isolation, quality of intimate relationships, pain and higher risk of abuse (Nosek, Howland et al., 2001). Men with disabilities may experience psychological distress from threats to sexual identity and masculinity and concerns about self-reliance, independence and employment (Marini, 2001).

Disabled individuals who are also lesbian, gay, bisexual or transgender face unique challenges. The larger society, and possibly their own families, are more likely to ostracize them (Olkin, 1999b), and like their heterosexual counterparts, they may have difficulty finding partners.

Many people with disabilities also live in poverty (Lustig & Strauser, 2007). Disability and poverty are reciprocal—disability increases the risk of poverty; being poor with decreased access to health care, transportation and assistive devices increases the risk of disability.

6. Support Resilience and Understand Disability-Specific Risk Factors

Higher education professionals can promote resilience and support the success of students with disabilities by involving them as partners in educational planning and by emphasizing student self-determination (Bannerman, Sheldon, Sherman, & Harchik, 1990; Gill et al., 2003). In order to promote student choice, a professional might train other service providers in active listening strategies or in ways to determine preferences of individuals with communication disabilities. Similarly, a higher education professional might provide organizational consultation and skills training to a student group on campus that is eager to advocate for social change (e.g., Hernandez, Balcazar, Keys, Hidalgo, & Rosen, 2006). Here, the higher education professional supports social networks to maximize the student's involvement in all appropriate decisions and ensures that the student receives appropriate services.

When working with disabled students, it is important for higher education professionals to understand that people with disabilities are often vulnerable to risk factors such as violence and abuse (Hassouneh-Phillips & Curry, 2002; Horner-Johnson & Drum, 2006; Hughes, 2005; Sullivan & Knutson, 1998). People with disabilities are at risk for abuse because they are perceived to be powerless, easily exploited and may be physically helpless, socially isolated, emotionally deprived and/or sexually naïve. Perpetrators have less risk of being discovered, and people with disabilities are less likely to be believed if they do report abuse or neglect (Andrews & Veronen, 1993; Nosek, Foley, Hughes, & Howland, 2001; Sobsey, 1994). Women with disabilities, especially older woman, are at elevated risk of abuse (Brownridge, 2006; Martin et al., 2006; Smith, 2008), and they experience abuse for longer durations than women without disabilities (Nosek, Foley et al., 2001). Although men with disabilities experience similar types of abuse, society often fails to recognize this (Saxton, McNeff, Powers, Curry, & Limont, 2006).

In addition to emotional, physical and sexual abuse, people with disabilities are vulnerable to disability-specific abuse. Violence against disabled individuals can include the withholding or excessive administration of medications, involuntary confinement, withholding or dismantling assistive equipment (e.g., wheelchairs) and withholding personal assistance for essential daily living activities such as eating and personal hygiene (Hughes, 2005; Nosek, Foley et al., 2001; Saxton et al., 2001). In institutional or community settings, disabled individuals who use personal assistance services experience a high incidence of neglect, verbal and/or physical abuse and financial exploitation at the hands of their assistants (Oktay & Tompkins, 2004; Powers, Curry, & Oschwald, 2002). Abuse and neglect may be the initial cause of a disability, may exacerbate an existing disability and may contribute to depression and other emotional difficulties (Kendall-Tackett, Lyon, Taliaferro, & Little, 2005; Mitchell & Buchele-Ash, 2000; Olkin, Abrams, Preston, & Kirshbaum, 2006).

Nosek, Hughes, and Taylor (2004) suggest that higher education professionals:

a) know the signs, symptoms and dynamics of disability-related violence, including the unique areas of vulnerability noted earlier;
b) screen for abuse and neglect and intervene appropriately;
c) document the history of abuse and neglect;
d) discuss safety planning with students, such as having a safe retreat, back-up personal care assistance and social supports;
e) maintain current contact information for accessible local domestic violence/ sexual assault programs and disability service providers (e.g., centers for independent living);
f) learn state mandatory reporting requirements for violence against people with disabilities including children, older adults and dependent adults and, when appropriate, involve the survivor throughout the reporting process; and
g) be aware of potential long-term consequences of reporting, including possible deterioration in quality of care and the need for accessible domestic violence shelters.

7. Become Familiar with the Role of Assistive Technology

Assistive technology is defined as equipment, products or systems that improve the functional capabilities of people with disabilities. Assistive technology includes ventilators that help people breathe; robotics to facilitate limb movement; vans with ramps or lifts for transporting people who use manual and power wheelchairs and scooters; baby-care equipment, adaptive eating utensils; hearing devices and text pagers; reading technology (e.g., Job Access with Speech [JAWS] computer screen-reading software; the Kurzweil Reader, which converts text to speech) for people with visual or learning disabilities and programs to simplify written language for individuals with neurodevelopmental disabilities (Vensand, Rogers, Tuleja, & DeMoss, 2000; Wehmeyer, 2006; Wehmeyer, Smith, & Davies, 2005). Computers with touch- and/or voice-activated programs and assistive devices allow users with communication disabilities to use a laser wand (usually attached to the person's head) to choose symbols or spell words, construct sentences and "speak" with a synthesized voice (Beukelman & Mirenda, 2005; Wehmeyer et al., 2005).

Though assistive devices help persons with disabilities in many ways, it is also important for higher education professionals to understand that this technology may have disadvantages as well. In addition to the opportunities it offers people with disabilities, it imposes the responsibilities of researching new technologies and assistive devices; learning to use new technology (Pell, Gillies, & Carss, 1999) and funding and maintaining equipment (NTFTD Report, 2004). Matching person with technology is best done by assessing milieu, personality and technology (e.g., Scherer, 2002, 2004). People may be frustrated when unavailable, unaffordable or inaccessible technology (e.g., some websites) limits their opportunities (Flowers, Bray, & Algozzine, 1999). While assistive technology may increase a person's independence, it may also pose a social barrier that makes the user seem too different or somehow deficient (Lupton & Seymour, 2000). Even when one person eagerly uses technology to attain objectives or enhance his life, another may find it overwhelming. Although not all people with disabilities and their families value, are interested in or are enthusiastic about assistive technology, understanding how it can affect a user's self-image, self-efficacy and coping and adaptation skills is important.

Finally, keeping up with the rapid advances in technology is difficult. Higher education professionals can check their state assistive technology center or refer their students to appropriate local assistive technology service providers or college and university disabled student services offices.

8. Integrate Disability-Affirmative Content into Health Promotion Work with a Focus on Self-Determination, Choice and Integration

Having a disability is not synonymous with disease or illness. In fact, disabled individuals often lead healthy and independent lives but may have a smaller margin of health and be at increased risk for preventable and/or manageable secondary health conditions that may affect their well-being and participation in community life (Kinne, Patrick, & Doyle, 2004; Pope & Tarlov, 1991; Ravesloot, Seekins, & White, 2005; WHO, 2001). These concerns include obesity, diabetes, high cholesterol and blood pressure, smoking and other health conditions.

Given that physical and mental health are intimately related and that health promotion programs and activities are conducted routinely on college campuses, higher education professionals can help students with disabilities understand how maintaining health and preventing secondary conditions can help them achieve life goals. For example, maintaining an exercise program and diet might prevent Type II diabetes and help students to obtain their goals more easily. When appropriate, higher education professionals can learn about their students' health issues, help their students understand the relationship between health and well-being and encourage students to practice healthy lifestyles that prevent both primary and secondary health problems (Gill & Brown, 2002; Heller, Hsieh, & Rimmer, 2002; Heller & Marks, 2002). Additionally, higher education professionals are encouraged to read the Surgeon General's "Call to Action to Improve the Health and Wellness of Persons with Disabilities" (2005), which states that professionals have a role in advancing the good health of persons with disabilities. The "Call to Action" discusses the challenges, strategies and research priorities required to help disabled individuals lead healthy and productive lives.

*9. Include a Focus on Disability within Faculty, Staff and Peer Leader
Training As Well As within Campus Climate Assessment*

Students with disabilities have the right to thrive within campus settings that are inclusive and that celebrate the diversity they bring to the university community. Higher education professionals, therefore, need to ensure that they are being inclusive of disability in the training opportunities created for faculty and staff members and peer leaders in a manner that helps these audiences understand the experience of disability. For example, disability topics can be included in diversity training courses, and disability can be integrated into experiential and interactive exercises that address human diversity. Beyond staff and peer leader training, it is critical to ensure that disability is a central component of programs and activities that educate all students about diversity in general and disability in particular.

In moving forward to create a culture of inclusion on college campuses, it is vital to evaluate how the construct of inclusiveness is being assessed and to ensure that the disability culture and experience on campus is being assessed. This means that college professionals should not be fearful or hesitant to ask about disability as a demographic variable on assessment tools, as long as the request for such information remains as voluntary as that for race/ethnicity, gender identity and sexual orientation and other variables; when possible, it would also be important to ensure the inclusion of students with disabilities in other forms of assessment, such as focus groups, qualitative interviews and assessment of the accessibility of campus environments and programs. Inclusion of assessment demographics related to disability as well as of the voices of students with disabilities can provide a clearer picture of the experiences of students and can offer avenues to better identify and address particular areas of need.

Conclusion

It is clear that higher education professionals are in a unique position to support the academic, work and life success of college students with disabilities in a number of critical ways. Higher education professionals can help disabled individuals become self-determining citizens of our diverse society. Second, higher education professionals may optimize the interaction between person and environment by collaborating with students who have disabilities and the systems that affect them. Third, higher education professionals may ensure validity, fairness and appropriateness of assessments by critically evaluating their own possible biases and ideas about disability. Fourth, rather than focusing on disability alone, higher education professionals can help the individual discover and balance personal strengths and limitations. Finally, higher education professionals can promote equal access and equal opportunity for persons with disabilities by using all appropriate accommodations in their procedures and practices. To achieve these goals, it is incumbent upon higher education professionals who work with students who have disabilities to maintain their skills and knowledge about disabilities by actively seeking disability-related training, education and consultation as needed.

References

ADA Accessibility Guidelines. (2005). Retrieved December 4, 2006, from www.access-board.gov/adaag/about/index.htm

American Psychological Association. (2010). *Publication Manual of the American Psychological Association*, 6th edition. Washington, DC: American Psychological Association.

Americans with Disabilities Act. (1990). Public Law 101–336. 42 U.S.C. § 12111, 12112.

Americans with Disabilities Act (ADA) Amendments Act of 2008. Public Law 110–325. 42 USCA § 12101.

Andrews, A. B., & Veronen, L. I. (1993). Special issue: Sexuality and disabilities: A guide for human services professionals. *Journal of Social Work and Human Sexuality, 8*, 137–159.

Bannerman, D. J., Sheldon, J. B., Sherman, J. A., & Harchik, A. E. (1990). Balancing the right to habilitation with the right to personal liberties: The rights of people with developmental disabilities to eat too many doughnuts and take a nap. *Journal of Applied Behavior Analysis, 23*(1), 79–89.

Beukelman, D. R., & Mirenda, P. (2005). *Augmentative & Alternative Communication: Supporting Children & Adults with Complex Communication Needs*, 3rd edition. Baltimore: Paul H. Brookes.

Blotzer, M. A., & Ruth, R. (1995). *Sometimes You Just Want to Feel Like a Human Being: Case Studies of Empowering Psychotherapy with People with Disabilities*. Baltimore: Paul H Brookes.

Brownridge, D. A. (2006). Partner violence against women with disabilities: Prevalence, risk, and explanations. *Violence Against Women, 12*(9), 805–822.

Bruyère, S. M., & O'Keeffe, J. (1994). *Implications of the Americans with Disabilities Act for Psychology*. Washington, DC: American Psychological Association.

Bryan, W. V. (2007). *Multicultural Aspects of Disabilities: A Guide to Understanding and Assisting Minorities in the Rehabilitation Process*, 2nd edition. Springfield, IL: Charles C. Thomas.

Chan, F., Gelman, J. S., Ditchman, N., Kim, J.-H., & Chiu, C.-Y. (2009). The World Health Organization ICF Model as a conceptual framework of disability. In F. Chan, E. Da Silva Cardoso, & J. A. Chronister (Eds.), *Understanding Psychosocial Adjustment to Chronic Illness and Disability* (pp. 23–50). New York: Springer Publishing Company.

Crawford, D. W., Jackson, E. L., & Godbey, G. (1991). A hierarchical model of leisure constraints. *Leisure Sciences, 13*(4), 309–320.

DePoy, E., & Gilson, S. F. (2004). *Rethinking Disability: Principles for Professional and Social Change*. Belmont, CA: Thomson/Brooks/Cole.

Dunn, D. S., & Andrews, E. (2015). Person-first and identity-first language: Developing psychologists' cultural competence using disability language. *American Psychologist, 70*, 255–264.

Dunn, D. S., & Dougherty, S. B. (2005). Prospects for a positive psychology of rehabilitation. *Rehabilitation Psychology, 50*(3), 305–311.

Federal Communications Commission. (2006). *What You Need to Know about TRS*. Retrieved December 7, 2006, from http://www.fcc.gov/cgb/dro/trs.html

Flack, J. M., Amaro, H., Jenkins, W., Kunitz, S., Levy, J., Mixon, M., & Yu, E. (1995). Panel I: Epidemiology of minority health. *Health Psychology, 14*(7), 592–600.

Flowers, C. P., Bray, M., & Algozzine, R. F. (1999). Accessibility of special education program home pages. *Journal of Special Education Technology, 14*(2), 21–26.

Gill, C. J., & Brown, A. (2002). Health and aging issues for women in their own voices. In P. H. Walsh, & T. Heller (Eds.), *Health of Women with Intellectual Disabilities* (pp. 139–153). Oxford, England: Blackwell. doi:10.1002/9780470776162.ch9

Gill, C. J., Kewman, D. G., & Brannon, R. W. (2003). Transforming psychological practice and society: Policies that reflect the new paradigm. *American Student Affairs Professional, 58*(4), 305–312.

Groce, N. (2005). Immigrants, disability, and rehabilitation. In J. Stone (Ed.), *Culture and Disability* (pp. 1–13). Thousand Oaks, CA: Sage.

Hahn, H. (1999). The political implications of disability definitions and data. In R. Marinelli, & A. E. Dell Orto (Eds.), *The Psychological and Social Impact of Disability* (4th edition, pp. 3–11). New York: Springer.

Hassouneh-Phillips, D., & Curry, M. A. (2002). Abuse of women with disabilities: State of the science. *Rehabilitation Counseling Bulletin, 45*(2), 96–104.

Hauser, P. C., Maxwell-McCaw, D. L., Leigh, I. W., & Gutman, V. A. (2000). Internship accessibility issues for deaf and hard-of-hearing applications: No cause for complacency. *Professional Psychology: Research and Practice, 31*(5), 569–574.

Heller, T., Hsieh, K., & Rimmer, J. (2002). Barriers and supports for exercise participation among adults with Down Syndrome. *Journal of Gerontological Social Work, 38*(1–2), 161–178.

Heller, T., & Marks, B. (2002). Health promotion for women with intellectual disabilities. In P. H. Walsh, & T. Heller (Eds.), *Health of Women with Intellectual Disabilities* (pp. 170–189). Oxford, England: Blackwell.

Hernandez, B., Balcazar, F., Keys, C., Hidalgo, M., & Rosen, J. (2006). Taking it to the streets: Ethnic minorities with disabilities seek community inclusion. *Journal of the Community Development Society, 37*(3), 13–25. doi:10.1080/15575330.2006.10383104

Horner-Johnson, W., & Drum, C. E. (2006). Prevalence of maltreatment of people with intellectual disabilities: A review of recently published research. *Mental Retardation and Developmental Disabilities Research Reviews, 12*(1), 57–69.

Hughes, R. B. (2005). Violence against women with disabilities: Urgent call for action. *The Community Student Affairs Professional, 38*, 28–30.

Hughes, R. B., Nosek, M. A., & Robinson-Whelen, S. (2007). Correlates of depression in rural women with physical disabilities. *Journal of Obstetric, Gynecologic, & Neonatal Nursing: Clinical Scholarship for the Care of Women, Childbearing Families, & Newborns, 36*(1), 105–114.

Jopp, D. A., & Keys, C. B. (2001). Diagnostic overshadowing reviewed and reconsidered. *American Journal on Mental Retardation, 106*(5), 416–433.

Katz, I., Hass, R. G., & Bailey, J. (1988). Attitudinal ambivalence and behavior toward people with disabilities. In H. E. Yuker (Ed.), *Attitudes toward Persons with Disabilities* (pp. 47–57). New York: Springer.

Kemp, N. T., & Mallinckrodt, B. (1996). Impact of professional training on case conceptualization of students with a disability. *Professional Psychology: Research and Practice, 27*(4), 378–385.

Kendall-Tackett, K., Lyon, T., Taliaferro, G., & Little, L. (2005). Why child maltreatment researchers should include children's disability status in their maltreatment studies. *Child Abuse & Neglect, 29*(2), 147–151.

Khubchandani, A. M. (2001). *Enhancing Your Interactions with People with Disabilities*. Washington, DC: American Psychological Association.

Kinne, S., Patrick, D. L., & Doyle, D. L. (2004). Prevalence of secondary conditions among people with disabilities. *American Journal of Public Health, 94*, 443–445.

Kosciulek, J. F. (1999). The consumer-directed theory of empowerment. *Rehabilitation Counseling Bulletin, 42*(3), 196–213.

Leigh, I. W., & Brice, P. J. (2003). The visible and the invisible. In J. D. Robinson, & L. James (Eds.), *Diversity in Human Interactions: The Tapestry of America* (pp. 175–194). New York: Oxford University Press.

Leigh, I. W., Powers, L., Vash, C., & Nettles, R. (2004). Survey of psychological services to students with disabilities: The need for awareness. *Rehabilitation Psychology, 49*(1), 48–54.

Lighthouse International. (2006). *Big Type Is Best for Aging Baby Boomers: A Case for Universal Graphic Design*. Retrieved December 7, 2006, from http://www.lighthouse.org/about/accessibility/bigtype_boomers.htm

Linton, S. (1998). *Claiming Disability: Knowledge and Identity*. New York: New York University Press.

Livneh, H. (1982). On the origins of negative attitudes toward people with disabilities. *Rehabilitation Literature, 43*(11–12), 338–347.

Livneh, H., & Antonak, R. F. (1997). *Psychosocial Adaptation to Chronic Illness and Disability*. Gaithersburg, MD: Aspen Publishers.

LoBianco, A. F., & Sheppard-Jones, K. (2007). Perceptions of disability as related to medical and social factors. *Journal of Applied Social Psychology, 37*(1), 1–13.

Lomay, V. T., & Hinkebein, J. H. (2006). Cultural considerations when providing rehabilitation services to American Indians. *Rehabilitation Psychology, 51*(1), 36–42.

Longmore, P. K. (1995). Medical decision making and people with disabilities: A clash of cultures. *Journal of Law, Medicine, and Ethics, 23*(1), 82–87.

Lupton, D., & Seymour, W. (2000). Technology, selfhood and physical disability. *Social Science & Medicine, 50*(12), 1851–1862.

Lustig, D. C., & Strauser, D. R. (2007). Casual relationships between poverty and disability. *Rehabilitation Counseling Bulletin, 50*(4), 194–202.

Mackelprang, R. W., & Salsgiver, R. O. (1999). *Disability: A Diversity Model Approach in Human Service Practice.* Pacific Grove, CA: Brooks/Cole.

Marini, I. (2001). Cross-cultural counseling issues of males who sustain a disability. *Journal of Applied Rehabilitation Counseling, 32*, 36–41.

Martin, S. L., Rey, N., Serte-Alvarez, D., Kepper, L. L., Meracco, R. E., & Prickers, P. A. (2006). Physical and sexual assault of women with disabilities. *Violence Against Women, 12*, 823–837.

Mason, J. (2007). The provision of psychological therapy to people with intellectual disabilities: An investigation into some of the relevant factors. *Journal of Intellectual Disability Research, 51*(3), 244–249.

McClain, L. (2000). Shopping center wheelchair accessibility: Ongoing advocacy to implement the Americans with Disabilities Act of 1990. *Public Health Nursing, 17*(3), 178–186.

Mehrabian, A. (1968a). Inference of attitudes from the posture, orientation, and distance of a communicator. *Journal of Consulting and Clinical Psychology, 32*(3), 296–308.

Mehrabian, A. (1968b). Relationship of attitude to seated posture, orientation, and distance. *Journal of Personality and Social Psychology, 10*(1), 26–30.

Mitchell, L. M., & Buchele-Ash, A. (2000). Abuse and neglect of disabled individuals: Building protective supports through public policy. *Journal of Disability Policy Studies, 10*(2), 225–243.

Nagi, S. Z. (1965). Some conceptual issues in disability and rehabilitation. In M. Sussman (Ed.), *Sociology and Rehabilitation* (pp. 133–136). Washington, DC: American Sociological Association.

National Council on Disability. (1996). *Improving the Implementation of the Disabled Individuals Education Act: Making Schools Work for All of America's Children* [Electronic Version]. Retrieved from http://www.ncd.gov/newsroom/publications/1996/96school.htm

National Federation of the Blind. (1993). *Resolution 93–01.* Retrieved October 29, 2009, from http://nfb.org/legacy/convent/resol93.htm

National Institute on Disability, Research, and Rehabilitation. (1999). *NIDRR Long-Range Plan 1999–2003.* Retrieved November 1, 2009, from http://www.ed.gov/rschstat/research/pubs/nidrr-lrp-99-03.doc

National Task Force on Technology and Disability. (2004). *Within Our Reach: Findings and Recommendations of the National Task Force on Technology and Disability.* Jackson, MI: Colonial Press.

Niemeier, J. P. (2008). Unique aspects of women's emotional responses to disability. *Disability and Rehabilitation, 30*, 166–173.

Nosek, M. A., Foley, C. C., Hughes, R. B., & Howland, C. A. (2001). Vulnerabilities for abuse among women with disabilities. *Sexuality and Disability, 19*(3), 177–189.

Nosek, M. A., Howland, C., Rintala, D. H., Young, M. E., & Chanpong, G. F. (2001). National study of women with physical disabilities: Final report. *Sexuality and Disability, 19*(1), 5–40.

Nosek, M. A., Hughes, R. B., & Taylor, H. B. (2004). Violence against women with disabilities: The role of physicians in filling the treatment gap. In S. L. Welner, & F. Haseltine (Eds.), *Welner's Guide to the Care of Women with Disabilities* (pp. 333–345). Philadelphia: Lippincott, Williams, and Wilkins.

Oktay, J. S., & Tompkins, C. J. (2004). Personal assistance providers' mistreatment of disabled adults. *Health and Social Work, 29*(3), 177–189.

Olkin, R. (1999a). The personal, professional and political when students have disabilities. *Women & Therapy, 22*(2), 87–103.

Olkin, R. (1999b). *What Psychotherapists Should Know about Disability.* New York: Guilford Press.

Olkin, R. (2002). Could you hold the door for me? Including disability in diversity. *Cultural Diversity & Ethnic Minority Psychology, 8*(2), 130–137.

Olkin, R., Abrams, K., Preston, P., & Kirshbaum, M. (2006). Comparison of parents with and without disabilities raising teens: Information from the NHIS and two national surveys. *Rehabilitation Psychology, 51*(1), 43–49.

Pell, S. D., Gillies, R. M., & Carss, M. (1999). Use of assistive technology by people with physical disabilities in Australia. *Disability & Rehabilitation, 21*(2), 56–60.

Peterson, D. B. (2005). International Classification of Functioning, Disability and Health: An introduction for rehabilitation higher education professionals. *Rehabilitation Psychology, 50*(2), 105–112.

Pope, A. M., & Tarlov, A. R. (1991). *Disability in America: Toward a National Agenda for Prevention*. Washington, DC: National Academy Press.

Powers, L. E., Curry, M. A., & Oschwald, M. (2002). Barriers and strategies in addressing abuses: A survey of disabled women's experiences. *Journal of Rehabilitation, 68*, 4–13.

Public Law 93–122. (1973). *United States Code, Section 504 of the Rehabilitation Act, 29 U.S.C. ' 794*.

Public Law 94–142. (1997). *Individuals with Disabilities Education Act 2004, 20 U.S.C. §§ 1400 et. seq.*

Pullin, D. (2002). Testing disabled individuals: Reconciling social science and social policy. In R. B. Ekstrom, & D. Smith (Eds.), *Assessing Disabled Individuals in Educational, Employment, and Counseling Settings* (pp. 11–31). Washington, DC: American Psychological Association.

Ravesloot, C., Seekins, T., & White, G. (2005). Living well with a disability health promotion intervention: Improved health status for consumers and lower costs for health care policymakers. *Rehabilitation Psychology, 50*(3), 239–245.

Reiss, S., Levitan, G. W., & Szyszko, J. (1982). Emotional disturbance and mental retardation: Diagnostic overshadowing. *American Journal of Mental Deficiency, 86*(6), 567–574.

Saxton, M., Curry, M. A., Powers, L. E., Maley, S., Eckels, K., & Gross, J. (2001). 'Bring my scooter so I can leave you': A study of disabled women handling abuse by personal assistance providers. *Violence Against Women, 7*(4), 393–417.

Saxton, M., McNeff, E., Powers, L., Curry, M., & Limont, M. (2006). We are all little John Waynes: A study of disabled men's experience of abuse by personal assistants. *The Journal of Rehabilitation, 72*, 3–13.

Scherer, M. J. (Ed.). (2002). *Assistive Technology: Matching Device and Consumer for Successful Rehabilitation*. Washington, DC: American Psychological Association.

Scherer, M. J. (2004). *Connecting to Learn: Educational and Assistive Technology for People with Disabilities*. Washington, DC: American Psychological Association.

Schultz, I. Z., Stowell, A. W., Feuerstein, M., & Gatchel, R. J. (2007). Models of return to work for musculoskeletal disorders. *Journal of Occupational Rehabilitation, 17*, 327–352.

Sinclair, J. (2007). *Why I Dislike "Person First" Language*. Retrieved October 29, 2009, from http://www.cafemom.com/journals/read/436505/

Smart, J. (2001). *Disability, Society, and the Individual*. Austin, TX: Pro-Ed.

Smart, J. E., & Smart, D. W. (2007). Models of disability: Implications for the counseling profession. In A. E. Dell Orto, & P. W. Power (Eds.), *The Psychological and Social Impact of Illness and Disability* (5th edition, pp. 75–100). New York: Springer.

Smith, D. L. (2008). Disability, gender, and intimate partner violence: Relationships from the behavioral risk factor. *Disability and Sexuality, 26*, 15–28.

Sobsey, R. (1994). *Violence and Abuse in the Lives of People with Disabilities: The End of Silent Acceptance?* Baltimore: Paul H. Brookes.

Strike, D. L., Skovholt, T. M., & Hummel, T. J. (2004). Mental health professionals' disability competence: Measuring self-awareness, perceived knowledge, and perceived skills. *Rehabilitation Psychology, 49*(4), 321–327.

Sullivan, P. M., & Knutson, J. F. (1998). The association between child maltreatment and disabilities in a hospital-based epidemiological study. *Child Abuse & Neglect, 22*(4), 271–288.

Taylor, S., & Epstein, R. (1999). *Living with a Hidden Disability*. Oakland, CA: New Harbinger Publications.

U.S. Census Bureau. (2000). *Census 2000 Summary File (SF 3)—Sample Data*. Retrieved August 22, 2006, from http://factfinder.census.gov/servlet/QTTableSF3_U_QTP21&-ds_name=DEC_2000_SF3_U

U.S. Department of Health and Human Services. (2005). *The Surgeon General's Call to Action to Improve the Health and Wellness of Persons with Disabilities*. Retrieved from http://www.surgeongeneral.gov/library/disabilities/

Uswatte, G., & Elliott, T. R. (1997). Ethnic and minority issues in rehabilitation psychology. *Rehabilitation Psychology, 42*(1), 61–71.

Vash, C. L., & Crewe, N. M. (2004). *Psychology of Disability*, 2nd edition. New York: Springer.

Vensand, K., Rogers, J., Tuleja, C., & DeMoss, A. (2000). *Adaptive Baby Care Equipment: Guidelines, Prototypes and Resources*. Berkeley, CA: The Looking Glass.

Wehmeyer, M. L. (2006). Universal design for learning, access to the general education curriculum and students with mild mental retardation. *Exceptionality, 14*(4), 225–235.

Wehmeyer, M. L., Smith, S. J., & Davies, D. (2005). Technology use and students with intellectual disability: Universal design for all students. In D. Edyburn, K. Higgins, & R. Boone (Eds.), *Handbook of Special Education Technology Research and Practice* (pp. 309–323). Whitefish Bay, WI: Knowledge by Design.

Wehmeyer, M. L., Smith, S. J., & Palmer, S. B. (2004). International review of research in mental retardation. In D. K. Davies, & S. E. Stock (Eds.), *Technology Use and People with Mental Retardation* (pp. 291–337). San Diego, CA: Elsevier Academic Press.

White, M. J., Nichols, C. N., Cook, R. S., & Spengler, P. M. (1995). Diagnostic overshadowing and mental retardation: A meta-analysis. *American Journal on Mental Retardation, 100*(3), 293–298.

Wilson, S. (2003). *Disability, Counseling, and Psychotherapy*. London: Palgrave.

World Health Organization. (2001). *The World Health Report—Mental Health: New Understanding, New Hope*. Geneva: World Health Organization.

Wright, B. A. (1983). *Physical Disability—A Psychosocial Approach*, 2nd edition. New York: Harper Collins.

Wright, B. A. (1987). Human dignity and professional self-monitoring. *Journal of Applied Rehabilitation Counseling, 18*(4), 12–14.

Wright, G. (1989). The miscommunication of nonverbal behavior of persons with physical disabilities and the implications for vocational assessment. *Vocational Evaluation & Work Adjustment Bulletin, 22*(4), 147–150.

4

Sexual Violence
Changing the Trajectory
KAREN S. MOSES

Introduction

National surveys of college students indicate that as many as 1 in 4 women and 1 in 16 men experience attempted and/or completed sexual assault while undergraduates in college (Cantor et al., 2015; Fisher, Cullen, & Turner, 2000; Krebs, Lindquist, Warner, Fisher, & Martin, 2007). These data have not improved in the past 15 years despite efforts to reduce risk and perpetration of sexual violence among this population. College students are considered at high risk for experiencing sexual violence, due to many factors within the environment. In recent years, national attention to improve safety and reduce risk among college students has contributed to enhanced efforts for prevention, response, policy and enforcement of sexual violence by colleges and universities.

Sexual violence is a societal issue being played out at college campuses. Professionals in higher education settings, whether based in student affairs, teaching, research, academic support or other settings, have the opportunity to influence students' college experience and their future lives. Information and skills that students learn in college, that contribute to safety and well-being, can have a ripple effect that benefits their families, communities and workplaces. This chapter offers a primer to create a campus climate that reduces the incidence of sexual violence and builds healthy relationships within the community of students, faculty and staff.

The first part of this chapter reviews key definitions, data and important facts and provides a brief description of current regulations influencing education, prevention, response, policy and enforcement regarding sexual violence in college. The second part of this chapter identifies methods for developing, implementing and evaluating an effective plan for sexual violence prevention among college students. The purpose is to provide a general understanding of the problem of campus sexual violence and to provide tools to change the trajectory such that sexual violence among college students is reduced meaningfully and that students can live and learn in an environment safe from sexual assault and abuse.

Definitions

Sexual violence describes a wide range of behaviors that involve sexual touch and/ or penetration that is performed without consent. In order to best understand what sexual violence includes, it is important to have a good working definition for consent.

Definitions for sexual consent vary; however, the primary characteristics included in the definition are similar. Sexual consent must be clearly given, meaning the desire to engage in any sexual activity must be communicated by the involved persons. Lack of a clear "yes," or silence, cannot be interpreted as consent. Sexual consent must be voluntary. Sex is not owed as an exchange for goods or services: acceptance of gifts, dinner, good grades, promotions and other benefits does not equal consent. Sex achieved through force, intimidation or coercion is assault. Sexual consent must be mutual, meaning that the involved parties have a say in whether various acts of sex are going to take place. Sexual consent must be active, meaning that communication about consent is ongoing and that partners check in with each other to make sure consent is still present. Consent given for a previous sexual encounter does not indicate consent for future encounters. Someone who is passed out or asleep cannot give consent. Someone who is under the influence of alcohol or drugs may not be able to give consent, depending on their level of intoxication. Someone who is under the age of 18 and those who are cognitively impaired cannot give consent.

The notion of affirmative consent has been taking hold in recent years. This takes sexual consent beyond the "no means no" standard to a "yes means yes" standard. In other words, all parties engaging in sexual activity together must affirm their consent through words or actions. Affirmative consent requires communication about engaging in sex up front, checking in with a partner to make sure she or he is in agreement about whether and how sex together is occurring and proceeding. California and New York state legislatures have passed laws requiring affirmative consent to be the standard for consent used by colleges and universities, and over 800 colleges use affirmative consent as the standard in sexual assault policies (Gray, 2014; Zaino, 2015).

Definitions of sexual consent help to clarify what consent means. However, these definitions include words such as "sex" and "sexual activity" without defining them. This could be problematic, as it assumes that there is agreement among the student population on the meaning of these terms. In fact, several studies have reported considerable variability in how college students define sex and what they consider sexual activities (Byers, Henderson, & Hobson, 2009; Gute, Eshbaugh, & Wiersma, 2008; Hans & Kimberly, 2011; Peterson & Muehlenhard, 2007; Sewell & Strassberg, 2015). Thus, it may be necessary for institutions to define sex and sexual activity to promote a more objective understanding of the definitions of consent, sexual violence and sexual misconduct.

Sexual assault includes rape (sexual penetration orally, anally or vaginally without consent); acquaintance rape (rape perpetrated by someone the victim knows or has met) and any unwanted sexual contact. Sexual violence includes a wide range of actions including sexual touch, harassment and assault that take place without consent. Intimate partner violence refers to physical, sexual or psychological harm committed by a current or former relationship partner or spouse. Intimate partner violence includes domestic violence, dating violence and stalking. Stalking refers to a pattern of repeated unwanted attention and contact that causes the victim concern or fear for their own safety or the safety of others. Intimate partner violence, its prevention and response overlap considerably with sexual violence. Definitions of sexual misconduct, sexual violence and consent vary from institution to institution, as do definitions for intimate partner violence, dating violence and stalking. It is important to become familiar with the definitions used by each specific college or university and to stay up-to-date with federal, state and local definitions, laws and ordinances.

Magnitude of the Problem

The proportion of college students who experience sexual violence has not changed much in the past 15 years. Over 15 years ago, a study completed for the National Institute of Justice found that 4.9% of college women surveyed (n = 4,446) had experienced attempted or completed rape during the past year (Fisher et al., 2000). The authors of the study estimated that between 20–25% (1 in 4 or 1 in 5) of female undergraduates will experience attempted or completed rape during their college years (Fisher et al., 2000). Another study prepared for the National Institute of Justice in 2007 (n = 5,446) found that 19.8% (about 1 in 5) of female college seniors surveyed had experienced completed non-consensual sexual contact by force or incapacitation (by alcohol or drugs) since entering college (Krebs et al., 2007). A recent 2015 survey commissioned by the Association of American Universities (AAU) (n = 150,072) found that 27.2% (about 1 in 4) of female college senior respondents had experienced unwanted sexual contact by force or incapacitation since entering college (Cantor et al., 2015). Authors explain that the higher rates among the AAU survey respondents can be attributed to the higher rate of non-consensual sexual touching found in their study (Cantor et al., 2015).

The American College Health Association–National College Health Assessment-II (ACHA-NCHA-II) provides national survey data annually for incidents of attempted and completed sexual assault. Table 4.1 provides data on the incidence of attempted and/or completed sexual assault and on non-consensual sexual touching, from the spring administration of the survey for the years 2010 to 2015. Spring 2010 data indicate that 3.3% of female students and 1.0% of male students experienced attempted or completed sexual assault during the past 12 months (American College Health Association, 2014). In spring 2015, that proportion had increased slightly to 4.4% of female students and 1.2% of male students (American College Health Association, November 20, 2015). Incidents of non-consensual sexual touching also increased slightly from 7.4% among female students and 3.5% among male students in spring 2010, to 9.8% among female students and 3.9% among male students in spring 2015 (American College Health Association, 2014; November 20, 2015). These data provide evidence that sexual violence among college students is increasing despite sustained national attention to this issue over the past several years.

Sexual violence can take a significant emotional toll on the victim. Victims may experience depression, anxiety, sleep disturbances, symptoms of post-traumatic stress disorder and other emotional/psychological symptoms (Centers for Disease Control and Prevention, 2015). This is sufficient reason to take action to prevent sexual violence from occurring. However, there are also academic implications.

TABLE 4.1 Proportion of the ACHA-NCHA-II National Reference Group who Experienced Attempted and/or Completed Sexual Intercourse and Non-consensual Sexual Touching in the Past 12 Months

In the past 12 months, experienced:	2010 (n = 95,712, 139 schools)	2011 (n = 105,781, 129 schools)	2012 (n = 99,666, 141 schools)	2013 (n = 123,078, 153 schools)	2014 (n = 79,266, 140 schools)	2015 (n = 93,034, 108 schools)
Attempted or completed sexual penetration (oral, anal, vaginal) without consent:						
Female	3.3	3.4	3.4	3.4	4.2	4.4
Male	1.0	1.0	0.9	1.2	1.1	1.2
Sexual touching without consent:						
Female	7.4	7.4	7.5	7.1	8.9	9.8
Male	3.5	3.1	3.0	3.2	3.3	3.9

Data from the ACHA-NCHA-II indicate sexual assault poses a serious barrier to academic performance. Among students surveyed from spring 2010 to 2015, between 12.5% to 17.9% of those who reported having experienced sexual assault during the previous 12 months indicated their belief that this resulted in a serious academic impact: They received a lower grade in a course, an incomplete or dropped course or experienced a significant disruption in thesis, dissertation or practicum work (American College Health Association, 2014; September 9, 2015; November 20, 2015). This places sexual assault among the top 6 serious academic impediments of the 30 examined on the ACHA-NCHA-II in spring 2015. As a comparison, other impediments in the top six serious academic impediments in spring 2015 include anxiety, attention deficit hyperactivity disorder, chronic health problems, depression and pregnancy (American College Health Association, November 20, 2015).

Who Are the Victims?

As Table 4.1 shows, a greater proportion of female college students report experiencing sexual violence than do male college students. This is consistent with data on sexual violence whether the victim is in college or not. Nineteen percent (19.0%) of undergraduate college women in the Campus Sexual Assault Study had experienced attempted or completed sexual assault since entering college, compared to 6.1% of undergraduate college men (Krebs et al., 2007). According to the AAU Climate Survey, 26.1% of senior females experienced sexual contact involving penetration or sexual touching as a result of physical force or incapacitation since entering college, compared to 6.3% of senior males (Cantor et al., 2015). Looking beyond the campus, the United States National Crime Victimization Survey data indicate that between 2010 and 2014, 84.2% of adult respondents who reported they had experienced rape or sexual assault were female (Bureau of Justice, 2015).

The AAU Climate Survey found additional groups of students at risk for sexual violence to include those who identify as transgender, genderqueer or nonconforming; questioning or not listed; lesbian, gay, bisexual, asexual or questioning and disabled (Cantor et al., 2015). Additionally, a greater proportion of freshmen experienced sexual violence than did undergraduates, and a greater proportion of undergraduate students experienced sexual violence than did graduate students (Cantor et al., 2015). In addition, the College Sexual Assault Study found sorority membership, having multiple sexual partners, attending off-campus parties, prior sexual violence victimization and alcohol use were associated with sexual assault (Krebs et al., 2007).

Who Are the Perpetrators?

In a 2011 national survey addressing sexual and intimate partner violence, female victims of sexual violence reported primarily male perpetrators: An estimated 99.0% reported male perpetrators of rape and 94.7% reported male perpetrators for other forms of sexual violence (Breiding et al., 2014). The majority of male victims of rape reported male perpetrators (79.3%), whereas females were more often the perpetrators of other forms of sexual violence reported by male victims (Breiding et al., 2014). Fisher et al. (2000) found that, in about 90% of attempted and completed sexual assaults reported by female college students, the victim and perpetrator know each other, and nearly half take place on a date. Similarly, Krebs et al. (2007) found that victims of incapacitated sexual assault reported the perpetrator was a friend (35.4%), an acquaintance (33.9%), a classmate or fellow student (27.1%) or a dating partner or spouse (18.5%) and that, in nearly 1 in 5 cases, college student victims of forced or incapacitated sexual assault were on a date with their assailant. Other perpetrator characteristics noted in the Campus Sexual Assault Study for forced and incapacitated sexual assault include fraternity membership (14.3% forced vs. 27.5% incapacitated), alcohol use prior to the incident (unknown for forced vs. 70.1% incapacitated) or White racial identity (57.1% forced vs. 79.9% incapacitated) (Krebs et al., 2007).

Although the majority of perpetrators are men, clearly not all men are sexual predators. Studies of college men indicate that between 5.9%–16% had engaged in behavior that met the criteria for attempted or completed rape, and 6.0%–30% had engaged in behavior that met the criteria for sexual assault (Abbey & McAuslan, 2004; Gidycz, Warkentin, & Orchowski, 2007; Lisak & Miller, 2002; Thompson,

Swartout, & Koss, 2013; Voller & Long, 2010). While these numbers suggest a disturbing proportion of the male college student population has committed rape and other acts of sexual violence, by far, the majority of college men have not committed such acts.

Surveys vs. Reports of Sexual Violence

Reports of sexual violence received by the police and the campus conduct office do not accurately represent the magnitude of the problem. The Campus Sexual Assault Study found that 12.9% of students who experienced forced sexual assault and 2.1% of students who experienced incapacitated sexual assault reported the incident to the police or campus security (Krebs et al., 2007). Usually a college or university will have a small number of reports of sexual violence each year, whereas the same institution may learn through confidential surveys of their students that about 2–4% of female students and 0.5–1.5% of male students annually have experienced attempted or completed sexual assault within the past 12 months (American College Health Association, 2014; September 9, 2015; November 20, 2015). These numbers can be staggering when accounting for enrollment size. For example, 3% of 10,000 is 300. At an institution with 10,000 female students, about 300 will have experienced attempted or completed sexual assault within the last 12 months. In contrast, the same institution may have received reports of 10–20 sexual assaults through the conduct office or campus security/police. Why the difference?

There are several reasons why the number of case reports varies so dramatically from the number of survey responses. Most victims of sexual assault in college know their attacker. This creates challenges that the victim must overcome in order to report their experience to the authorities. Some internal dialogue may include "Whose side will my friends take?" "I don't want to get my friend in trouble" or "Maybe it's my fault in some way (didn't say a verbal 'no,' gave wrong signals, got too drunk)." Imagine how hard it might be to make a report of sexual assault about someone with whom a student has socialized or who has been thought of previously as a friend.

Some victims initially do not recognize their experience as sexual assault. They may mistakenly believe that sexual assault must include physical violence or force. They may not have learned that consent for sex must come without coercion. They may have been impaired by alcohol or drugs, thus unable to give consent for sex. They may explain away their experience as their own fault for not saying "no" more clearly or blame themselves for doing something to lead on their assailant.

Additionally, victims may not want to talk about their experience; it is very difficult to describe a traumatic sexual assault experience over and over again to various authorities and support services. This is the basis of a term used to describe the process of reporting and reliving the experience of sexual violence: re-victimizing the victim. Furthermore, some students are aware that the system can be slow to process their complaint. Ultimately, reports to the police rarely result in criminal charges against their attacker. The potential for not getting results may make it seem not worth the effort of reporting.

It is natural for friends, family and first responders to encourage a victim to make a police report or to report the incident to campus authorities. The student has been harmed. A crime has been committed. There is an alleged perpetrator at large who could inflict harm on other members of the student community. However, it is very important to ensure that it is the victim's choice to make a report; it is the victim's right to control what happened to his or her body that was violated through an act or acts of sexual violence. Therefore, a college professional's actions and words should empower a victim to become a survivor who makes her or his own decisions about what actions to take next. It is vital to present options for support, reporting and services that could benefit the survivor and then to let that person decide which actions to take.

At the same time, it is important that incidents of sexual assault and other forms of sexual violence are reported to police and/or campus authorities. For many perpetrators, the current incident is not likely to be their first or their last act of sexual violence. One way to stop sexual violence is to prevent a perpetrator from repeating the offense with other victims. Educating victims about the benefits and challenges of reporting an experience of sexual violence can help them to make an informed decision on how to proceed. In this context, it is important to balance the needs of the victim for safety, healing and empowerment with the needs of the community for safety. Many institutions have developed processes for victims and witnesses to make anonymous reports so that they can report their experience on their own terms, while taking steps to make the perpetrator accountable for his or her actions.

Regulations

The *Clery Act* was established in 1990 following the rape and murder of Lehigh University student, Jeanne Clery, in her residence hall by another student in 1986. The Clery Act requires all colleges and universities that receive federal funding to inform the public about crime on campus and in the surrounding area, and of their efforts to improve campus safety, through a publically accessible annual security report. Within this report, institutions must outline specific policies and procedures such as dissemination of timely warnings; emergency notifications; options for survivors of sexual, domestic and dating violence and stalking and campus crime-reporting processes (Clery Center for Security on Campus, 2015b).

Additionally, the Clery Act requires that institutions provide survivors of sexual assault, domestic violence, dating violence and stalking with options such as changes to their academic, transportation, living or working situations and assisting them with notifying local law enforcement, if the victim/survivor chooses to do so (Clery Center for Security on Campus, 2015a). It also addresses the rights of both parties in campus disciplinary processes pertaining to these acts of violence.

The campus security report includes data about crimes from campus security and police, local police and campus disciplinary offices. Data is also included from various campus partners such as women's centers and violence prevention programs, as these offices may receive reports from their clients that were not made to other offices. Student services professionals may be involved in providing data or assistance with the preparation of the annual security report. All faculty and staff should review the annual security report and become familiar with trends in crime data for their institution.

To learn more about the Clery Act, visit the Clery Center for Security on Campus at http://clerycenter.org/. The U.S. Department of Education's Campus Safety and Security Data Analysis Cutting Tool (http://ope.ed.gov/security/) makes it possible to compare campus crime statistics for institutions across the nation, allowing prospective students and their parents to view the campus crime data from institutions they are considering attending (U.S. Department of Education, 2015). This tool is designed to make it easier for families to consider campus security and safety in their decision on which school to attend.

The *Campus Sexual Violence Elimination (SaVE) Act* is included in the 2013 reauthorization of the *Violence Against Women Act*. The Campus SaVE Act requires colleges and universities to include a broader range of incidents in their annual security report than was previously required for the Clery Report: domestic and dating violence and stalking in addition to acquaintance rape and sexual assault. Under this act, institutions must guarantee victims enhanced rights, provide for standards in institutional conduct proceedings and provide campuswide prevention education programming across required topics (Violence Against Women Reauthorization Act of 2013, 2013).

Title IX protects people from discrimination based on sex in education programs or activities that receive federal financial assistance (U.S. Department of Labor, 2015). Title IX falls under the civil rights laws and is enforced through the Office for Civil Rights (U.S. Department of Education, Office for Civil Rights, 2015). A *Dear Colleague Letter* published in April 2011 by the Office for Civil Rights brought significant change in how Title IX is implemented in institutions of higher education (U.S. Department of Education, Office for Civil Rights, 2011). This letter specifies that sexual harassment of students, including acts of sexual violence, are forms of sexual discrimination prohibited by Title IX.

The *Dear Colleague Letter* outlines schools' obligations to respond to acts of sexual harassment and sexual violence, discusses proactive efforts schools can take to prevent sexual violence and provides examples of remedies and enforcement strategies for responding to sexual violence (U.S. Department of Education, Office for Civil Rights, 2011). The *Dear Colleague Letter* resulted in interest, training and activities; changes in policies and procedures; assignment of Title IX coordinators and deputy coordinators and heightened attention to prevention. Student services personnel should be aware of their institution's policies for responding to disclosures of sexual harassment and sexual violence, how to provide appropriate support for students who have had these experiences and what to do or where to find information should an incident or situation be observed by or reported to them.

Prevention of Sexual Violence

The Centers for Disease Control and Prevention (CDC) identifies sexual violence as a public health issue and addresses sexual violence through primary prevention methods and interventions that aim to reduce sexual violence at the population level, such as for the entire campus, rather than by just influencing individual health or safety (Centers for Disease Control and Prevention, 2014). It is widely recognized that sexual violence is a complex issue influenced by multiple factors and that it affects individuals and communities. This type of problem lends itself to the use of the socio-ecological approach.

Socio-Ecological Approach

The socio-ecological approach focuses on population- and individual-level risk and protective factors across multiple dimensions of the environment or "ecology" in which a problem exists. The CDC uses a four-level social-ecological model to address sexual violence prevention. This framework serves as a guide to help campus planning teams think beyond individual risk reduction strategies and develop a comprehensive plan to prevent sexual violence that addresses behavioral norms, beliefs, policy and social systems that together create the conditions that lead to sexual violence (Centers for Disease Control and Prevention, 2004).

The socio-ecological model described by the National Association of Student Personnel Administrators (NASPA) incorporates dimensions specific to the campus environment and serves as a useful planning tool for institutions of higher education (National Association of Student Personnel Administrators, 2004). The NASPA model considers risk and protective factors influenced by characteristics of the individual, the physical setting, the human aggregate, the organization and the social climate or surrounding community. The following are examples of factors influencing sexual violence that fall within each dimension of the NASPA socio-ecological model.

- Individual factors (characteristics of the individual)—gender, first-year freshman, high-risk drinking, drug use, attitudes and beliefs that support sexual violence, past history of sexual assault
- Physical setting factors (characteristics of the physical setting)—proximity to local drinking establishments and parties where alcohol is served, proximity to liquor stores and access to alcohol
- Human aggregate factors (characteristics of the various groups represented)— unhealthy group norms around drinking, sexual expectations, peer pressure, limited peer support for bystander intervention
- Organizational factors (characteristics of the institution)—lack of policies defining sexual misconduct, lack of enforcement of policies, inadequately trained resident assistants/security officers, limited budget allocated for sexual violence prevention, limited awareness by faculty and professional staff of how to incorporate prevention into their work

- Social climate/surrounding community factors (characteristics of the surrounding community)—lack of local enforcement and prosecution by local authorities, limited training among bartenders and serving staff on how to identify and reduce risk among patrons

When using the socio-ecological model to develop a comprehensive plan to reduce sexual violence among students, the campus planning group considers risk and protective factors within each dimension. Planning centers around identification of priority risk and protective factors and use of evidence-based and theory-based approaches to reduce risk and/or advance protection. For example, studies indicate high-risk drinking is an individual risk for both perpetration and victimization (Abbey, 2008; Krebs et al., 2007). The college campus physical setting is often surrounded by drinking establishments. There may be particular groups within the human aggregate who host alcohol parties yet do not take action to reduce risk of sexual violence at social events. Perhaps campus policy or local statutes about underage drinking are not clearly articulated to new students, thus resulting in weak compliance and increased risk of sexual violence associated with drinking. These observations framed within the socio-ecological model could result in a plan to address high-risk drinking as a way to reduce sexual violence risk.

Another example: It could be that the individual student does not feel comfortable in the role of active bystander. There may be a perception that peer support (human aggregate) for stepping up to prevent potential harm is lacking or that the social norm on campus or in an individual's reference group is to stay out of other people's business. The institution may not have identified bystander intervention as a skill to promote. Faculty and staff may not understand their role in mentoring and role modeling bystander action. The social climate and laws may make it difficult to intervene due to concerns about liability, whether real or perceived. These observations could result in a plan to strengthen bystander intervention skills, establish a normative expectation that students care and intervene when someone is in harm's way, train faculty and staff to model active bystander behaviors and form partnerships with local bars to engage staff in bystander intervention and support for active bystanders in their places of business.

One advantage of using the socio-ecological model is that it facilitates development of a comprehensive plan that includes action across the multiple dimensions, or areas of influence, within the model. The socio-ecological model serves as a tool for the planning group to use to understand the interplay between the multiple dimensions, identify priority risks they will address, determine protective factors that already exist within the individual and the environment, consider which groups to target for education and training, discuss which policies and procedures to establish and determine how to partner with the surrounding community on the issues identified.

Primary Prevention, Risk Reduction and Outreach

Prevention strategies span the continuum from before the problem takes root to the onset of symptoms to avoidance of harm due to the symptoms that have emerged. Primary prevention aims to stop a problem before it starts. Secondary prevention aims to reduce risk or the impact of the problem once symptoms are evident. Tertiary prevention aims to reduce the impact of an illness or injury, once it has taken place.

When applied to sexual violence, primary prevention means preventing the initial perpetration of sexual violence (Centers for Disease Control and Prevention, 2014). Interventions intended to impact knowledge, attitudes and behaviors that address the root causes of sexual violence contribute to its primary prevention. Such interventions could include education and skill building sessions focused on healthy relationships, sexual wellness, communication, asking for and giving consent, interrupting oppressive words and actions to build a climate of respect, as well as fostering healthy student norms for these skills and values (Perry, 2005).

Secondary prevention of sexual violence addresses risk and protective factors that influence the potential for victimization (Centers for Disease Control and Prevention, 2014). These interventions aim to reduce risk and empower individuals and groups to take action to reduce the likelihood that they or their peers will experience sexual violence. Such interventions include personal safety tips, self-defense classes, action steps to stop sexual violence when it is already in progress or likely to occur, strategies to protect a drink and other self and community protection strategies. Laws, policies and enforcement against acts of sexual violence can also reduce risk under the umbrella of secondary prevention.

In the case of sexual violence, tertiary prevention helps to reduce subsequent risk after an incident. This type of prevention helps individuals and communities reduce the risk that sexual violence will be perpetrated again by the assailant or experienced again by the victim.

Outreach and awareness programs describe sexual violence and its impact on survivors and the community and may be used within the context of primary, secondary or tertiary prevention. These interventions provide information about sexual violence, its impact on survivors and the community, what to do in when someone you know experiences sexual violence and promote campus and community victim resources. Such interventions focus on raising awareness about the magnitude of the problem and its root causes and provide resources for more information and support (Perry, 2005). Outreach and awareness programs can motivate participants to engage in additional learning opportunities leading to greater potential for individual and collective knowledge, attitude and behavior change.

A comprehensive plan incorporates strategies across the prevention continuum with a focus on primary prevention. Just as with heart health, it is clear that, the earlier in the continuum that successful prevention occurs, the better the outcomes for individuals and communities. Using this heart model, a comprehensive program would facilitate physical activity and healthy eating habits among children and youth (primary prevention); provide prescription medicines for high cholesterol, diabetes and high blood pressure to reduce risk (secondary prevention) and teach community members to call 9–1–1 if someone is observed having a heart attack (tertiary prevention).

Universal, Selective and Indicated

A comprehensive plan to reduce the incidence of sexual violence accounts for the various influences across the socio-ecological model to determine what strategies to implement across the continuum of prevention, as well as to identify which groups will receive what interventions. Universal, selective and indicated refer to the group the intervention aims to impact (Centers for Disease Control and Prevention, 2014).

A universal approach to campus sexual violence prevention targets the general student population, regardless of risk. An example of a universal approach used by some colleges and universities is requiring online sexual violence education for all incoming freshmen. Selective approaches are directed to those at elevated risk for sexual violence perpetration or victimization; since students referred to the dean of students for a violation of the campus alcohol policy may be at heightened risk for experiencing or perpetrating sexual violence, an appropriate selective approach could be an alcohol education program that includes an exploration of the connections between alcohol and sexual violence risk. Indicated approaches address students who have already experienced or perpetrated sexual violence. A self-defense class designed to empower victims to protect themselves and to build their confidence following an attack would be an indicated approach as would mandated counseling sessions for those found responsible for sexual misconduct.

Prevention Education Requirements

It is important to meet the prevention requirements set forth by law, as well as to be responsive to and appropriate for the specific needs of the institution and the student body. The *Dear Colleague Letter* provides a general guide for prevention. However, the Campus SaVE Act requires specific educational components to be covered. Specifically, the SaVE Act requires colleges and universities to provide programming that addresses sexual violence, which includes rape, acquaintance rape, domestic and dating violence, sexual assault and stalking. Programs must include primary prevention and awareness programs for all incoming students and new employees, as well as ongoing prevention and awareness programs for students and faculty (Violence Against Women Reauthorization Act of 2013, 2013).

The SaVE Act further requires primary and ongoing prevention and awareness programs to include:

1. A statement that the institution prohibits these acts of sexual violence
2. The definition of domestic violence, dating violence, sexual assault and stalking for the appropriate jurisdiction
3. The definition of consent in reference to sexual activity for the appropriate jurisdiction
4. Safe and positive options for bystander intervention in such instances
5. Information on risk reduction to recognize warning signs of abusive behavior and how to avoid potential attacks

There are many ways in which to provide this information. Colleges and universities can use an online module or course to meet these requirements. Such programs are scalable to the institution's enrollment numbers and can help ensure that the educational requirements are met. It is important to look closely at each program to determine whether the information and format are a good fit with the overall plan and approach of the institution. Information on whether the program has produced short-term and/or sustained change in knowledge, attitudes, behavior intentions and behaviors leading to a reduction in rates of sexual violence among student participants should influence selection. Having students review the products can provide insight on how students receive the educational approach and whether the education is a good fit for the institutional culture.

How Can We Ensure That Campus Prevention Efforts Will Be Effective?

If campus personnel are serious about sexual violence prevention, it is vital to go beyond meeting the minimum education requirements and ensure that the methods used actually result in meaningful change. A starting place to find evidence-based methods is to review the literature to see what may work to change behavior among college students. Several studies shed light on what works with college students.

A meta-analysis of 69 college sexual violence prevention program evaluation studies suggests that interventions for college students are more effective when they are longer, presented by professionals, include content addressing risk reduction and gender-role socialization or provide information and discuss myths and facts about sexual assault (Anderson & Whiston, 2005). Researchers note that these results are limited in that most published evaluation studies measure knowledge and/or attitudes immediately following the intervention, with positive results. Fewer studies assess behavioral intentions or behavior change in follow-up surveys or measure program effect on victimization or perpetration of sexual violence (Anderson & Whiston, 2005).

A systematic review of 140 sexual violence prevention studies also suggests that longer interventions have a more positive impact, while one-hour programs for college students did not have lasting effects (DeGue et al., 2014). The majority of studies examined in this review were implemented on college campuses (70%), with the remainder conducted in high schools (14.3%), middle schools (7.1%) and other settings (8.6%). DeGue et al. (2014) found that 27.9% of the interventions had positive effects on all outcomes that were measured, 21.4% had no significant effects, 41.4% had a mixture of positive and null effects (no effect) and 6.4% found at least one harmful effect, such as an increase in risk behaviors. Of those studies that examined sexually violent behavior after the intervention, 47.6% ($n = 10$) showed no effect, and 4.8% ($n = 4$) showed significant positive effects (DeGue et al., 2014). Two programs found to be effective to reduce sexually violent behavior were developed for middle school and high school students and had not been tested with the college population.

A recent study of a sexual assault resistance program for university women is worth mentioning. The Enhanced Assess, Acknowledge, Act Sexual Assault Resistance program included four 3-hour sessions designed to improve women's assessment of their risk of sexual assault and develop strategies to reduce perpetrator advantages; assist women to access and resist unwanted sexual behaviors; engage women in self-defense training focusing on sexual assault situations involving acquaintances and attackers larger than the woman; explore sexuality and relationships and develop strategies for sexual communication. The researchers found that the risk of completed rape was significantly lower over a period of one year among the freshmen women who participated in the training (Senn et al., 2015). Compared to the control group, a smaller proportion of participants in the training experienced completed rape (5.2% participants vs. 9.8% controls) and attempted rape (3.4% participants vs. 9.3% controls) within one year of the training (Senn et al., 2015). This appears to be a very promising risk reduction program.

Active bystander interventions extend responsibility to the entire community to notice and intervene in situations that promote oppression at the root of sexual violence and stop acts of sexual violence in process (Moynihan & Banyard, 2008). Such programs engage students in stopping sexual violence before it occurs. For example, a student may observe someone trying to get another person drunk with the intention of having sex with that person. An active bystander is primed to intervene in a safe and effective manner. Strategies range from finding a friendly way to get the potential perpetrator or victim to leave with their friends, asking someone else to help deter the situation or calling 9–1–1 if the situation is potentially dangerous.

Studies of the bystander approach to address violence against women in a college population show positive changes in knowledge, attitudes and bystander behaviors among college men and women (Banyard, Moynihan, & Plante, 2007; Coker et al., 2011; Moynihan & Banyard, 2008). Programs such as Green Dot, Bringing in the Bystander and Step Up! have been developed for use with college students and show promise as effective strategies to reduce sexual violence on campus.

Although a comprehensive, multidimensional plan for sexual violence prevention based in the socio-ecological model is recommended, most studies evaluate a single program aimed to change knowledge, attitudes, behavior intentions and/or behaviors among students. There are few evidence-based programs for the college student population that have been examined in a peer-review process and no registry for evidence-based sexual violence prevention interventions for college students. Thus, it is incumbent upon the planning group to use the principles of effective prevention to plan interventions and to evaluate both individual programs and ongoing trends to determine the impact of the overall plan.

The CDC recommends that prevention strategies be based on the principles of effective prevention outlined by Nation et al. (2003). This serves as a guide when evidence-based interventions for the population are lacking. Effective prevention strategies are comprehensive, developmentally appropriate, culturally relevant and theory driven; they utilize varied teaching methods, have sufficient dosage, build on supportive positive relationships, are administered by well-trained staff and include outcome evaluation (Nation et al., 2003). When adhering to these principles, it is more likely that the strategies implemented will work together to have the desired outcome—a reduction in incidence of sexual violence.

Sexual Violence Prevention: Taking Action for Change

Effective sexual violence prevention requires a systematic planning process that involves a cross section of constituents and disciplines working together to create change. Campus-specific data enables the planning group to be strategic in their design and to address sexual violence where change is most needed. All aspects of planning, implementation and evaluation are strengthened through institutional supports. This section of the chapter identifies methods for developing a comprehensive plan, tips for implementing key strategies and evaluating a comprehensive plan for sexual violence prevention among college students.

Planning

A comprehensive plan cannot be developed or implemented in a silo or a single unit of the institution. Instead, a *planning group involving multiple sectors and disciplines* engaged in a collaborative planning process is needed (Langford, 2005). The planning group should be assembled to represent key members of the student and staff who are positioned to effect a change: students who are passionate about sexual violence prevention; members of student government; faculty experts in prevention and sexual violence; health, wellness, counseling and/or conduct staff; campus and/or local police; an evaluator; program staff for at risk groups such as athletes, fraternities and sororities, and lesbian, gay, bisexual and transgender students; decision-makers and other key stakeholder groups such as alumni, parents and community agency representatives. The collaborative workgroup should use a *systematic planning process* to create a comprehensive plan that maps out key strategies based on identified risk and protective factors across the socio-ecological influences of the campus. Such a planning process involves using campus data to determine risk behaviors and at-risk groups, reviewing literature to gain an understanding of what works and what might work to change behavioral outcomes, mapping out what is currently done and what will be done in the future to achieve strategic goals, articulating strategic goals and actions that will be taken to reach them and incorporating evaluation to measure success and engage in quality improvement of the plan and its component parts.

Strategic and targeted plans are based on data that reveal the most serious problems, the factors that contribute to them and the assets that exist locally that help to mitigate them (Langford, 2005). The same survey used to monitor trends can be used to identify problems related to sexual violence and which sub-groups of students are most affected. For example, an analysis of the institution-specific ACHA-NCHA-II data can show which groups are most likely to experience attempted or completed sexual assault and non-consensual sexual touching relative to high-risk drinking. Information compiled for the Clery Act and Title IX reports contain information on incidents as well as assets. Additional surveys can be developed to determine students' knowledge, attitudes, behaviors and skills regarding consent, communication, bystander actions and norms.

Environmental scans can help planners to see how the campus environment shapes attitude and behavior norms promoting or preventing sexual violence. Polices addressing sexual harassment, community norms for bystander intervention, local and campus enforcement practices for harassment and sexual misconduct cases and advertisements in the student and local papers can all serve as indicators of how the environment supports and/or suppresses sexual violence. This information can be used to develop programs, policies and messages designed to address the campus environment. Subsequent environmental scans can be done to evaluate the degree of change achieved.

Institutional support can play a significant role in sexual violence prevention efforts. Plans must be supported by infrastructure, institutional commitment and systems (Langford, 2005). Resources and processes are needed to support development, implementation and evaluation of a comprehensive plan. Often institutions provide a budget or staffing to implement the plan. However, support may be provided in other meaningful ways, such as the president or chancellor approving the plan and expecting activation of the plan by all relevant departments, by implementing recommended policy, by providing approval for a campuswide climate survey, by providing staff support to put up and maintain a new website or by agreeing to require online education for all new students.

The Logic Model

A key component of planning is to determine what outcomes the plan aims to achieve, which individuals or groups the plan aims to impact and how these outcomes and impacts will be advanced. Strategies may include awareness activities, education, bystander skills training, social marketing and media campaigns, peer education, activism, policy change and improved enforcement practices. All of the strategies, taken as a whole, should be mapped out to show how they are intended to work together to achieve the desired outcomes. This mapping-out process can be done by creating a logic model that shows how each separate intervention works together with all the planned interventions to achieve the desired goals. The Centers for Disease Control and Prevention guide to developing logic models, Making Logic Models Work for You, can aid the work group in this process (Gervin, 2013).

A logic model begins with the end in mind. Figure 4.1 provides a sample logic model with the end, or outcome, being a decrease in sexual violence perpetration and victimization among students. Products leading to this outcome might include new or revised policies that define affirmative consent or require mandatory education of new students. Short- and mid-term outcomes might include an increase in confidence, skill and performance as an active bystander or a reduction in high-risk drinking. Activities or strategies might include mandatory education of freshmen, peer involvement in educating students, police officer training or policy review. What might be needed to fulfill these activities to reach the desired

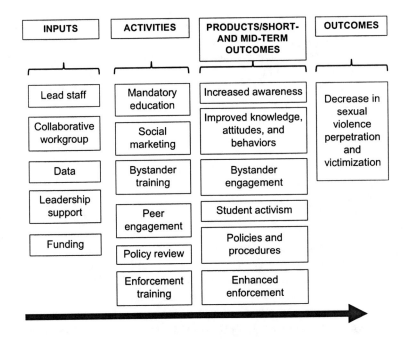

INPUTS	ACTIVITIES	PRODUCTS/SHORT- AND MID-TERM OUTCOMES	OUTCOMES
Lead staff	Mandatory education	Increased awareness	Decrease in sexual violence perpetration and victimization
Collaborative workgroup	Social marketing	Improved knowledge, attitudes, and behaviors	
Data	Bystander training	Bystander engagement	
Leadership support	Peer engagement	Student activism	
Funding	Policy review	Policies and procedures	
	Enforcement training	Enhanced enforcement	

Figure 4.1 Sample Sexual Violence Prevention Logic Model

outcomes are the inputs: a collaborative work group led by a coordinator position with administrative and funding support and relevant data to engage in this work together. The logic model should be developed based on the needs of the institution, data-based decision making, relevant theory and best-practices and implementing strategies that logically will contribute to the outcomes sought. A logic model can help keep the work group focused on the outcomes. Ideas and projects that do not logically and intentionally contribute to the goals can more easily be discarded when the plan is mapped out in a logic model.

Tips for Implementation

Sexual violence prevention addressing the college student population is evolving. Although the number of evidence-based programs for college students is limited, many strategies have been used to reduce sexual violence among college students in the past 30–40 years. What has been learned over the years is reflected in the approaches that are being used in today's institutions of higher education.

Education to reduce risk of sexual violence often includes risk reduction strategies or protective behaviors to avoid victimization. Safety tips can empower individuals to take actions to reduce their own risk of sexual assault; these include messages such as stick with your friends, arrive and leave the event together, use text alerts or apps to let your friends know where you are and what you are doing, lock your doors, stay within your alcohol limits and protect your drink. New evidence of the effectiveness of a sexual assault resistance program including self-defense tactics shows promise (Senn et al., 2015).

In promoting risk reduction strategies, it is important to use language that clearly places the responsibility for sexual violence on the perpetrator, regardless of whether or not a victim used the recommended safety strategies. Campus professionals must be careful not to set victims up to be blamed by their fellow students, by adjudicators or by themselves for their victimization.

Bystander intervention strategies, discussed earlier in this chapter, must go beyond education to engage students and staff in training sessions that provide time to practice recognizing, analyzing risk and responding appropriately to a wide array of situations. It is important to stress safety, as there are times when the best course of action is to call 9–1–1 or to bring the issue to a campus authority. Efforts to engage students as active bystanders can be extensive, including awareness activities, social marketing campaigns, peer education, policy enhancement and other strategies. Bystander intervention programs typically extend beyond sexual violence prevention: The aim is to create prosocial campus norms that reduce risk within the student community. The skills learned and reinforced in such programs apply to alcohol risk, dating violence, disordered eating, distress and bullying, as well as assisting when someone needs help with a door, a flat tire or a ride home.

Sexual violence is interrelated to many other health and safety issues relevant to the college population. Bystander intervention is just one example of a strategy designed to provide a skill set that is of benefit in sexual violence prevention and other aspects of student life. With creative planning, interventions and communications designed to reduce sexual violence risk or perpetration can be *woven into education* about alcohol and drugs, sexual wellness, building healthy relationships and other areas of interest to students.

Students bring an array of identities to their college experience that influence the campus norms including their race/ethnicity, sexual orientation, gender identity, age, faith, veteran status, country and region of origin. There exist unique *cultural influences* within each specific campus, college, residence hall, club, team or other group. When working with students, it is important to use language, examples, images and message delivery systems that are relevant to the students addressed. It is important to acknowledge that *sexual violence impacts all groups*, to share data and information and to plan programs and activities that support this reality. For example, women and men; transgender, gender-queer or nonconforming; lesbian, gay, bisexual, asexual and questioning students are victims and survivors of sexual violence. Using gender-inclusive language, examples, activities and policies can help foster trust and respect among students who identify with these groups.

Undergraduate students are those at greater risk of sexual violence victimization and perpetration. Thus, it is important to consider the *developmental needs* of the traditional-aged college student when planning and implementing sexual violence prevention strategies. For example, new freshmen are transitioning from the protection of their families and communities to independent living. They are in a new environment, developing a new peer group, exploring new behaviors and developing new habits. They are in a period of life that has a strong focus on making connections relationally and sexually. A developmentally appropriate program for this population may discuss social pressures, develop skills for communication about sex and consent, use peer influence to enhance use of bystander intervention strategies, engage students in leadership to build norms for respect within their peer group, provide training for staff and resident assistants that reinforces positive norms, builds trust and opens communication avenues with their students to influence and model expected behaviors.

Regardless of the group that is the focus of a prevention effort, it is critical to *engage group members* to help design and adapt programs and messages to fit their group. These individuals can provide perspectives on how to communicate with their group, how to engage them, who should facilitate the intervention and how to deliver the education. How one engages a class of mixed freshmen should look and feel different than how one engages student athletes, female engineering students, international students, Hispanic students, fraternities and sororities, graduate students or faculty. By engaging group members in the planning process, buy-in from members of the group is garnered, and critical knowledge is gained to help meet the needs of the group and its individual members.

Changing student norms about consent, bystander intervention and tolerance for sexual aggression involves *engaging peer leaders*. While theories and evaluation studies provide information about the most recent findings and best practices, students provide information about the campus norms, the cultural norms, peer pressures and perceptions and the reality of their student experience. They are positioned, not just to improve program planning, but to influence other students, particularly students within their close peer groups. It is important that higher education professionals engage peer leaders intentionally, with specific outcomes for the peer leaders and their peers as the focus of their involvement.

Men are a growing influence in sexual violence prevention. *Involving college men* as peer leaders in sexual violence prevention is particularly important, as they are positioned in their peer relationships to influence other college men. As mentioned previously, most college men do not rape or commit acts of sexual violence. These men can serve the community as effective peer leaders, advocates for policy change, coordinators of outreach and awareness activities, active bystanders and catalysts that change the culture of violence that exists in society. Men are best positioned to change the culture and social norms of men. Thus, it is essential to engage male staff and students in sexual violence prevention.

In order to be effective, peer leaders need to receive *adequate training and mentoring* that matches their role. Training should provide a foundation of knowledge of the topic, comfort facilitating the program, competence with answering participant questions and dealing with common challenges that may arise during implementation whether they are facilitating a program in the residence halls or staffing an information table at the student union. Their training must prepare them to listen and respond, facilitate and guide discussion and respond appropriately to disclosures. Well-trained staff are a key to effective prevention whether the staff are paid students, student volunteers or professional staff (Anderson & Whiston, 2005; Degue et al., 2014).

Research indicates that *longer education programs or those with multiple sessions* show more positive results over time (Anderson & Whiston, 2005; DeGue et al., 2014). However, it can be challenging to get approval to devote even a single class session for sexual violence prevention when faculty are pressed to use all classes allotted to them to cover course material. The college environment demands that a systematic and intentional approach is used to assure that students have sufficient exposure to sexual violence prevention education to influence and maintain the desired behaviors. It may be necessary to infuse sexual violence prevention into a wide variety of educational programs, activities, social media communications, peer education efforts and other programs to achieve the dosage needed to reinforce prosocial attitudes and behaviors to sustain them over time.

Evaluating Outcomes

Evaluation is essential in determining how to improve program design, activities, delivery and all components of the program to garner positive outcomes. Each intervention used should incorporate an evaluation process that goes beyond counting the number of participants or asking if they "liked" the program or would recommend it to another student.

Evaluation helps determine whether the interventions are working, how to improve results, which activities to keep using, which to improve and which to stop. Evaluation provides insight to whether knowledge, attitudes, behavior intentions and/or behaviors are changed. Intention to change a behavior can be measured immediately following a program, using a pre- and post-test design. A follow-up evaluation that takes place a month or more after the intervention can be used to examine whether the interventions have resulted in long-lasting behavior change. This type of evaluation was lacking in a review of prevention programs (DeGue et al., 2014).

Ultimately, a comprehensive plan to reduce sexual violence among students will include several interventions. It is important to evaluate each element of the institution's plan to ensure that the education, messages, activities, policies, enforcement practices and other interventions work together to result in the desired community norms and lead to a reduction in the incidence of sexual violence.

One way to examine the impact of a comprehensive prevention plan is to monitor trends using a random sample survey. For example, the American College Health Association–National College Health Assessment-II can be used to monitor experiences of sexual violence among the student population over time (American College Health Association, 2016).

Evaluation is a necessary component of a comprehensive plan to reduce sexual violence perpetration and victimization among college students. It is essential to include a skilled evaluator or researcher in the planning group or as a consultant to the planning group. For those who lack evaluation experience, or do not have the resources for evaluation, it may be helpful to partner with a member of the faculty or a graduate student to plan and implement the evaluation.

Conclusion

This brief overview of the problem and prevention of sexual violence among college students was written to raise awareness, provide a planning structure and information about what might work. The overall aim is that current and future professionals in higher education will be compelled to engage in the work to end sexual violence among our students.

The rate of sexual violence among college students has remained stable over the past 15 years or longer despite ongoing prevention programs. This reality has a significant impact on the academic and personal lives of our students. Professionals in higher education have the unique opportunity to change this trajectory through a well-planned comprehensive sexual violence prevention effort. Examples of interventions and programs that are effective at reducing perpetration and victimization among college students are limited. To make a difference will require collaboration and a dedication to the principles of effective prevention. Evaluation and dissemination of programmatic and institutional successes and challenges in prevention will support efforts across the nation and around the world to address this pervasive problem.

References

Abbey, A. (2008). *Alcohol and Sexual Violence Perpetration*. Harrisburg, PA: VAWnet, a project of the National Resource Center on Domestic Violence/Pennsylvania Coalition Against Domestic Violence. Retrieved from http://www.vawnet.org/applied-research-papers/print-document.php?doc_id=1586

Abbey, A., & McAuslan, P. (2004). A longitudinal examination of male college students' perpetration of sexual assault. *Journal of Consulting and Clinical Psychology, 72*(5), 747–756.

American College Health Association. (September 2, 2014). *Unpublished analysis of the American College Health Association-National College Health Assessment-II data for the proportion of students who experienced attempted and/or completed sexual assault for the national reference group in Spring 2010, 2011, 2012, and 2013*. Provided by email to this author by the research office of the American College Health Association.

American College Health Association. (September 9, 2015). *Unpublished analysis of the American College Health Association-National College Health Assessment-II data for the proportion of students who experienced attempted and/or completed sexual assault for the national reference group in Spring 2014*. Provided by email to this author by the research office of the American College Health Association.

American College Health Association. (November 20, 2015). *Unpublished analysis of the American College Health Association-National College Health Assessment-II data for the proportion of students who experienced attempted and/or completed sexual assault for the national reference group in Spring 2015*. Provided by email to this author by the research office of the American College Health Association.

American College Health Association. (2016). *Publications and reports: ACHA-NCHA II*. Retrieved from www.acha-ncha.org/reports_ACHA-NCHAc.html

Anderson, L. A., & Whiston, S. C. (2005). Sexual assault education programs: A meta-analytic examination of their effectiveness. *Psychology of Women Quarterly, 29*(4), 374–388. doi:10.1111/j.1471–6402.2005.00237.x

Banyard, V. L., Moynihan, M. M., & Plante, E. G. (2007). Sexual violence prevention through bystander education: An experimental evaluation. *Journal of Community Psychology, 35*(4), 463–481.

Breiding, M. J., Smith, S. G., Basile, K. C., Walters, M. L., Chen, J., & Merrick, M. T. (2014, September 5). Prevalence and characteristics of sexual violence, stalking, and intimate partner violence victimization—National Intimate Partner and Sexual Violence Survey, United States, 2011. *Morbidity and Mortality Weekly Report*. Retrieved from http://www.cdc.gov/mmwr/preview/mmwrhtml/ss6308a1.htm

Bureau of Justice. (2015). *Bureau of Justice Statistics*. Retrieved from http://www.bjs.gov/index.cfm?ty=nvat

Byers, E. S., Henderson, J., & Hobson, K. M. (2009). University students' definitions of sexual abstinence and having sex. *Archives of Sexual Behavior, 38*(5), 665–674.

Cantor, D., Fisher, B., Chibnall, S., Townsend, R., Lee, H., Bruce, C., & Thomas, G. (2015). *Report on the AAU Campus Climate Survey on Sexual Assault and Sexual Misconduct*. The Association of American Universities. Rockville, MD: Westat.

Centers for Disease Control and Prevention. (2004). *Sexual Violence Prevention: Beginning the Dialogue*. Atlanta, GA: Centers for Disease Control and Prevention.

Centers for Disease Control and Prevention. (2014). *Preventing Sexual Violence on College Campuses: Lessons from Research and Practice*. Prepared for the White House Task Force to Protect Students from Sexual Assault. Retrieved from https://www.notalone.gov/assets/evidence-based-strategies-for-the-prevention-of-sv-perpetration.pdf

Centers for Disease Control and Prevention. (2015). *Sexual Violence: Consequences*. Retrieved from http://www.cdc.gov/violenceprevention/sexualviolence/consequences.html

Clery Center for Security on Campus. (2015a). *Summary of the Campus Sexual Violence Elimination (SaVE) Act*. Retrieved from http://clerycenter.org/campus-sexual-violence-elimination-save-act

Clery Center for Security on Campus. (2015b). *Summary of the Jeanne Clery Act*. Retrieved from http://clerycenter.org/summary-jeanne-clery-act

Coker, A. L., Cook-Craig, P. G., Williams, C. M., Fisher, B. S., Clear, E. R., Garcia, L. S., & Hegge, L. M. (2011). Evaluation of Green Dot: An active bystander intervention to reduce sexual violence on college campuses. *Violence Against Women, 17*(6), 777–796. doi:10.1177/1077801211410264

DeGue, S., Valle, L. A., Holt, M. K., Massetti, G. M., Matjasko, J. L., & Tharp, A. T. (2014). A systematic review of primary prevention strategies for sexual violence prevention. *Aggression and Violent Behavior, 19*, 346–362. doi:10.1016/j.avb.2014.05.004

Fisher, B. S., Cullen, F. T., & Turner, M. G. (2000). *The Sexual Victimization of College Women*. Washington, DC: National Institute of Justice.

Gervin, D. (2013, September). *Making Logic Models Work for You*. Retrieved from the Centers of Disease Control website at http://www.cdc.gov/dhdsp/pubs/docs/CB_September_2013.pdf

Gidycz, C. A., Warkentin, J. B., & Orchowski, L. M. (2007). Predictors of perpetration of verbal, physical, and sexual violence: A prospective analysis of college men. *Psychology of Men & Masculinity, 8*, 79–94.

Gray, E. (2014, August 28). California passes first-ever bill to define sexual consent on college campuses. *Time*. Retrieved from http://time.com/3211938/campus-sexual-assault-consent-california/

Gute, G., Eshbaugh, E. M., & Wiersma, J. (2008). Sex for you, but not for me: Discontinuity in undergraduate emerging adults' definitions of "having sex." *Journal of Sex Research, 45*(4), 329–337.

Hans, J. D., & Kimberly, C. (2011). Abstinence, sex, and virginity: Do they mean what we think they mean? *American Journal of Sexuality Education, 6*(4), 329–342.

Krebs, C. P., Lindquist, C. H., Warner, T. D., Fisher, B. S., & Martin, S. L. (2007). *The Campus Sexual Assault Study*. Washington, DC: National Institute of Justice.

Langford, L. (2005). *Preventing Violence and Promoting Safety in Higher-Education Settings: Overview of a Comprehensive Approach*. Newton, MA: Educational Development Center.

Lisak, D., & Miller, P. M. (2002). Repeat rape and multiple offending among undetected rapists. *Violence and Victims, 17*(1), 73–84.

Moynihan, M. M., & Banyard, V. L. (2008). Community responsibility for preventing sexual violence: A pilot study with campus Greeks and intercollegiate athletes. *Journal of Prevention & Intervention in the Community, 36*, 23–38.

Nation, M., Crusto, C., Wandersman, A., Kumpfer, K. L., Seybolt, D., Morrissey-Kane, E., & Davino, K. (2003). What works in prevention: Principles of effective prevention programs. *American Psychologist, 58*, 449–456. doi:10.1037/0003-066X.58.6-7.449

National Association of Student Personnel Administrators. (2004). *Leadership for a Healthy Campus: An Ecological Approach for Student Success.* Washington, DC: National Association of Student Personnel Administrators. Retrieved from http://www.longwood.edu/assets/health/leadership_for_a_healthy_campus.pdf

Perry, B. (2005). *What's in a Name: Outreach or Primary Prevention? Moving Upstream: Virginia's Newsletter for the Primary Prevention of Sexual Violence.* Retrieved from http://www.communitysolutionsva.org/files/Moving_Upstream_1–2_1.pdf

Peterson, Z. D., & Muehlenhard, C. L. (2007). What is sex and why does it matter? A motivational approach to exploring individuals' definitions of sex. *Journal of Sex Research, 44*(3), 256–268.

Senn, C. Y., Eliasziw, M., Barata, P. C., Thurston, W. E., Newby-Clark, I. R., Radtke, L., & Hobden, K. L. (2015). Efficacy of a sexual assault resistance program for university women. *The New England Journal of Medicine, 372*(24), 2326–2335.

Sewell, K. K., & Strassberg, D. S. (2015). How do heterosexual undergraduate students define having sex? A new approach to an old question. *Journal of Sex Research, 52*(5), 507–516. doi:10.1080/00224499.2014.888389

Thompson, M. P., Swartout, K. M., & Koss, M. P. (2013). Trajectories and predictors of sexually aggressive behaviors during emerging adulthood. *Psychology of Violence, 3*(3), 247–259. doi:10.1037/a0030624

U.S. Department of Education. (2015). *The Campus Safety and Security Data Analysis Cutting Tool.* Retrieved from http://ope.ed.gov/security/

U.S. Department of Education, Office for Civil Rights. (2011). *Dear Colleague Letter.* Retrieved from http://www2.ed.gov/about/offices/list/ocr/letters/colleague-201104.html

U.S. Department of Education, Office for Civil Rights. (2015). *Office for Civil Rights: Title IX and Sex Discrimination.* Retrieved from http://www2.ed.gov/about/offices/list/ocr/docs/tix_dis.html

U.S. Department of Labor. (2015). *Title IX, Education Amendments of 1972.* Retrieved from http://www.dol.gov/oasam/regs/statutes/titleix.htm

Violence Against Women Reauthorization Act of 2013 (PL 113–4, 7 March 2013). *127 United States Statutes at Large* (pp. 54–160). Retrieved from http://www.gpo.gov/fdsys/pkg/PLAW-113publ4/pdf/PLAW-113publ4.pdf

Voller, E. K., & Long, P. J. (2010). Sexual assault and rape perpetration by college men: The role of the big five personality traits. *Journal of Interpersonal Violence, 25*(3), 457–480. doi:10.1177/00886260509334390

Zaino, J. (2015, July 21). *Changing Definitions of Sexual Consent on College Campuses.* Blog U, University of Venus. Inside Higher Ed. Retrieved from https://www.insidehighered.com/blogs/university-venus/changing-definitions-sexual-consent-college-campuses

Part III
Intellectual Wellness

5

Time Management
Finding Balance to Do It "All"

MICHAEL P. MCNEIL

Time is the coin of your life. It is the only coin you have, and only you can determine how it will be spent. Be careful lest you let other people spend it for you.
—Carl Sandburg

Introduction

Known to some as time management and to others as life balance, most people can recall the feeling of wanting just a little more time in the day to get things done. The honest, if difficult to accept, truth is that no one needs more time in a day; however, most people may need some guidance in determining how to use the available time.

"The concept of time management is generally defined in terms of clusters of behavior that are deemed to facilitate productivity and alleviate stress" (Lay & Schouwenburg, 1993, p. 648). Effective time management strategies increase academic performance (Campbell & Svenson, 1992) and are frequently suggested by academic assistance personnel as aids to enhance achievement for college students. Although many campus efforts promote the importance of starting assignments well in advance of due dates, breaking down large assignments into a series of smaller ones and keeping a regular schedule to complete these smaller tasks, these strategies are oft ignored by students, resulting in increased distress as exams and deadlines approach (Brown, 1991).

Considering the generalized experiences of today's college students, the millennial generation has a unique relationship with the idea of balance and time management. If asked, it would not be surprising to hear students say they have no problems with time management. However, a close look at choices and how time is spent may say otherwise. These students hail from a generation where parents overscheduled their kids, instilled a can-do-it-all mentality and lacked role modeling to teach balance, especially when it comes to time choices. Possessing a tendency to be hyper-involved, these students often mistake choices with opportunities thinking they are all "necessary" and are driven by an internalized fear of missing out (FOMO). Young people today have a tendency to want to do everything and simply cannot fathom the concept of missing something. As a result, these young people may be quick to trade what they perceive as discretionary time (like sleep) so as to stay "connected."

Faculty members tend to have views different from students on how students should spend their time when compared to student views. For example, faculty may cite the concept that for every hour spent in class, two additional hours should be devoted to course-related activities (assignments, reading, etc.) in each week. By extension this means a 3-credit class will be about 9 hours of work per week (3 hours in the classroom and 6 hours outside of the classroom on course-related efforts). Additionally, faculty members were more likely than students to expect students to make academic pursuits a time priority over other tasks and to hold them accountable for time-based choices (Collier & Morgan, 2008).

Administrators often find themselves puzzled by the seeming availability of time in the schedule of students, yet also observe a lack of accomplishment and continuous procrastination among the population. The difference between theoretical schedules envisioned by academic and student affairs administrators and the student realities of managing time open many interesting discussions and serve as opportunities for role modeling and mentoring.

This chapter seeks to explore the current state of affairs regarding time management; identifies the impact on student lives as well as misperceptions (multitasking, FOMO) and offers strategies for students, faculty and administrators. Given that the lack of time management skills has been associated with lower academic performance (ACHA, 2015; MacCann, Fogarty, & Roberts, 2012; Proctor, Prevatt, Adams, Reaser, & Petscher, 2006), anyone involved in post-secondary education is encouraged to make time to read this chapter and develop a priority list of how to address time management issues (in oneself and with others).

State of Affairs

Time, the use of or perceived lack of, is contributing to challenges for students. According to a survey of more than 93,000 college students who participated in the American College Health Association–National College Health Assessment (2015), 86% of respondents reported feeling overwhelmed by all they had to do, and 82% reported feeling exhausted (not from physical activity). While the survey questions do not explicitly link these two ideas to time management, it is hardly a stretch to see the connection.

The ACHA instrument asks about time working for pay and volunteering, both time factors for college students. As summarized in Table 5.1, student respondents reported spending varying levels of time on the respective activities.

TABLE 5.1 Non-Academic Time Use

Number of Hours Spent per Week	Zero	1–20	21–39	40+
Work for Pay	41%	36%	17%	3%
Volunteering	62%	37%	2%	0.1%

(ACHA, 2015)

As can be seen, notable proportions of the population are neither volunteering nor working, so how exactly are college students using their time beyond academics? It must the acknowledged that the data is primarily drawn from undergraduate respondents so the experience may be different at the graduate level. However, one might also posit that undergraduates are the population that struggle most with managing time. Higher education professionals should investigate this further because of the limited data that clearly indicates all of the areas of non-classroom time utilization among students.

Looking at other time-related questions on the ACHA-NCHA survey, three academic impediments have solid relationships with time management. Among the respondents, more than 11% of students reported Internet use/computer games, 9.1% reported extracurricular activities, and 13.9% reported work negatively affected their academic performance in the last 12 months. Given these are likely non-curricular in nature, students are self-reporting areas related to time that are resulting in negative outcomes. By comparison, only 3.2% of students reported that learning difficulties are negatively impacting academic performance (ACHA, 2015). With time management being associated as a skill-based challenge for those with learning disabilities, it is interesting to see that non-learning focused factors may be negatively impacting greater proportions of the student population.

Students who spend considerable time on video games (including online games) may struggle with overall time management and also tend to have lower GPAs (Anand, 2007). Students reported sacrificing other responsibilities and self-care behaviors in order to prioritize time on the playing of games. While one researcher postulates that video game players may be dealing with a form of addiction, the relationship to struggles with time management is clear (Anand, 2007).

Looking at some specific populations, the issues of time management continue to appear, but manifest themselves in different ways. Misra and McKean (2000) and Macan, Shahani, Dipboye and Phillips (1990) found that female students were more effective with time management (perceived and measured); however, age (or year in school) was not a factor with time management skills. Students with Attention Deficit Hyperactivity Disorder (ADHD) had more difficulty with time management than peers with Learning Disabilities (LD) or no conditions. Students generally struggled with the ability to manage and self-regulate time (Reaser, Prevatt, Petscher, & Proctor, 2007). Students with lower GPAs tended to use time management as part of their study skills set less frequently than those with higher GPAs. This also held true for a subset of students diagnosed with learning disabilities (Proctor et al., 2006). The use of time management as a study skill has been widely established to support student academic success so it is interesting to see that struggling students are failing to use one of the most easily accessible tools to improve academic performance.

Among community college students, time management may be a more important predictor of success for part-time students when compared to those studying full time. Researchers also found the predictive nature of good time management to academic success among older students (MacCann et al., 2012). With more life experience, or competing non-academic priorities (as frequently seen in part-time students), the embracing of time management as a necessary strategy for success can be seen.

While Reis, Hébert, Díaz, Maxfield and Ratley (1995) found that poor time management led to underachievement (students who did not know how to handle unstructured time tended to be less academically successful), Balduf (2009) found that the issue does not originate in college. High achieving high school students facing academic challenges in college lacked a number of key skills that were contributing to the lack of success. Key among the issues was a lack of time management skill.

Another way to consider the current state is to apply the generational lens. Counting from birth, by the time a millennial student leaves college, he or she will have:

- Spent 10,000 hours playing video games
- Sent and received more than 200,000 e-mails and instant messages (IMs)
- Spent 20,000 hours watching TV
- At most, spent 5,000 hours reading books

(Wolfe, 2009)

Seeing these numbers suggests that academic and co-curricular goals may be second, third or even further down the time-priority list of college students.

Time Conflict

Trying to determine exactly where the time concerns originate is likely a literal waste of time. Each student brings a unique set of experiences to campus, and although college professionals may try to categorize and generalize, it may be difficult to really understand this issue. Whether it is lack of balance, not having previous guidance on the choice of time expenditures or relation of time spent now to later success, there are opportunities for students, faculty and administrators to explore and understand issues of time (real and perceived). That being said, here are a few ideas on where to begin:

How Do You Use Your 1,440?

This critical question is often lost on college students. Very few have any ideas regarding the meaning of 1,440. When prompted, you might hear a guess of a tax form (that's the 1040), if anything. Walking students through the math will yield the realization that there are 1,440 minutes in a day (60 minutes in an hour × 24 hours in a day).

Consider this—you have a bank account that receives a deposit at exactly midnight, and you have 24 hours to make decisions and use that money. The following midnight any remaining funds are removed, but one second later you get a new day's allocation, and the process starts all over. **This is time.** Each person has the same 1,440 minutes in their day's bank and has the ability to decide what and how it is spent and what ends up being wasted. It's not to say any unused time is a waste, or that time spent in pursuit of non-critical tasks is less valuable, but to show that we each have the same to spend and that it is our choices that define the time and balance we experience.

Previously Overscheduled

Prior to enrolling in higher education, large portions of schedules for many students were controlled by authority figures. Parents likely drove wake and sleep times (or the recommendation of), schooling drove notable portions of the day, and "free time" was frequently driven by family expectations.

Lack of Self-Determination with Time Management

These newly enrolling college students came of age in a time when parents/caregivers were taking them to events such as soccer, ballet or piano lessons after school; this was followed by homework and then bedtime. They may not have been given the opportunity to truly have self-determination on how time was utilized and thus never developed the experience and self-efficacy to know how to create balance with time.

Instant Gratification

Much has been said about generational shifts and that the contemporary generation of traditional-aged college students have never learned patience (Coomes & DeBard, 2004). With technology, rapid television news cycles and other quick reward drivers, these young people have not learned that time does not need to always be driven by the immediate "need" and that patience is a key that helps create perspective and may influence future time-related decisions. Some refer to this as self-induced Attention Deficit Disorder (ADD).

First-Generation Students

Collier and Morgan (2008) found that first-generation students were more likely to report problems related to time management than students with family members who had previously attended college. Helping first-generation students understand the relationship of time to academic pursuits and how the use of time may be different from past academic settings may provide opportunities to address the discrepancy between the use of time and indicators of academic success.

Multitasking

There was a time when multitasking was considered a desired skill (Ellis, Daniels, & Jauregui, 2010). College students, driven in part by the online, on-demand, always available world are well known for playing music, talking on the phone, writing a paper and watching an online video all at the same time. In the past few years, a greater amount of literature has emerged helping highlight the challenges of multitasking and bringing to light that productivity and quality both suffer. The desire to do more in the same amount of time is resulting in lower quantity and quality of the person's effort (Junco & Cotton, 2011; Lepp, Barkley, & Karpinski, 2014).

Fear of Missing Out

As noted in the beginning of this chapter, students often fear that they may miss out on some opportunity or potential gain. Their multitasking appears based on their self-ascribed ability to "do it all" and their perception that they just cannot miss out.

Campus professionals may find the "fear of missing out," found in the boxed text, helpful in discussions with students. These may be included as part of social media, campaigns, websites or other approaches to help students reorient their views about time and their priorities. Personnel may also find it insightful to assess their students' perspectives on these and related items.

FOMO!

Suffering from FOMO (fear of missing out)? Always find yourself saying YOLO (you only live once)? Here are a few ways to refocus:

- **Do you.** In other words, be yourself! Consider making a list of things that you enjoy and that make you happy, including people with which you enjoy spending time. Do you prefer to stay in and bake cookies over going to a party? Or would you rather go to a museum than to the mall? Remember that it's OK if you don't have the same experiences as everyone else, as long as what you're doing makes **you** happy!
- **Look out for the green-eyed monster (a.k.a. jealousy).** Some research suggests that constantly tracking what other people are doing on social media might increase jealousy, which may then increase feelings of depression or the feeling that life is unfair. Consider reading "Struggling with Low Self-Esteem" in the *Go Ask Alice!* archives for some tips on keeping the green-eyed monster at bay and increasing self-confidence.
- **Take it one day at a time.** If your FOMO seems to be brought on by a recent transition—going to college, moving to a new place, etc.—remember to give yourself a little time and space to adjust. You might doubt whether you made the right choice or if you'll make friends; you may even question whether you'll succeed. These are all normal feelings, and research suggests that FOMO amongst college students might be related to the desire to be autonomous or feel competent in a new environment. As you settle into your new space (literally and figuratively), feelings of jealousy, inadequacy or anxiety about missing out may start to fade.
- **Give social media (and your phone) a rest.** Technology is great for connecting us with others, but constantly being "connected" can also lead to anxiety. A good rule of thumb is to spend more time with friends and family in the real world than in the virtual world. An idea you may consider is to set aside just one or two hours a day where you don't look at or check any email, social media or other technology.

- **Plan an adventure.** Whether you decide to spend a semester abroad or just try a new cuisine for lunch, consider finding ways to push yourself out of your comfort zone or beyond just the typical day-to-day happenings. Rather than feeling bummed about missing out on other people's exciting lives, you can focus on making your own life exciting—in little ways or big ways!

Adapted and Reprinted with Permission from Go Ask Alice!
Columbia University (2015)

Impacts on College Students

The impacts of poor time management by students range from the academic to personal. Balduf (2009) found the lack of studying material early in a term contributed to time management issues. As a result, students will focus on the most immediate academic concerns, one issue at a time. This constantly behind feeling leads to a vicious cycle of stress that may manifest itself in any number of ways. Time management is a predictor of academic stress and learning time management may help reduce academic stress.

Students, including first-generation students, tend to approach time allocations for post-secondary study based on the time they perceive as being available rather than considering the amount of time that is necessary to complete the work and master subjects (Collier & Morgan, 2008). This discretionary approach to time may lead to lower academic performance measures (i.e., grades) and a focus on process (earning the degree) rather than on true learning.

Conflicts in time between academic considerations and employment, family and other life aspects were reported by students, and students perceive faculty as not being aware of responsibilities outside of coursework (Collier & Morgan, 2008). These differing perceptions may further stress and contribute to an ongoing time-stress-learning conflict. Additionally, "time demands of academic life may have induced students to reduce time-consuming health behaviors, such as getting enough sleep" (Clement, Jankowski, Bouchard, Perreault, & Lepage, 2002, p. 257). One example includes working students trying to find time to focus on academics and sacrificing sleep; another example involves students in highly competitive environments feeling pressure to enroll in a higher-volume course load while not reducing their social involvement, thus resulting in less time available for healthier behaviors like sleep.

Overcoming Procrastination

A chapter on time management would be incomplete without addressing procrastination. Essentially, procrastination is not a result of people being lazy, as people often invest the time, close to a deadline, to complete the required task or assignment. By completing what is expected, they are demonstrating that laziness is not the issue. Rather, the employment of delaying tactics when faced with a task or responsibility is more about values, priorities and the ability to apply oneself. In essence, procrastination is actually a factor of time choice expenditure and prioritization of options. Procrastination is an acknowledgement of what the individual believes is important, with activities that are delayed actually being viewed by an individual as less important than undertakings on which time is expended earlier.

Some people believe that they perform better under pressure while others enjoy the thrill of working against a clock. Of course, people share these statements most frequently when not engaged in a rush of activity to complete a required task. Procrastination may be a self-protective concept used by students to ensure a feeling of being "busy" and "not having enough time." In reality, procrastination is choice, one that may be rooted in psychological origins or a result of never having learned about balance and time-choice.

To address and overcome procrastination takes more than desire; it requires significant effort and willingness to not give up if not successful on the first try. In working with students, whether as a student affairs professional, a faculty member, an academic advisor, an administrator or some other role, consider using the following five steps.

Self-awareness is learning to recognize when and why procrastination is happening and is a key first step. If a person cannot identify the root causes of the procrastination choices, then they are likely to continue to use the same patterns of procrastination behavior. Despite the tenants of chaos theory, procrastination change is unlikely to occur without self-awareness and reflection.

Making a change decision is like a New Year's resolution. People may promise to stop procrastinating without a real plan or even belief that a plan can be successful. Once a student approaches the change decision, it is important to understand why and how life will be better once a new non-procrastination way to completing tasks and assignments is in place. This change decision process also allows the student to identify immediate and longer-range rewards that can come with change.

Identifying strategies is key, as not every approach to overcoming procrastination will be right for every person or situation. Much like tools in a toolbox, having a range of options and the right tools for addressing procrastination is necessary to successfully overcome the challenge. Encourage students to work with teaching and learning centers, academic advisors and fellow students who have overcome procrastination to learn different strategies that may be applied to a given situation.

Staying on task helps a person focus the desired change. As with most change processes, setbacks and challenges along the way often occur. For procrastination, there is a familiarity to delaying work on an assignment or responsibility, and this can put internal psychological pressure to continue with the procrastination behavior. A pattern of having past successes, despite procrastinating, can be difficult to change. Having a support system (people), reminding oneself of the reasons for change (learning, feeling less rushed, etc.) and a reward for success (e.g., more true free time without thinking about what you "should" be doing) can all help people stay on track. Be aware that most people slip back at some point in a change process. It's not failure; it's an opportunity to try another tool that supports moving forward.

Rewards assist by encouraging students to set shorter- and longer-term rewards that help reinforce the new non-procrastination behavior. Encourage them to call a valued friend or family member after completing a task ahead of schedule and share how nice it feels to not be rushed. Suggest that they have—even schedule—the time to watch a favorite show or read a book they've been meaning to get to. Perhaps just being able to take a 10-minute break and do a short walk, free from a racing mind can be helpful. Rewards are as unique to the person as the reasons for procrastination.

Addressing Procrastination

Assess—What feelings lead to procrastinating, and how does it make you feel? Are these positive, productive feelings? Do you want to change them?

Outlook—Alter your perspective. Looking at a big task in terms of smaller pieces makes it less intimidating. Look for what's appealing about or what you want to get out of a task or assignment.

Commit—If you feel really stuck, start simply by committing to complete a small task, any task, and write it down. Finish it and reward yourself. Write down on your schedule or "to do" list only what you can completely commit to and, if you write it down, follow through. By doing so, you will slowly rebuild self-trust that you will really do what you say you will, which so many procrastinators have lost.

Surroundings—When doing work, choose wisely where and with whom you are working. Repeatedly placing yourself in situations where you don't get much done and are easily distracted—such as studying in bed, at a café or with friends—can actually be a kind of procrastination, a method of avoiding work.

Goals—Focus on what you want to do, not what you want to avoid. Think about the productive reasons for doing a task by setting positive, concrete, meaningful learning and achievement goals for you.

Be Realistic—Achieving goals and changing habits takes time and effort; don't sabotage yourself by having unrealistic expectations that you cannot reasonably meet.

Self-talk—Notice how you are thinking and talking to yourself. Talk to yourself in ways that remind you of your goals and focus on positive self-talk habits and language. Instead of saying, "I wish I hadn't . . ." say, "I will. . . ."

Un-schedule—If you feel really stuck, you probably won't use a schedule that is a constant reminder of all that you have to do and is all work and no play. So, if your many attempts to make a schedule have failed miserably, make a largely unstructured, flexible schedule in which you slot in only what is necessary. Keep track of all the time you spend working toward your goals, tally it up and reward yourself for it. This can reduce feelings of being overwhelmed and increase satisfaction in what you get done.

One Piece at a Time—Breaking down big tasks into little ones is a good approach. A variation on this is devoting short chunks of time to a big task and doing as much as you can in that time with few expectations about what you will get done. In short, it'll be easier to complete the task because you've gotten started and removed some of the obstacles to finishing.

Adapted from Understanding and Overcoming Procrastination, Dominic J. Voge, 2007, and The McGraw Center for Teaching and Learning, Princeton University, 2012. Reprinted with Permission.

Recommendations

Students

Convincing students they may have challenges with time management is difficult enough. If willing to engage, there are a number of ideas that can help promote a balanced sense of time that supports the personal and academic goal achievement of college students.

Students are encouraged to develop time management priorities for creating a balanced, health-promoting and sustainable schedule. The recommended order for adding time to a blank schedule is 1) sleep (7–9 hours per night), 2) meals (2–3 hours a day), 3) classes and academic work (classroom hours + 5–8 hours per class per week) and 4) everything else. Sleep and meals come before classes as proper sleep and good nutrition are both contributors to success in the academic arena. Like Maslow's hierarchy of needs, the scheduling of sleep and meals before all others is driven by sleep and nutrition providing support to effectiveness of all tasks that follow in a schedule.

These priorities for time management are not impacted by variables such as full-time or part-time student status, age, hours spent working or volunteering. Linking back to the concepts of being over involved, setting unrealistic schedules, glorifying "busy," and the fear of missing out, students may overschedule when adding more than sleep, meals and academics. While not suggesting that students should only focus on academics and directly connected items, post-secondary education is a time of life that should be focused primarily on learning. The co-curricular opportunity to learn about balance that supports immediate and long-term goals is an important lesson for students as well. Students can do it all; but it does not need to be in the same day, week, month, semester, year or academic experience.

Recognizing that some students will be required to work full time or part time, there are opportunities to focus on balance. The typical convention of a four-year plan for undergraduate study may not hold true for these students. If that is the case, students should be encouraged to focus on what type of balanced time/life approach will support reaching graduation, not how many semesters/years it will take. Research also shows that working may help students develop better time management skills (Reid & Moore, 2008).

Similar ideas hold true for students with family responsibilities. Due to these needs, there may not be enough time to take a full course load each term. Like working students (or perhaps working students with family obligations), the focus needs to be on learning and success, not the days/months/years to reach degree completion.

Though finding the right blend of time management tips may vary from student to student, there are a number of strategies from which to choose. Consider the following Time Management Tips and try them on for size. Maintain those that are working and drop those that do not contribute to personal time management goals.

Time Management Tips

There are students with great potential struggling with making time to address academics. Some students have a to-do list just too long for the time in a day. The tips that follow are intended to synthesize strategies and options available to assist students in being successful with time choices that support the achievement of personal and academic goals. Insert these tips in a syllabus, share them in print materials (posters, flyers, etc.), post them on departmental websites or social media shares and use them to openly discuss the role of successful time management in student group meetings and classroom conversations.

Time Management Tips

- *Plan*—Keep a weekly planner to help stay organized.
- *Write*—Jot down reminders for key items (including assignments).
- *Goals*—Set more specific goals that include timeframes rather than broad ideas like "graduate."
- *Dislike*—If procrastination is a problem, do the most difficult or distasteful task first. Getting it over with can help reduce anxiety.
- *Pieces*—Divide up large projects into subprojects. It makes them less intimidating, reduces procrastination and allows a sense of accomplishment even before the project is complete.
- *Daily*—Complete at least one task each day, even if that's a small part of a larger project.

> - *Worry*—Schedule time to worry. Try not to worry about Task B when working on Task A. Schedule Task B and worry about that task at that time and not before.
> - *Disconnect*—Turn off phones, social media, etc. when working on academics. If this is a struggle, consider adding software or apps that prevent use of select functions when on.

Faculty

While many higher education professionals have used previous academic experiences and testing as predictors of success in college, studies have established that time management may predict achievement related to academic quality and college GPA (Britton & Tesser, 1991; Macan et al., 1990). Faculty members are wise to consider the role that time plays in student success. Perhaps higher education professionals may be wise to embrace what Chickering and Gamson (1987) said when they noted that students need help with learning time management. "Allocating realistic amounts of time means effective learning for students and effective teaching for faculty" (p. 4).

Students may have very different concepts of the amounts of time needed to be successful with academic pursuits at the college level. Collier and Morgan (2008) explored the similarities and differences between student and faculty expectations. Their study found that "discussions among groups of faculty and groups of students highlight important differences regarding issues of time management and specific aspects of coursework" (p. 425).

Faculty members are wise to begin each term with a frank conversation on the role and amount of time needed to demonstrate learning and success. Offering reminders of key assignment due dates, discouraging procrastination and holding students accountable to deadlines are all basic strategies to help promote effective time management. "If students do not understand professors' expectations about how many hours a week they should study, then students may not allocate sufficient time to master key course skills or to identify and retain key content areas" (Collier & Morgan, 2008, p. 442). Further, encourage students to use time between classes to make progress on academic responsibilities and assignments.

Other key strategies to promote time/life management include:

- Model balance when it comes to time. This can be most easily demonstrated when returning graded assignments in a timely manner.
- Make major assignments due in parts. This offers opportunities to give feedback along the way and makes grading the finished product easier for faculty members.
- Provide guidance on deadlines. Reminders help, and frequent reminders reduce the number of people asking for extensions.

- Be intentional with spacing assignments. Faculty members teaching upper division courses are encouraged to work with colleagues who are likely teaching the same students to not make all assignments due in the same short timeframes. Students will feel less pressure, faculty will have fewer items to grade at once and likely there will be fewer complaints from students.
- Do not allow late assignments to earn credit. It sends the message that time management is important to success. Read and provide feedback on late submissions (relative to learning) but do not grant full or even reduced credit.
- Hold office hours. When office hours are not used by students, the use of time is less efficient for faculty and students alike. Encourage students to use office hours to help answer questions on assignments, readings or other issues before submitting.

Activity: Building a Healthy, Balanced Schedule

Recommended time management priorities for creating a balanced, health-promoting and sustainable schedule:

1. Sleep
2. Meals
3. Classes
4. Academic Prep (studying, homework)
5. Work (if necessary to remain enrolled)

These priorities for time management are not impacted by variables like full-time or part-time student status, age, hours spent working or volunteering, etc.

Challenge yourself. Take an empty weekly or monthly calendar noted with 24 hours per day. Create a schedule using the priority list, stopping initially after the first four categories. Use 7–9 hours for sleep, 30 minutes each for breakfast and lunch, 1 hour for dinner. After the first four categories have been included, the remaining time is yours. How much time allocated to any additional activities is determined by the individual (e.g., work if required to stay in school).

While this may feel aspirational, give it a go. Compare how you actually spend your time in a week (keep a time journal perhaps) to the plan created using this approach. Identify the discrepancies and make a plan for how you might address them. If you try, be ready for the realization that many of us are not terribly efficient with our time and that multitasking often leads to individual tasks taking longer.

Administrators

Administrators may seem to have less influence on issues of students' time, although this is somewhat of a misnomer. It is the student affairs administrators that often take the lead on first welcoming students to campus, also known as orientation. Although not complete without support from academic colleagues, the tone set during orientation is a starting framework for students adjusting to the time demands of campuses. "Time management is the most difficult part of the transition from high school to college" (Reid & Moore, 2008, p. 255). High school is very structured, and the unstructured nature of college may make it difficult for students to adjust successfully. Administrators are wise to revisit the structure of orientation as students frequently mention orientation as being overscheduled; during this period, there is little free time, after which the sense of structure is wholly removed, and students may be at a loss for how to approach time management. Replacing non-essential sessions with one on time management may also help focus students' attention on the issue earlier in their post-secondary career. Perhaps finding a better sense of time balance as students transition to campus can begin to set the framework for the college experience.

With college campuses being highly complex, often bureaucratic organizations, administrators should investigate the amount of time students spend trying to learn how to get even simple things accomplished. The perceived lack of time control that manifests in students may have a relationship to how successful they are with time management. Given that some students will have a preference for disorganization and that this factor alone is associated with academic stress, administrators are wise to consider opportunities to streamline the complexity of tasks to facilitate more time-efficient student functions (registration, paying bills, submitting forms, etc.). Embracing scheduling and planning, along with promoting a perceived control over time among students is associated with student success (Macan et al., 1990).

Campuses are wise to consider limiting the number of leadership roles each student may have or the number of organizations to which a student belongs and ensuring that there are structural and advisor-supported efforts that help with co-curricular involvement/development without overscheduling students. Grayson (1996) noted that among first-year students not performing to expected levels, when those students invested in academically related extracurricular activities, they were more likely to have increases in GPA than those who focused on socially related options. Refocusing to limited co-curricular and academically related options might help address time management challenges as well as promote broader student success.

Administrators can also model time balance through a series of actions including:

- Having an "activity hour" in each standard day to provide space for clubs and organizations to meet. Having just one per week is insufficient as it results in too many items scheduled at exactly the same time, creating time conflicts and pressures for students.

- Balance the types of classes across a day and the days of the week. If too many classes of a similar nature are scheduled back-to-back, it may create pressures and prevent faculty from working together to support a temporally balanced approach to learning.
- Add time between class start and end times. If classes are too close together, it may create the feeling of rushing. Careful spacing facilitates opportunities for student engagement with faculty before and after class (rather than running to the next class) as well as gives students an opportunity to make the mental transition from one topic to the next. To accomplish this element, it becomes essential to use more of the day for academic courses to accommodate the spacing.
- Set realistic limits on how many courses can be taken per term. While some students may be able to balance an above-average workload, limits on the number of courses promote balance in students.

Conclusion

Today's society glorifies the idea of "busy." Too much to do, not enough time and starting requests with "I know you are busy, but . . ." just validate that one person's time is more important than anything else and that polite, if validating, requests can get a person to further sacrifice balance to add yet another item to the to-do list. These pressures are contributing to a social expectation, nay a social requirement, that individuals must always be doing "more." It is time to bring about the end of the false "busy" and return people to lives of wholeness, balance and meaningful purpose. Next time someone says "I know you must be busy" quickly interject "just like everyone else" to shift from the falsely glorified "busy" and begin a real conversation about shared experiences on time and how to use choice of time expenditures to bring an evenness to life.

The higher education community has an opportunity to correct the overscheduled and managed time of the current generation and offer lessons in priority, goals, balance and develop an unhurried sense of time. Unstructured time need not feel unfamiliar and uncomfortable but can be seen as discretionary opportunities to pursue hobbies and interests knowing that key priorities and responsibilities are safely accounted for in the wise time schedules of students. It is important that college professionals not procrastinate in making a renewed focus on time balance a key part of the college student learning experience.

References

American College Health Association. (2015). *American College Health Association-National College Health Assessment (ACHA-NCHA) Spring 2015 Reference Group Data Report.* Retrieved from http://www.acha-ncha.org/docs/NCHA-II%20WEB_SPRING_2015_REFERENCE_GROUP_DATA_REPORT.pdf

Anand, V. (2007). A study of time management: The correlation between video game usage and academic performance markers. *CyberPsychology & Behavior, 10,* 552–559.

Balduf, M. (2009). Underachievement among college students. *Journal of Advanced Academics, 20,* 274–794.

Britton, B. K., & Tesser, A. (1991). Effects of time-management practices on college grades. *Journal of Educational Psychology, 83,* 405–410.

Brown, R. T. (1991). Helping students confront and deal with stress and procrastination. *Journal of College Student Psychotherapy, 6*, 87–102.

Campbell, R. L., & Svenson, L. W. (1992). Perceived level of stress among university undergraduate students in Edmonton, Canada. *Perceptual and Motor Skills, 75*, 552–554.

Chickering, A. W., & Gamson, Z. F. (1987, March). Seven principles for good practice in undergraduate education. *AAHE Bulletin*, 3–7.

Clement, M., Jankowski, L. W., Bouchard, L., Perreault, M., & Lepage, Y. (2002). Health behaviors of nursing students: A longitudinal study. *Journal of Nursing Education, 41*, 257–265.

Collier, P. T., & Morgan, D. L. (2008). "Is that paper really due today?" Differences in first generation and traditional college students' understandings of faculty expectations. *Higher Education, 55*, 425–446.

Columbia University. (2015). *Oh no! I've got FOMO (fear of missing out)!* Retrieved from http://goaskalice.columbia.edu/answered-questions/oh-no-ive-got-fomo-fear-missing-out

Coomes, M. D., & DeBard, R. (2004). A generational approach to understanding students. *New Directions for Student Services, 106*, 5–16. doi: 10.1002/ss.121

Ellis, Y., Daniels, B., & Jauregui, A. (2010). The effect of multitasking on the grade performance of business students. *Richard in Higher Education Journal, 8*, 1–10.

Grayson, J. P. (1996). *Under- and Over-Achievement in First Year*. Toronto, Ontario, Canada: Institute for Social Research.

Junco, R., & Cotton, S. R. (2011). Perceived academic effects of instant messaging use. *Computers & Education, 56*, 370–378.

Lay, C. H., & Schouwenburg, H. C. (1993). Trait procrastination, time management, and academic behavior. *Journal of Social Behavior and Personality, 8*, 647–662.

Lepp, A., Barkley, J. E., & Karpinski, A. C. (2014). The relationship between cell phone use, academic performance, anxiety, and satisfaction with life in college students. *Computers in Human Behavior, 31*, 343–350.

Macan, T. H., Shahani, C., Dipboye, R. L., & Phillips, A. P. (1990). College students' time management: Correlations with academic performance and stress. *Journal of Educational Psychology, 82*, 760–768.

MacCann, C., Fogarty, G. J., & Roberts, R. D. (2012). Strategies for success in education: Time management is more important for part-time than full-time community college students. *Learning and Individual Differences, 22*, 618–623.

Misra, R., & McKean, M. (2000). College students' academic stress and its relation to their anxiety, time management, and leisure satisfaction. *American Journal of Health Studies, 16*, 41–51.

Princeton University. (2012). *Understanding and Overcoming Procrastination*. Retrieved from https://www.princeton.edu/mcgraw/library/for-students/avoiding-procrastination/procrastination.pdf

Proctor, B. E., Prevatt, F. F., Adams, K. S., Reaser, A., & Petscher, Y. (2006). Study skills profiles of normal-achieving and academically-struggling college students. *Journal of College Student Development, 47*, 37–51.

Reaser, A., Prevatt, F., Petscher, Y., & Proctor, B. (2007). The learning and study strategies of college students with ADHD. *Psychology in the Schools, 44*, 627–638.

Reid, M. J., & Moore, J. L. (2008). College readiness and academic preparation for postsecondary education. *Urban Education, 43*, 240–261.

Reis, S. M., Hébert, T. P., Díaz, E. I., Maxfield, L. R., & Ratley, M. E. (1995). *Case Studies of Talented Students Who Achieve and Underachieve in an Urban High School (Research Monograph 95120)*. Storrs: University of Connecticut, National Research Center on the Gifted and Talented.

Voge, D. (2007). Classroom resources for addressing procrastination. *Research and Teaching in Developmental Education, 23*, 88–96.

Wolfe, I. S. (2009). *Geeks, Geezers, and Googlization*. Lancaster, PA: Author.

6

Financial Wellness

A Campuswide Responsibility

BRYAN ASHTON

Introduction

The landscape of higher education has seen rapid changes over the last few years, including changes in the way that information is delivered to students (such as the rise of Massive Open Online Courses), the type of students attending college (including the rise of new traditional—non-traditional—students) and arguably most importantly the way that individuals perceive the value of higher education. One is hard pressed to regularly visit any mainstream media outlet and not see stories related to the rising cost of higher education and the subsequent rise in student loan debt being assumed by students and recent graduates. These concerns appear to grow even further when looking at the increase in the number of individuals defaulting on their student loans and the increased length of repayment on these loans, which is leading to a delayed financial life for many recent graduates ("Life Delayed," 2013). The idea of a delayed financial life is often quantified through lack of savings (both for emergency and for retirement), delayed homeownership and delayed starting of a family. It is important for higher education professionals, whether student affairs professionals, faculty, academic advisors, administrators or others, to understand the context through which its audience views the services provided. Increasingly, that context is related to the cost and perceived value that is returned to the student for that cost. This means that increased focus must be paid to how individuals finance higher education and the effects that financing has on their daily lives, both while they are enrolled in school and as they leave the institution to transition into the world as alumni and as productive adults and leaders in the country and the world.

Fairly well documented are the continual rise in the price tag of education (to the student) and the subsequent impact on the larger institutional metrics including average student borrowing and the cohort default rates that it creates (Holland, 2015). As such, this chapter takes a slightly different approach to understanding the role of finances in a college student's life. The focus is on the impact of these changes, the impact that finances have on the individual and ways that higher education professionals can assist students navigate the complex world of money during their time in higher education and beyond.

Identifying the Problem

Research findings generated through the National Student Financial Wellness Study show that substantial work remains to be done with educating students around their finances. When asked a series of five financial knowledge questions, students answered three questions (60%) correctly on average. These numbers are compounded by data that shows a limited number of students have received financial education while in school, whether at the secondary school or higher education level. Less than one-third (30.6%) of respondents, from a sample size of 18,795 across 52 institutions of higher education, received any financial education in high school, with only 13.2% (of survey respondents) receiving that education in a form that was more than a one-time event. Unfortunately these numbers only get worse when looking at students in the collegiate setting; there, only 22.8% of students have received some form of financial education with only 7.5% (of survey respondents) of those students receiving it in a format that lasted longer than a one-time event (Center for the Study of Student Life, 2015a).

In conjunction with the limited exposure to financial management training, the environment around financial management has also made it increasingly more difficult for individuals (of all ages) to manage spending and focus on the future financial lives they will have. Years ago, individuals would write checks and balance their checkbooks afterwards or pay using cash. Both of these methods of payment create a feeling of attachment to the actual act of spending. According to the Federal Reserve System, debit cards are the fastest growing segment of the transaction market (Federal Reserve System, 2013). Transactions are now conducted with various forms of "plastic" or online payment methods, removing much of the attachment that a person has to money. This is shown in students' financial behaviors. The national study cited earlier shows that just over 22% of students report that they follow a weekly or monthly budget (Center for the Study of Student Life, 2015a).

All in all, the combination of limited financial literacy, modest financial education efforts and the changing landscape surrounding financial transactions has increasingly caused financial stress among students. Across a range of variables, student financial stress remains at high levels:

- 72.0% of students feel stressed about their finances in general
- 50.5% worry about the ability to pay monthly expenses
- 59.8% of individuals worry about having enough money to pay for school

Additionally, data from a statewide assessment of student finances shows that students self-report that their financial situation is having an impact on their ability to perform while in school. Results show that over one-quarter of students in four-year institutions have reduced their class load, and approximately one-third have considered dropping out of college, based on the amount of money owed; these rates are higher among students in two-year institutions. Effects on individuals to perform academic work are cited by between 28% and 37% of survey respondents (Center for the Study of Student Life, 2011).

Given that focus on student finances has generally been through lenses of student loan debt and the cost of education, it is easy to assume that issues related to student finances would reside within a campus's office of financial aid. While some aspects of financial affairs are found there, it is becoming clear that the implications of student finances extend far beyond the amount of borrowing and truly impacts student wellness overall, including academic performance.

Rise in Collegiate Programs

As individuals have increasingly looked at higher education with a focus on finances, there has been a rise in pressure on institutions of higher education to reduce the cost of the education they are providing, with the federal government often leading the charge (Lewin, 2013). This pressure presents many challenges, as very often the cost of structure of higher education institutions is deeply ingrained, with substantial movement to reduce costs relying on large programmatic cuts or shifts in state/private support. Given this reality, there has been an additional focus on the institutions' responsibility to help support a student financially. This is coupled with an increasingly common understanding that individuals are entering into large financial decisions (going to college) without having the adequate information to make the decisions and understand the long-term implications of those decisions. As such, there has been increased agreement among administrators about the need to begin to address the shockingly low level of financial literacy in their student body and to assist students with managing their financial challenges (Inceptia, 2013).

This attention has led to a large increase in the number of campuses that are looking to tackle issues related to collegiate financial wellness. These programs have attempted to address a variety of primary metrics, including student loan debt, student financial knowledge and student loan default rates. To address these topics, collegiate financial wellness programs have taken numerous approaches by designing interventions to reach their student population. These approaches include the distribution of information via online approaches including one-time modules and semester-long courses, presentations and workshops; one-on-one coaching/counseling and occasionally curricular options. Higher education has traditionally used one- or two-time interventions to engage students in financial information and attempt to build financial capability. This inability to sustain engagement, and the idea that shorter engagement leads to less desirable outcomes, has prompted topics of conversation around metrics for these interventions as programs attempt to define their impact and set learning outcomes related to the delivery of financial literacy information. Despite increased recognition by administrators around the value of sustained engagement in financial topics, there is also a very real understanding that challenges are presented by the difficulty related with scaling these interventions. Included in these challenges are the cost of scaling interventions (normally in terms of the staff time associated with delivering the intervention) and the idea of potentially delaying graduation or increasing costs for students by requiring them to take a semester-long course.

Despite some of these challenging factors, an increased consumer pressure remains to provide real-world skills for students, which has led, and will continue to lead, to an increase in collegiate financial literacy initiatives. This focus is not only on the employability of graduates but also on the responsibility of institutions to help students manage their finances given the high cost of higher education (as cited earlier). As programs related to student money management continue to grow, they will be faced with many of the same problems that have plagued financial education in a variety of populations, including unclear metrics, lack of evidence-based practice and a challenging population of learners. However, there are many promising practices and opportunities appropriate for higher education professionals of all types, whether student affairs professionals, faculty members, administrators, academic advisors or others. These approaches can individually and collectively help engage and support students with their financial issues, both for a healthy college experience as well as for their lives following college.

History

Financial education programs have existed in a variety of forms on college campuses for a few decades. These programs often began as extensions of academic units, specifically those academic programs charged with producing students trained in the consumer sciences and individuals who were interested in pursuing the Certified Financial Planner (CFP) route. These programs provided (and still provide) an amazing opportunity for students to be trained in financial topics; they put that training to use helping students on their own campus make better financial decisions.

As these academic (CFP prep) programs gained traction, also found has been an increase in the number of students working to support fellow students in a 1:1 peer coaching role. These students were trained to provide interventions, similar to those peer educators in other areas of health promotion (alcohol and other drugs) but were still traditionally housed in the academic programs that they supported. Only recently has the trend been to engage these programs in other areas of the institution, such as the financial aid office, the Chief Financial Officer's office and the student affairs division.

The relocation of these initiatives into these centralized offices provides a lens to look at the experience from the students' perspective, predict points of student financial strain and provide targeted, just-in-time interventions to support these efforts. While there are pros and cons to each administrative home for a program, the important point is that there is no one home that can provide total ownership of the issue, as financial wellness truly is a campuswide area of concern. Table 6.1 below looks to outline many of the pros and cons of specific administrative homes for programs.

Wherever a financial education program is housed administratively, many different types of interventions can be delivered. Research has suggested (based on student desires) that three main avenues exist through which campuses should deliver financial education, including online interventions, in person through

TABLE 6.1 Assessment of Programmatic Home Options for Financial Education

Program Home	Pros	Cons
Academic Program	• Expertise for the program is often available in the program • Access to students for peer-to-peer coaching • Opportunity to provide semester-long classes • Easy to provide curricular options and conduct research and assessment activities	• Difficult to connect with students outside of the classroom • Difficult to expand beyond general financial literacy to financial behavior and financial aid • Challenges with connecting with other campus departments
Student Affairs	• Strong understanding of the holistic student experience • Ability to access students through multiple touch points (e.g., housing, student organizations) • Broadens the conversations beyond just finances and has broader access to referral networks	• Need to be strongly linked to enrollment management/financial aid • Need to be involved in policy conversations and financial aid conversations • Need to develop academic ties for effective peer-to-peer programs
Financial Aid	• Strong access to financial aid information and policies • Good understanding of student debt issues and campus trends • Access to just-in-time interventions	• Easy to focus on only financial aid literacy • Tend to be quick interactions driven by time to service • Tough to create campuswide focus
Chief Financial Officer	• Great senior administration buy-in (and often funding) • Support to move across the institution • Can make substantial business practice changes	• Difficult to reach students • Issues with creating goal congruence across campus • Disconnected from many points of the student life cycle

one-on-one coaching and in person through group workshops (Goetz, Cude, Nielsen, Chatterjee, & Mimura, 2011). More broadly, campuses are delivering this education through seven different channels in an effort to reach a wide variety of students:

1. *Online modules* provide a scalable option to help meet students where they are and allowing for the access to information when and where a student may need it. These are often targeted at enhancing knowledge gain of students using them and provide broad coverage over a variety of topics. Many institutions

are placing this type of programming as part of their pre-enrollment routine or in a first-year seminar course.

2. *Presentations and workshops* have been a very traditional means of delivering financial education. These can take a variety of forms but currently have been focused on specific topics (such as repaying debt, moving off campus or budgeting in the first year) and include hands-on worksheets and activities. This allows them to leave with customized information related to their own financial situation.

3. *One-on-one coaching/counseling* has become increasingly popular to reduce the stigma around receiving financial education and allow for a personalized experience that can assist in creating a financial plan to proactively addressing finances and respond to negative financial events. These sessions are often conducted with trained student volunteers or trained staff and cover a wide variety of topics.

4. *Static website resources* have traditionally been included with information provided by financial aid offices to help students make more informed borrowing decisions. While these resources may not have the highest level of engagement, they serve as a trusted source of information in an era of information overload.

5. *Just-in-time education* provides a great opportunity to provide relevant information to a student when they need it. Since concerns exist about the retention of financial information over the long term, students can be provided with the relevant financial education during the time of decision making to assist in making the most appropriate decision.

6. *Curricular offerings* are often seen as one of the most effective, but most difficult to scale, interventions. These provide the opportunities for students to be immersed in a full semester of personal finance, learning specific financial topics and working to provide the alignment of those topics to their individual situations.

7. *Business practices* have a large impact on student finances, even when institutions may not realize it. In line with a public health environmental approach, institutions are beginning to review their business practices (everything from how loans are packaged, to class drop procedures and satisfactory academic progress) to make sure that students are supported financially throughout. Indiana University implemented a revision of business practices (in addition to a financial literacy intervention) and saw a $44 million reduction in borrowing over a two-year time period (Indiana University, 2015).

Many programs provide support to students who encounter any of a variety of different challenges. Four areas are identified as being of particular importance for student support:

1. Assist students in developing financial capability: Provide resources to help students grow their financial knowledge, develop healthy attitudes around financial topics and implement sound financial behaviors.

2. Address students' financial stress: Financial stress is a reality for the majority of students at campuses across the country (Center for the Study of Student Life, 2015a). Work to help students manage this stress to healthy levels, assist in the students' development of sound financial behaviors and strive to help students manage stress that may be distracting from their ability to succeed academically.

3. Provide just-in-time education to enhance decision making: Individuals are increasingly making financial decisions without the necessary information to make an informed decision. Look at points in time when individuals are making financial decisions and provide them with the necessary information and resources to make an informed decision. Do this while knowing that many students have not received financial education, and even if they have, there may have been some atrophy in the knowledge gained.

4. Support students in financial crisis: Unfortunately, financial crisis is a reality for many Americans, and being enrolled in a college or university does not prevent this. This may be caused by job loss, injury or illness or any of a number of other factors, but the end result is serious financial strain and change in financial circumstance. Strive to support students through these financial shocks and attempt to help them manage cash flow during these times and beyond.

Very often these services are targeted at helping students in three different ways:

1. Being proactive allows college professionals to reach students in their first or second year and help them to understand their current financial standing and identify any potential roadblocks that may create financial concern in the future. This is a great way to identify barriers to graduation related to finances when there is still time to make adjustments to the individual's financial plan.

2. Being reactive in supporting students is a necessity on college campuses. Many situations in college (and in life) that cause severe stress are driven by financial events. Some of these events are avoidable, but many come about as a result of "life happens" or unexpected events that arise. When these situations emerge, it is important that institutions have emergency aid and assistance programs in place. It is also important to provide adequate financial coaching to help students weather the transition.

3. Finances are an incredibly misunderstood topic, and very few people receive formal education on their finances. Because of this, there are often unanswered questions. Thus, it is important to provide a confidential, unbiased place where individuals can go to seek support as they develop their financial plan and navigate their financial life.

Challenges to Program Implementation

As with any relatively new field, there are inherent challenges as programs and services develop. Program planners need to make sure that the appropriate level of service is provided and that programs are developed in an effective manner that assist students throughout the campus community. These challenges often begin at the inception of a program and persist throughout the time that the program is developing. This starts with developing the unit on campus where the program should be based. As noted previously, many areas on campus exist where programs and services related to financial wellness can be housed: student affairs, financial aid, business and finance and academic units. All of these locations have pros and cons and many may seem like a natural fit on a college campus. Finding the right home for a program is a campus-by-campus discussion, and one that is often plagued with politics, financial considerations and other inherent campus issues. Despite these challenges, it is important to note that regardless of where a program is housed, it should not be viewed as ownership or exclusivity. Ownership of this issue must truly be campuswide, as it allows for the campus to take an environment-based approach and support students across a wide variety of units.

Another challenge that is often difficult to remove from the conversation about where a program is located is the development of the appropriate program metrics. These metrics can be difficult to establish and are often driven by the different constituencies represented in the program leadership. Some common metrics include increased financial knowledge, increased student retention, reduction in students' account payable balances, changes in student borrowing behaviors and reduction in student loan default rates. It is important to note that many of these metrics have numerous contributing factors and may be difficult to accurately assess. However, it is still important for campus administrators and program heads to come to a common understanding around the metrics of success of a campus-based initiative or program.

There are additional challenges that emerge once a program has been developed. These challenges include figuring out how to create a sustained interaction with students, reaching the students who need the support the most and engaging the campus community in delivering the information (regardless of job function). When looking at effective interventions around student finances, the aim is to consistently try to establish a relationship with a student that extends beyond a one-time intervention. This is true of many other health promotion topics and is very important with the issue of financial wellness. Because of this, it is helpful to assess the student life cycle and identify different points in time that may be helpful to provide various financial education points. It can be beneficial to look at the student experience and identify which offices and processes have the most impact with students at risk for financial stress and attempt to integrate interventions into those areas. Finally, the importance of financial wellness as a campuswide issue cannot be overstated. Ways of engaging various offices, and the important role of faculty and academic advisors in understanding the nature and scope of student financial issues and stressors, should be examined. There is a need to work to engage other units of campus in understanding their role in student finances and help them examine ways in which they can aid the broader mission of enhancing student financial wellness. As these programs continue to mature and expand, it is hoped that these challenges will be lessened.

What Works?

Many emerging trends exist in higher education that have worked to support students as they manage their financial lives. Highlights of these include the following:

- Provide an opportunity for financial interventions to be holistic in nature. Finances, like many other areas of student wellness, are truly interconnected with various areas of a student's life. If a student is presenting with financial concerns, often these concerns are either driven by another wellness area of concern (e.g., addiction, emotional distress, relationship difficulties) or that the financial situation is causing some other wellness concerns (e.g., poor nutrition, increased stress/anxiety, drug or alcohol abuse).
- Unfortunately many individuals hold financial interventions to unrealistic standards. A one-time intervention with a student is unlikely to have substantial long-term impact on knowledge gain or behavior change (regardless of the subject matter). Because of this it is important to look at opportunities to continuously reinforce topics related to student finances and provide ongoing reinforcement of key financial topics. This could include a re-education process when students take out loans after their first year or a realistic introduction to budgeting conversation at the beginning of each year to assist with understanding financial commitments.
- Due to the holistic nature of student finances, it is important to include the campus community in the conversation and map the student life cycle, thus allowing for recognition of the various opportunities for integration of just-in-time education that is timely and relevant to students. Examples of just-in-time education include:
  - Working with students to provide financial coaching and connection to government assistance/benefits during a Volunteer Income Tax Assistance Clinic (VITA) as they are filing their taxes (see online Resources section).
  - Providing enhanced options for entrance and exit counseling related to a student's loans accumulated while in school.
  - Working with students to provide a template to budget for the transition from a residence hall to an off-campus residence, which often presents challenges related to students' ability to manage cash flow (a much larger financial refund is normally issued, with the intent that the sum lasts over an entire semester).
  - Assisting students who are behind with their payments to the institution or who are seeking emergency support to manage their current financial situation but also exploring opportunities to plan to avoid similar situations in the future.
  - During the application process, assisting students by walking through the process of budgeting for their entire degree. This allows them to see how much funding they will be responsible for (either by themselves or with family support) and also identifies which forms of financial aid may not be guaranteed every year. This can help to assist with potential retention issues that may arise through a lack understanding of the total cost of a degree.

- Higher education institutions often shy away from mandating certain interventions; however, with financial wellness, there is room for mandates, soft mandates and even incentivized interventions. This may include mandating individuals going through the emergency aid process to receive financial coaching (please note that there are specific regulations related to federal student aid) or waiving late fees associated with the late payment of tuition if a student completes a plan to become current with the institution.

Best Practice Case Studies

The field of financial education programs on college campuses is still in its relative infancy. Given this, many questions exist related to the effectiveness of specific programs and the best practices for developing a program on campus. However, some practices are emerging as potential best practices on numerous campuses, of all sizes, across the country. A few of these practices are included below:

Peer Financial Coaching

Challenge: One of the largest challenges seen with delivering financial information is moving beyond the stigma often associated with discussing money. Studies have shown that parents are more likely to talk with their kids about sex than certain money topics (T. Rowe Price, 2013), which presents challenges when it comes to engaging individuals in conversations about money. Because of this, campuses have searched for ways to present financial information in non-threatening ways and begin to develop the comfort talking about money and developing a financial plan.

Opportunity: Campuses have looked toward peer financial coaching as a mutually beneficial partnership. First and foremost, the student body has access to well-trained peer educators that are relatable and able to reduce the stigma associated with discussing money. Additionally, these students have credibility in their ability to recommend suggestions for alterations to their financial lives, as they are intimately familiar with the challenges facing their fellow students. The peers delivering the financial coaching are trained to work with different clients in a one-on-one setting and are trained to have very difficult conversations. This training is transferable into numerous career fields of interest to students and is viewed as a strong asset in the employment search process with numerous recruiters.

Outcome: Peer financial coaching is showing many positive outcomes in early assessment of certain programs. This includes an increase in students' awareness of their financial situation, an increase in self-efficacy of students when it comes to managing their finances and short-term increases in financial knowledge and positive financial behavior. Additionally, students report comfort in meeting with a peer coach as it relates to reducing the stigma associated with discussing personal finances.

As one financial coach at Ohio State explains:

Today's college student values family and friends as a way of support and help. Increasingly college students have turned to their friends to share advice, take help and support each other on many facets of life such as career choices, education choices, financial well-being etc. In spite of the strong friendships and support systems, students sometimes are afraid to share the financial problems with their 'close' ones due to their assumption of being judged. This is where professionally trained peer-to-peer coaching becomes so effective.

At Scarlet and Gray Financial, peer to peer coaching has been so effective by offering a friendly, judgment free, and professional environment to students who are in need of help in the area of financial wellness. The idea that one student coach can help and guide another student client on a personal level while giving the client a reassurance of complete confidentiality and friendly environment makes it a wonderful experience for the student client. The coach embodies the passion to help and the client comes with a need for help, which makes it a win-win situation for both the individuals and results in an effective coaching. The emotional, intellectual, and similar experiences of college experiences of the students can help them connect, share problems, and trust each other, which can catapult the relationship to a deeper level, fostering problem solving, and improved results.

(Nikhil Aggarwal—Peer Financial Coach, The Ohio State University)

Emergency Loans

Challenge: Many institutions traditionally offer an emergency loan, such as through operational budgets, reserve funding or an institutional endowment, to students in need of immediate and unanticipated financial assistance. This loan can be seen as a loan of last resort and could have limits on it, such as the ability to access it only once per academic year. If this is offered, campus administrators would benefit from exploring why students were taking the loan, what resources could help support students beyond the financial assistance and if there were ways to avoid students needing to access the loan in the future.

Opportunity: Because the loan was derived from institutional funds, the institution maintains the opportunity to alter the application requirements to include additional resources that could help provide more holistic support.

Outcome: Institutions may include a financial coaching requirement to the process of applying for the loan. Through this coaching appointment, students are able to take a holistic look at their finances, set financial goals and develop the appropriate cash flow plans. Further, students can become connected to other campus and community resources to help reduce the burden of their financial emergency. These appointments can lead to an increased connection to campus-based resources and an increased understanding of how to develop a financial plan that can assist with managing their money in the future.

Mandated Interventions

Challenge: Finances, for many, present a situation where ignorance can be bliss. However, there is a great opportunity to plan a sound financial future when individuals have the time and coaching to help facilitate these activities. Many students are unaware of their current financial standing (including how much money is being borrowed). Numerous opportunities exist to assist students to recognize where they stand financially and allow them to begin to develop a financial plan.

Opportunity: Institutions can support students' financial wellness through mandatory interventions for various situations.

1. Many institutions look to integrate financial interventions prior to students coming to campus or within the first few weeks of an academic term. These interventions include online modules that can be completed from the comfort of a student's home but may also incorporate an in-person session that explains the management of finances during a student's first year or gives an in-depth overview of the student loan process.
2. Institutions are also looking to integrate mandatory financial literacy programs into specific co-curricular programs including bridge programs, scholar programs/learning communities and student organizations. These interventions take many forms but have the benefit of being integrated often after students have been enrolled for some time in higher education.
3. Campuses are also looking to provide financial interventions as part of an emergency support process. This includes building financial interventions into the application process for emergency institutional aid, developing interventions for those on payment plans and working with those who have past due balances.

Outcome: Institutions can combine online and in-person tools to provide a holistic intervention to individuals during different checkpoints in their financial lives. Institutions have found success in providing yearly or semester recaps of individual student loan balances. These letters have shown reductions of student borrowing and also make students more aware of their finances. Integration of financial coaching into emergency loan application processes or as part of a co-curricular program can help students pause and reflect on their current financial standing and make modifications to enhance their short- and long-term financial wellness.

Financial Advisory Board

Challenge: At many universities, a large number of departments and individuals are either already providing some form of financial intervention or see the value of this in their work. While this is great news for the buy-in needed to truly create a campuswide initiative, it can present challenges when it comes to finding a home for an initiative without creating issues with individuals feeling the need to own the efforts.

Opportunity: These passionate and talented individuals all bring different perspectives to the table around the financial challenges of students, which is incredibly helpful in determining the types of interventions that a campus needs and the metrics associated with success. These individuals can contribute to the drafting of a common vision for campus-based financial wellness efforts and can ideally contribute to finding the appropriate home for a wellness initiative, a home that provides the opportunity for shared ownership across campus.

Outcome: A successful activity for many campuses (of all sizes) is the convening of a financial wellness advisory board, which serves to connect individuals from across campus and create a space to have true inter-departmental conversations about student finances. The result may be a document that sets a shared strategic plan including outcomes, priorities and partnership strategies to drive support from all corners of the campus to support the mission of enhancing students' financial wellness.

Campuswide Concerns

Students are coming to campus with a wide variety of concerns, and they continue to face numerous challenges. These challenges are presenting concerns for administrators and other campus leaders, who look more critically at how to enhance student success. Financial challenges are increasingly topping these areas of concerns; some examples include:

- Students are feeling stress as they watch the amount of money they borrow for their degree increase. This stress, often compounded by the decrease in average earnings for many degrees (and increased un-/under-employment rates) has many students questioning the economic return of the degrees they will be receiving.
- Additionally, students report high levels of financial stress related to meeting their monthly expenses (defined as the "needs" including housing, food and utilities). This day-to-day stress is similar to the stress felt by many Americans as they work and live paycheck to paycheck. This can create challenges related to students' ability to focus on their academic pursuits.
- Students increasingly report that the amount of money they owe and their current financial situation causes them to work more hours. While working on campus can provide some positive outcomes, students are increasingly working more hours, thus having an impact on their academic performance. As students work more, they may reduce their course load or distract their focus from their academic studies; this can often increase the time to complete the degree and increase the spending on education in the long run. Additionally, many of the jobs held by students are part time and spilt across multiple employers, thus providing additional challenges of scheduling and balancing course loads.
- One of the leading causes of student financial stress, after the amount of money students owe, is generated by the idea that students do not have enough money to participate in the activities of their peers. This stress is often driven by perceived differences in socio-economic status and can be addressed by working to create financially inclusive communities and programs for the student body.
- Purchasing required course materials—65% of students report not purchasing required course materials due to personal financial constraints (U.S. PIRG Education Fund & The Student PIRGS, 2014).

- Alcohol consumption—An emerging tie is found between increased alcohol consumption and financial stress, something that creates some concern as these high-risk behaviors continue to show signs of being tied together (Center for the Study of Student Life, 2015b, p. 16).

Not only do these micro-level concerns represent the interconnectedness of student financial issues with other wellness issues, they also show that numerous departments across campus have interactions, directly or indirectly, with students' financial situations. These include faculty members who select required course texts and course assignments (which may impact student work schedules), to academic advisors who help define a student's time to earn a degree (and therefore impact an individual's debt levels), to career advisors who assist students in navigating the complex process of post-collegiate earnings (therefore affecting repayment). They also include student affairs practitioners who influence the integration of different socio-economic backgrounds throughout the campus and set or define experiences that may be cost-prohibitive for some students. It is important to look at the opportunities offered to students (no matter how great they may be) and assess the financial feasibility of them for students. Some opportunities that often present financial challenges for students include study abroad, sorority and fraternity life, service trips (at times) and participation in floor/residence hall activities. These costs may be driven by the actual price and may also be driven by indirect costs such as lost wages, child care and transportation expenses.

In line with the issue of student finances being a campuswide issue, an environmental approach is essential; this utilizes all higher education personnel as front-line ambassadors for financial wellness. This begins by having personnel willing to engage in conversations around finances with students, thus helping raise the awareness of students' current financial situations as well as reducing the stigma around talking about money and finances.

As noted, one of the most stigmatized and awkward conversations that someone can have is around money. This is shown through the T. Rowe Price study (referenced earlier) that outlines the many topics (including drugs and sex) that parents would rather discuss with their kids before topics related to money. Because of this significant gap, higher education professionals have the opportunity, and perhaps the obligation, to engage students in conversations around money; this may be the first time many students have had these conversations. Some natural spaces and personnel appropriate for having initial conversations about money include:

- Academic Advising: This includes talking about the value of obtaining a degree on time (thus helping reduce debt, decrease the amount of interest that accrues on loans and promoting a student beginning to earn sooner). It also includes conversations around dropping courses and its impact on financial aid.
- Faculty Office Hours/Student Performance Conversations: Students are increasingly working more hours, with an increase in those working 20+ hours per week (Perna, 2010). They are also likely to not purchase required textbooks or course materials because of finances. Engaging in conversations around

these topics can serve as a starting point for broader financial discussions with students. In addition to having those conversations about financial topics in a one-on-one setting, it is also beneficial to have up-front conversations about finances on the first day of class and potentially include financial resource information on a course syllabus. This can include the acknowledgement that students may often have competing obligations (work, involvement and class) and may also extend to acknowledging the high price of supplemental materials (books) with a recognition that the faculty members have done everything possible to reduce associated conflicts and costs.

- Survey Course Instructors: Survey courses are a great time to begin to address student financial concerns. First-year integration courses very often focus on helping students develop an academic plan (hopefully with the intent of assisting that student to finish within the generally allotted time to graduate). It is equally as important to help students figure out the financing plan for their education. This can be integrated into the degree planning, as it flows nicely given the many financial repercussions from prolonging the time to degree. Among these are that many merit- and need-based aid allocations do not extend beyond the normal time to degree, federal student aid provides borrowing limitations and individuals may not have planned for out-of-pocket expenses to pay beyond the advertised time to graduate. Additionally for many traditional-aged students, this may be the first time that they are managing their lives independently.

- Career Services Advisors: The new reality of higher education, including consumers' focus on return, is that the tie between the cost of education and expected salary afterwards is expected to be linked. This has caused an increased focus on the return on investment (or ROI) of a degree. Additionally, when thinking about the financial obligations that students assume to attend higher education (e.g., with loans) there is a need to make sure that those obligations can be repaid in a way that does not impact students' ability to live the life that they desire. While career decisions should not be driven solely by the financial fit of a career, it is important to structure conversations around major/career exploration to include the financial fit of a potential career.

- Financial Aid Administrators: Financial aid administrators have one of the most obvious connections to student finances as they, and their counterparts, are often the ones working directly with students to finance the educational experience, borrow specific amounts and navigate financial challenges that may impede students' ability to meet financial obligations. In this setting, it is important to recognize that a student's financial situation is typically much broader than a statement of account; thus, asking open-ended questions can help uncover specific topics that may lend themselves to campus-based referrals and may also help understand the underlying concern that is driving the borrowing or financial concerns. In addition to supporting the student in a holistic way (for example, if the borrowing is to support others), there is also a need for financial aid administrators to be well versed in the borrowing vehicles and repayment options available to students so they can provide the just-in-time education that is needed.

- Student Affairs Professionals: Student affairs professionals play what has been a relatively ambiguous role in a student's financial life; that is, historically, most professionals, whether residence halls or activities personnel, have not engaged in finance-oriented discussions with students. However, many touch points related to students' finances do exist, and these are crucial to understanding how students assimilate into a campus environment. First, it is important to understand the context of the campus environment and how differences in socio-economic status may impact students' financial stress, specifically as it relates to their fit on campus. Further, but in the same vein, it is important to realize how student programs, and costs associated with these programs, can influence an individual's experience. However, just as important as these two areas, is the student affairs professionals' ability to engage in conversations around money with the students with whom they interact. Often student affairs professionals are the individuals with whom students develop the closest relationship, which gives these professionals the ability to reduce the stigma of talking about money by having open-ended and broad conversations about money. This may include conversations around the balance of hours worked or the idea of taking out loans; it may lead to individuals uncovering some underlying financial issues, which can be referred to campus or community resources (such as food banks) to support.

It is important to note that, as professionals have these conversations, they build a certain relationship with the student along the way, particularly because of the often-sensitive nature of this "new" topic. This can be done sharing personal experiences as they relate to managing finances (including mistakes), acknowledging the financial challenges that many students face and using small wins (such as talking about major/career) as a catalyst for a broader conversation about money. Additionally, it is important to note how professional actions, such as policy decisions, might affect students. These include the cost to participate in various activities (such as fraternity and sorority life) as well as the cost of textbooks or lab fees students are asked to purchase.

This is not to ask that every higher education professional become a Certified Financial Planner. Instead, it is modeling the way to show that there are safe spaces on campus to discuss finances, referring to available campus resources where students can address more in-depth problems and issues; it is also being aware of how actions and services affect students' financial well-being.

Summary Action Steps

Research and discussions are ongoing to understand in greater depth how student finances impact the academic experience and the broader student experience, both while students are enrolled as well as following graduation. However, there is strong research to suggest that this is an issue that is connected to a variety of other wellness issues (such as stress and drug/alcohol use) and that there is a connection as it relates to student persistence and retention. For these reasons, there has been a well-founded increase in the extent to which campuses are addressing this issue and doing so in a holistic manner.

Based on the current experience of professionals nationally who are dealing with financial wellness, the following is a summary of steps that campus professionals can take to help address this issue:

- Begin by analyzing ways that student finances are impacted during the time a student is enrolled on campus. In many cases, a working group on student financial wellness can map out different points in time that students make financial decisions and when they may encounter financial challenges.
- Help all campus professionals recognize where their work intersects with the areas of student finances. At times, it is also helpful to think about the student challenges personally encountered and how they may be impacted by financial situations (i.e., a student wanting to increase or decrease student employment hours and/or a student who is missing class or work often by being sick).
- Begin to engage students in conversations around their finances by recognizing signs of financial stress and by being willing to engage in conversations to support these students. This does not mean providing specific financial advice (in fact, it is best to leave this to the financial specialists), but it does require being open to nudging students to discuss their financial situation.
- Advocate for a campuswide service to help students with issues related to money. Such a service should look to address the following:
  - Proactively educate students about their finances (building financial knowledge in the student body)
  - Support students in financial crisis
  - Serve as an area for help-seeking students to have conversations related to various financial topics and help to grow healthy financial attitudes and behaviors
- Work to enhance professionals' own financial wellness to become more comfortable in having broad, finance-based conversations. This includes:
  - Setting financial goals. Financial goals are the life blood of a financial plan. Almost every goal an individual has incorporates some form of financial implications. By working to recognize these goals, and the subsequent financial implications, a person can create short-term and long-term financial goals that will allow for the development of a financial plan. These goals should take on a SMART goal format (Specific, Measurable, Achievable, Results Focused and Time Bound).
  - Following the understanding of individualized financial goals, it is important to understand current financial settings. This is accomplished by completing a few steps:
    - Develop an understanding of currently held assets. This may include checking/savings accounts, investment accounts, retirement accounts, house, a paid-off vehicle and other possessions.

    o Determine specific liabilities (often debt); this includes student loan debt, mortgage and any other outstanding debt. It is important to not only know the balances but the interest rates and repayment timetables on these products. Even if this looks scary, getting all liabilities in the same place is the first step to developing a plan to pay off these debts.

    o Check personal credit score, as these are "grades and transcripts" of a person's financial life. It is important to check the credit report to make sure it is error free. Further, it is helpful to review the credit score to understand how creditors and others view an individual's finances.

    o Finally, it is often helpful to track spending for a few weeks to get a better feeling for where money goes. Professional financial advisors often work with clients to record (by paper and pencil if possible) what they spent each day and where they spent it. This provides a better idea of current money habits and also provides an opportunity for reflection to address where realignments of spending may be feasible, thus better meeting personal goals and priorities.

  o The next step is to then develop a financial plan (including a budget) that is aligned with personal goals and priorities. These goals and priorities that influence individualized spending will vary from person to person, as will the vehicle to actually get there.

  o Consulting with a professional financial advisor, enrolling in online or in-person financial education courses and talking with various community resources may be a good way to begin this process.

Conclusion

In an ideal world, students would not need to worry about their finances as they pursue their degree, which would allow full focus on academic dreams. However, that unfortunately is not a reality in the near future. Campuses have been moving toward a campus environment that supports students financially and helps them manage their finances beyond just paying their tuition and fees. This truly takes a campuswide approach, and each and every practitioner, staff member and faculty member has a stake in assisting students to think critically about how they support students and their financial wellness. This support has ripple effects across a student's life and can remove many of the large barriers related to student success and completion.

References

Center for the Study of Student Life. (2011, September). *Ohio Student Financial Wellness Survey: Student Loans, Credit Cards, and Stress.* Retrieved from http://cssl.osu.edu/posts/documents/09-01-11-ohio-financial-wellness-report-final-no-watermark.pdf

Center for the Study of Student Life. (2015a, July). *National Student Financial Wellness Study: National Descriptive Report.* Retrieved from http://cssl.osu.edu/posts/documents/nsfws-national-descriptive-report.pdf

Center for the Study of Student Life. (2015b, July). *Wellness Assessment: Physical Wellness.* Retrieved from http://cssl.osu.edu/posts/documents/physical-wellness-report.pdf

Federal Reserve System. (2013, December). *The 2013 Federal Reserve Payments Study*. Retrieved from https://www.frbservices.org/files/communications/pdf/general/2013_fed_res_paymt_study_summary_rpt.pdf

Goetz, J., Cude, B. J., Nielsen, R. B., Chatterjee, S., & Mimura, Y. (2011). College-based personal finance education: Student interest in three delivery methods. *Journal of Financial Counseling and Planning, 22*(1), 27–42.

Holland, Kelley. (2015, June). *The High Economic and Social Costs of Student Loan Debt*. Retrieved from http://www.cnbc.com/2015/06/15/the-high-economic-and-social-costs-of-student-loan-debt.html

Inceptia. (2013, January). *College Students Are Put to the Test: The Attitudes, Behaviors and Knowledge Levels of Financial Education*. Retrieved from https://www.inceptia.org/PDF/Inceptia_Financial AptitudeAnalysis_researchbrief.pdf

Indiana University. (2015). *IU Leader Testifies about Success of University's Financial Literacy Efforts*. Retrieved from http://news.iu.edu/releases/iu/2015/06/financial-literacy-testimony.shtml

Lewin, Tama (2013, August). *Obama's Plan Aims to Lower Cost of College*. Retrieved from http://www.nytimes.com/2013/08/22/education/obamas-plan-aims-to-lower-cost-of-college.html?_r=0

Life Delayed: The Impact of Student Debt on the Daily Lives of Young Americans. (2013). Retrieved from http://www.asa.org/site/assets/files/3793/life_delayed.pdf

Perna, Laura W. (2010, July). *Understanding the Working College Student*. Retrieved from http://www.aaup.org/article/understanding-working-college-student#.VrqaGfkrLIV

T. Rowe Price. (2013, March). *5th Annual Parents, Kids & Money Survey*. Retrieved from https://corporate.troweprice.com/Money-Confident-Kids/images/emk/2013-PKM-Survey-Results-Report-FINAL-0326.pdf

U.S. PIRG Education Fund & The Student PIRGS. (2014, January). *Fixing the Broken Textbook Market*. Retrieved from http://www.uspirg.org/sites/pirg/files/reports/NATIONAL%20Fixing%20Broken%20Textbooks%20Report1.pdf

Part IV
Physical Wellness

7

Disordered Eating
A Critical Need to Address on Campus
BRIDGET GUERNSEY RIORDAN

Introduction

College professionals in various roles have been educated and prepared to help students succeed and thrive on their campuses. However, one hidden epidemic exists that often receives little attention in the public media, in awareness efforts and with campus policies and programs. In fact, while up to 1–3% of students report this as getting in the way of their academic progress, even that comparatively low number represents thousands and thousands of students. The issue is also one that is often not discussed or even addressed as many professionals aren't sure what to do and don't know how to react. The issue is disordered eating. The data indicate that disordered eating is often a hidden epidemic at colleges and universities.

This chapter discusses various types of disordered eating, eating disorders and their characteristics, the factors that may lead to an eating disorder and how eating disorders have an impact on those who have them as well as on the community. Special attention will be given to what student affairs professionals as well as other campus personnel can do to help prevent students from developing eating disorders, how to assist students who may have eating disorders and what treatments are proving effective for treating individuals with eating disorders. For the purpose of this chapter, the term "disordered eating" will be used to describe the broader scale of abnormal eating patterns while "eating disorders" will be used in reference to professionally diagnosed disorders such as anorexia, bulimia, binge eating and other non-specified eating disorders. In addition, this chapter will explore the widespread problem of disordered eating and dispute the myth that it only affects certain populations.

Why the Topic of Disordered Eating Is Important
for College Professionals

College professionals know the importance of taking care of the basic needs of their students. Food is a basic human need. Food is the fuel required to operate the body, the sustenance of life. When looking at Maslow's Hierarchy of Needs, food along with air, drink, shelter, warmth, sex and sleep all factor in as basic level human physiological needs (Burton, 2012). A person cannot survive without food. And as Maslow found, the basic need for food is required for a person to progress to other levels of significant development that include security, friendship, achievement and self-fulfillment. All of these areas of development are what college personnel promote when they discuss developing students and how students will go through these processes while at their institutions. Aside from boasting about updated residence halls, high-security access and a multitude of food offerings, colleges have long marketed themselves as the place for preparing students for complex problem solving, building strong communication skills, enhancing leadership skills and developing well-rounded global citizens. Without the first level of needs adequately satisfied, such as sound nourishment, it is very difficult for students to grow in the other areas and become prepared for the post-college world. However, simple food consumption can be complicated for many. And when individuals use food consumption as something they overly control or manipulate, the normal process of eating and the basic need for food takes on a new meaning and significance. One of the lowest levels of the Maslow hierarchy can falter. Food can become the enemy.

During the college years, food is extremely important for students to maintain energy and good health, which will assist them in succeeding in and out of the classroom. Healthy eating commonly results in healthy students. Colleges emphasize their on-campus food venues, healthy options and variety of offerings. Unfortunately, even if students choose healthy foods, healthy eating patterns may not run concurrently with this choice. Food may be used as a way to limit body weight, soothe emotions, strive for perfection or control the environment. And the resulting impact can create severe health problems such as malnourishment, severe weight gain and a number of psychological disturbances. All the healthy food offered may be nonconsequential when students use it in an unhealthy way. Food can hurt.

Within the college community, students experience stress brought on by multiple new experiences, academic pressures and being away from home. Unfamiliar surroundings require strong coping skills, and many students are not equipped with these skills. These stressors can exacerbate insecurities and the need for self-control. Disordered eating, which can be brought on by stress, often emerges in adolescence; this means that many college-aged students arrive at their college communities with disordered eating problems. The numbers are disturbing. According to data gathered from the National Association of Anorexia Nervosa and Associated Disorders, college students are particularly impacted by disordered eating in startling numbers.

- 95% of those who have eating disorders are between the ages of 12 and 25.
- 86% report onset of eating disorder by age 20.
- 91% of women surveyed on a college campus had attempted to control their weight through dieting. Nearly one-quarter (22%) dieted "often" or "always."
- 25% of college-aged women engage in bingeing and purging as a weight-management technique.
- Over one-half of teenage girls and nearly one-third of teenage boys use unhealthy weight control behaviors such as skipping meals, fasting, smoking cigarettes, vomiting and taking laxatives.

- The mortality rate associated with anorexia nervosa is 12 times higher than the death rate associated with all causes of death for females 15–24 years old (NEDA, 2015).

Even those who aren't experiencing disordered eating when they arrive on campus can react to stress by altering their eating patterns and possibly falling into the trap of an eating disorder, a challenging mental health issue. And as many mental health experts report, mental health problems are an impairment to focused, engaged and effective learning (Keeling & Hersh, 2011).

The Evolution of Disordered Eating in the Mental Health Field

Although anorexia nervosa was first noted as an illness in the late nineteenth century (Striegel-Moore & Bulik, 2007), research on broader eating disorders did not enter mainstream discussion until the 1970s. British psychiatrist Gerald Russell was credited with introducing bulimia nervosa into the nomenclature in 1979. In the United States, the 1983 death of Karen Carpenter, Grammy-winning lead singer of The Carpenters, was attributed to a heart attack brought on by a long struggle with anorexia nervosa. Many reports over the years noted Carpenter's thin frame, but only those close to her realized the extent of her illness. The 32-year-old singer's death put a face on anorexia nervosa and brought an increased awareness of the dangers associated with it (Latson, 2015). Throughout the 1980s and 1990s as researchers explored the psychological and behavioral changes within the college student population, eating disorders emerged as a growing issue. In 1998, noted higher education researchers Arthur Levine and Jeannette S. Cureton reported a 58% increase in eating disorders amongst college students over the previous 20 years.

Anorexia and bulimia, always in the forefront of eating disorder research, often included discussions about binge eating. Finally, in 2013, binge eating disorder (BED) was formally recognized as a medical condition when it was included in the *Diagnostic and Statistical Manual of Mental Disorders* (DSM-5), the medical resource prepared by the American Psychiatric Association. DSM-5 serves as the standard classification of mental disorders used by mental health professionals in the United States. Binge eating disorder gained a valuable spokesperson in 2015 when Monica Seles, former #1 world-ranked tennis star, revealed that she had struggled with binge eating for several years. Her public announcement and testimonial on the Binge Eating Disorder website prompted a great deal of media attention and talk show discussion giving the disease needed exposure and recognition.

Recent research suggests that while up to 3% of the general population may have a clinical eating disorder, such as anorexia nervosa or bulimia, up to 50% of the population may exhibit disordered eating patterns such as severely restricting certain foods or overloading on proteins (Gottlieb, 2014). Because the statistics show that traditional college-aged students are at a vulnerable age for disordered eating as well as eating disorders, student affairs professionals, faculty members and other college professionals must carefully examine this critical phenomenon and how it is impacting college communities.

What Does Disordered Eating Mean? How Are Eating Disorders Defined?

As reported by Striegel-Moore and Bulik (2007), the core features of eating disorders include disturbance in body image (e.g., overvaluation of thinness, weight or shape concerns), over- or under-control of eating (e.g., severe dietary restriction, binge eating) and extreme behaviors to control weight or shape (e.g., compulsive exercise, purging). It is important to note that anorexia nervosa was first noted in DSM-I in 1952, however, binge eating was not mentioned until 1987. The current classifications are anorexia nervosa, bulimia nervosa and binge eating disorder (BED). Eating disorders that combine elements of several diagnostic classifications are considered "other specified feeding or eating disorder" (OSFED) (NEDA, 2015). What distinguishes persons with disordered eating from persons who have an eating disorder is typically the degree to which they engage in the behavior. Gottlieb (2014) noted that individuals with disordered eating often exhibited some of the same behaviors as those with eating disorders; however, they did so with less frequency and/or lower intensity. Disordered eating on its own is troubling and can be quite serious although the impact may not be as extreme as experienced by someone with a diagnosed eating disorder. Nevertheless, those with disordered eating are vulnerable and can be at risk for subsequently developing a full-blown eating disorder.

Each eating disorder has distinct characteristics. In addition, a combination of eating disorders may impact an individual. In some cases, individuals may exhibit more than one eating disorder either simultaneously, such as a person who binge eats and also is bulimic, or while experiencing disordered eating, a person may fluctuate between anorexia and bulimia. Currently recognized eating disorders are characterized as follows:

Anorexia nervosa describes the set of behaviors that include voluntary self-starvation, severe food restriction and a distorted perception of body shape and/or size. Biological consequences of anorexia are thinning of bones, brittle hair and nails, dry and yellowish skin, growth of fine hair all over the body (lanugo), mild anemia, muscle wasting and weakness, severe constipation, low blood pressure, slowed breathing and pulse, damage to the structure and function of the heart, brain damage, multi-organ failure, lower than normal internal body temperature (which causes a person to feel cold all the time), lethargy, sluggishness, feeling tired all the time and infertility.

Bulimia nervosa is the term that describes a pattern of behaviors including food binging and purging with practices of self-induced vomiting, excessive and/or compulsive exercising and laxative and/or diuretic abuse. Biological symptoms of bulimia are chronically inflamed and sore throat, swollen salivary glands, worn tooth enamel as a result of exposure to stomach acid, acid reflux and other gastrointestinal problems, intestinal distress and irritation from laxative abuse, severe dehydration from lack of fluids, broken blood vessels in the eyes, abrasions on knuckles and electrolyte imbalance (which can lead to dizziness and/or heart attacks).

Binge eating disorder (BED) is characterized by recurrent episodes of binge eating (on average, at least once a week for three months) and abnormally consuming large amounts of food, more food than a person would normally eat in a similar period of time and under similar circumstances. As reported through the DSM-5, further diagnosis of binge eaters include the following eating patterns: eating episodes marked by feelings of lack of control, eating too quickly (even when not hungry), feelings of guilt, embarrassment or disgust and binge eating alone to hide the behavior.

Although a large amount of food may be consumed during a binge, those with binge eating disorder do not typically use vomiting or over-exercise to counter their binge eating. Binge eating disorder biological symptoms include weight gain, obesity and obesity-related diseases such as heart disease and diabetes.

Other specified feeding or eating disorder (OSFED) is the category often used to acknowledge other eating behavior patterns outside of anorexia, bulimia and binge eating disorder. It also covers eating behaviors, such as night eating, that do not fit perfectly into one of the other categories. Biological symptoms vary based on the eating problem. Individuals exhibiting night eating may consume more than 50% of their daily caloric intake in the evening and/or throughout the night (Miller, 2013). In recent years, the category of other specified disordered eating has been scrutinized as many psychologists believe it is more beneficial for patients to be diagnosed with a specific disorder.

What Characterizes Someone with Disordered Eating?

A number of characteristics are present in individuals who have disordered eating. They include perfectionism, low self-esteem, extreme criticism of themselves and their bodies, intense fear of gaining weight, fear of being fat, weight loss (or weight gain in binge eating), excessive exercise, preparing or buying food (but not eating it), solitary eating and denial of any problem. In most disorders, guilt, secrecy and isolation are also present.

In many cases, eating disorders occur together with other psychiatric disorders like anxiety, panic, depression, obsessive-compulsive disorder and alcohol and other drug abuse problems. As Striegel-Moore & Bulik reported (2007), certain personality traits make a person more apt to develop an eating disorder. Perfectionism is often cited and can cause someone to take more extreme measures to conform. A person with high social anxiety may be more impressionable and bothered by social feedback and, thus, may resort to drastic eating measures to fit in. Someone who is highly impulsive may be susceptible to binge eating.

Often times the fear of getting fat is so overwhelming for anorectics or bulimics that they are willing to experience extreme discomfort such as severe hunger pain, constant thirst, fatigue and physical changes in hair and skin. Bulimics may withstand hours in the bathroom vomiting or defecating, resulting in broken blood vessels, damaged teeth or exhaustion. A person with obsessive-compulsive disorder may not be able to stop the damaging eating behavior. In addition, the eating disordered person must hide their behavior with food in order to avoid criticism, interference and social ostracism. Isolation and secrecy are resulting behaviors.

Who Is Most Likely to Exhibit Disordered Eating?

Research has found that those with eating disorders have a number of traits in common. One of the most common traits is age at onset. Typically, the first occurrence of anorexia and bulimia is during adolescence. However, many cases are cited with elementary school children (NEDA, 2015). Adolescents may be vulnerable due to the bodily changes that occur with the onset of puberty. Pre-pubescent weight gain may hamper the self-image of still-developing pre-teens and teens. For the first time, a pre-adolescent may feel fat or chubby. In order to maintain the thin ideal, individuals may overly control their eating. Depending on the age of puberty onset, these feelings and possible dangerous eating patterns can carry on throughout high school and college, making the college student population extremely susceptible to disordered eating. As noted, eating disorders commonly emerge in adolescence; however, an exception to this occurs with binge eating disorder whose onset can occur well into adulthood (Striegel-Moore & Bulik, 2007).

Socioeconomic status is often a predictor of disordered eating. In countries that value thinness, a thin body image is associated with wealth within a culture where heavier people are associated with the working class; subsequently, higher-income individuals are found to be more susceptible to anorexia. The desire to be thin and socially acceptable among one's peers takes precedence over healthy eating.

Throughout much of the research concerning anorexia and bulimia is a reference to the overall preponderance of women who are diagnosed with eating disorders. Some estimates show between 35–57% of adolescent girls use crash dieting, fasting, self-induced vomiting, diet pills or laxatives to control their weight (NEDA, 2015). Much of this is attributed to the emphasis on thinness for the female body image and the societal expectations placed on women to be within that ideal. These expectations affect girls as well as women. Forty-two percent of girls in first to third grades want to be thinner (Collins, 1991). Overall, it is estimated that up to 10% of adolescent girls and young women have eating disorders. Growing up with the thin ideal is a reality that can be dangerous.

Females are well-documented with eating disorders in the research. However, caution must be taken to keep the disease from only being considered a female problem. As Dr. Kelly Klump noted, "It's not uncommon even in this day and age to see eating disorders referred to as 'choices by vain girls who just want to be skinny'" (Novotney, 2009). Although a high percentage of those suffering from eating disorders are females, the number of males with eating disorders is considerable. Males comprise approximately 10–15% of people with anorexia or bulimia. In addition, males may be underdiagnosed because their eating disorder may be caused by another behavioral factor. Muscle dysmorphia, becoming pathologically preoccupied with muscularity, affects more men than women and may cause those with it to follow extremely restricted diets with no carbohydrates and protein overload (Novotney, 2009). They may overuse protein powders or similar products to bulk up or resort to bulimia to maintain a sleek frame. Males may also appear very healthy and fit and do not fit the female stereotype long associated with eating disorders. They are also less likely to seek medical treatment for disordered eating issues.

The numbers are even higher for men who identify as gay. Homosexual males may be at elevated risk because of gay culture's increased emphasis on physical appearance relative to that of heterosexual male culture (Striegel-Moore & Bulik, 2007). In looking at male sexuality and eating disorders, Feldman and Meyer (2007) reported that a higher percentage of gay (15%) than heterosexual males (5%) had diagnoses of eating disorders. They noted that the high prevalence may be due to the sociocultural perspective that places social and cultural norms of an ideal, and typically unattainable, body image on gay men that subsequently influences their eating behaviors. Also noted by Feldman and Meyer was that studies focusing on lesbian women show varying results with the overall determination that lesbian women and heterosexual women have similar levels of eating disorders.

Often eating disorders have been considered a disease of White, affluent females. However, recent research shows growing numbers among persons of color. Acculturation, when people modify their culture to adapt to another culture, causes some populations to take on the desire to be thin as demonstrated in the majority culture; it is a way to fit into the mainstream culture. Living in the United States, with Western culture norms, has had a negative effect on some populations. African-American and Latina women were found just as likely to engage in binge eating as Caucasian women (White & Grilo, 2005). Latinos were reported to have significantly higher rates of eating disorders if they spent more than 70% of their lives in the U.S. Diagnosing Latinos may be more challenging because they are prone to use binge eating over caloric restrictions; thus, they do not appear skinny despite their problematic eating behaviors (Novotney, 2009). Asian-American women tend to be at risk for eating disorders due to issues with perfectionism and need for high achievement (McConville, 2014). One of the challenges of helping persons of color who have eating disorders is the differences in the way they approach mental health issues. Many cultures do not acknowledge mental health problems nor is there acceptance regarding seeking help for mental health issues.

A population that is beginning to get more attention regarding eating disorders is college student-athletes. Many student-athletes share some of the same traits as those susceptible to eating disorders, including perfectionism, compulsiveness and weight control. According to the National Collegiate Athletic Association (NCAA) Sports Science Institute, in some sports, especially those sports where weight or appearance may be a factor in eligibility or judging performance, such as figure skating and gymnastics, athletes may have a higher incidence towards eating disorders than athletes in other sports (NCAA, 2013). Attention must be paid to balance performance enhancement with healthy eating habits.

What Societal Influences Contribute to Disordered Eating?

The "selfie" may be one the largest contributors to narcissism and vanity ever. And the selfie users pay a price. The ultimate "selfie" shows its creator as terrific looking and, of course, thin. Selfies have become the ultimate form of self-expression, and people will take photos in exotic settings and even doing everyday tasks like eating and exercising. Of course, they won't be shared unless the person looks fantastic in the eyes of the owner—hair perfect, eyes ahead and body fit and trim. As the selfie generation and the need for self-promotion grows, it's a wonder how anyone can fight the urge to be thin.

Although selfies are relatively new, brought on by the abundance of cell phone cameras and smart phones in use, social pressure to be thin has existed throughout the history of American culture. Influences, such as an emphasis on feminine beauty and the objectification of the female body, have been shown to be risk factors for the development of an eating disorder (Striegel-Moore & Bulik, 2007). And it starts early. Barbie dolls are popular gifts for little girls. With her teeny, tiny waist and perfectly lean thighs, Barbie epitomizes the notion that thin is the ideal. Over time, Barbie has gone from stewardess to pilot, but throughout it all, her body has remained unrealistically thin. Of course, the emphasis on beauty takes a toll as estimates show between 40–60% of girls ages 6–12 are concerned about their weight or becoming fat; this is a concern that remains throughout life (Smolak, 2011). Also, of note over the past 20 years and not to be left out are the male action figures that have developed increasingly larger biceps and well-pronounced abdominal muscles. Female and male body ideals have become increasingly well-defined.

Constant exposure to the thin ideal is everywhere. Magazine titles shout out, "Lose 10 Pounds in 10 Days," "7-Day Slim Down," "Burn Fat Like Crazy," "How to Eat Like a Man and Lose Weight," "Faster Weight Loss," "Indulge Without the Bulge," "Flat Abs & Lean Legs" and "Ditch the Diet, Drop the Pounds! We Tell You How." Television shows such as *The Biggest Loser* exploit persons who struggle with obesity and have them compete to see who can lose the most weight in the shortest period of time through extreme dieting and excessive workouts. The show's popularity is evidenced by its run of over 16 seasons. And, of course, the show emphasized that participants were happier because now they were thinner.

One must also be thin in order to look good in current clothing styles. The fashion industry has long been known to showcase rail-thin models. In the current modeling industry, "large size" models are the same size as the average American woman. Twenty years ago department store women's dress sizes started at size 4. However, now it is common to see size 0 as well as size 00. Also, male models must have perfect abdominal muscles and be muscular and trim. In fact, if someone photographed does not look thin enough, he or she can be artificially enhanced through the art of Photoshopping to look even thinner. As scientist Dr. Michael Lutter noted, "The most obvious environmental cause is the Western ideal of thinness and beauty. In cultures in which thinness is prized, there are much higher rates of eating disorders" (Bidwell, 2013).

Another contributor to disordered eating may be the plethora of high-fat, sugar-enhanced, salt-induced food currently marketed for Americans through fast food restaurants and processed foods. Oregon Research Institute psychologist Eric Slice studied brain activations after subjects drank a chocolate milkshake. He found that those who showed greater activation of the key reward regions of the brain reported increases in bulimic behavior. "If children are exposed to a high-fat, high-sugar diet early in development, they develop a strong preference for and craving for these foods that doesn't otherwise emerge, and that this is what sets people up for bulimia" (Novotney, 2009).

Although having an eating disorder can be a very isolating experience, family dynamics can also play a role in their formation. As psychologist Judy Scheel reported in "When Food Is Family," a number of attachment issues can influence a child towards developing an eating disorder. The attachment issues include:

- Child feels criticized, shamed or blamed, treated like a scapegoat.
- Child is not valued for individual traits or is expected to live up to family ideal or be perfect. Parent values child by what she/he does and not who she/he is.
- Child is brought into conflict between parents.
- Parent is "controlling," "over-involved," or "overprotective." Parent doesn't allow child to work problems out on her/his own.
- Parent is regularly overindulgent, unable to tolerate child being upset or angry.
- Family only accepts positive emotions and suppresses negative emotions.
- Parent is unavailable emotionally or has unresolved conflicts from his/her own childhood and brings them to the relationship with the child.
- Parent is jealous of child and is disappointed child doesn't emulate parent.
- Family does not identify or discuss emotions, fails to talk about emotions surrounding significant events such as divorce, death, moving or other issues.

Scheel explains that the family dynamic may not be completely to blame for the child's eating disorder but may be one of the underlying causes. Scheel also notes that attachment is different than love. Many parents may deeply love their children even though attachment issues make the relationship problematic. Even though many college students form a new family of friends and community when they come to college, they don't leave their biological or custodial families behind. They just bring their family problems with them (Hornbacher, 2006).

Another family issue that has an impact on disordered eating is whether or not families eat dinner together. Families that share meal times have personal interactions and can often hold one another accountable for healthy eating practices. Solitary eating is a factor in many eating disorders as it supports the secrecy needed to maintain the unusual eating behaviors associated with disordered eating. In her book, *Wasted: A Memoir of Anorexia and Bulimia*, Maya Hornbacher explained her own family eating dynamics and how they impacted her multi-year downward spiral with eating disorders.

Studies indicate that conflict at mealtime can exacerbate eating-disordered behavior. On the cultural front, there is some evidence that the specifically modern trend of solitary eating in general leads to "weird" eating, food choices that would not be made in a family or social eating situation: people eating alone tend to eat what one might call "comfort foods," or in my case 'binge foods": high in carbohydrates, high in salt and fat, low in their capacity to satiate actual physical hunger and likely to cause eating well past the point of fullness. While my own family ate dinner together every night, as I got older, I ate alone more often—and ate more carbohydrates, sugar, and fat.

(2006, p. 24)

Aside from the family dynamics, some evidence suggests that heredity may play a part in why certain people develop eating disorders. Through a study of single families that experienced eating disorders across generations, researchers found that family members with mutations in two different genes, ESRRA and HDAC4, had a 90% and 85% chance, respectively, of developing an eating disorder. Scientists found that, when the genes worked properly, the brain worked to increase a person's desire for food when they needed more calories. However, when the genes were mutated, which is rare, they worked to block a person's desire to eat (Bidwell, 2013). This finding will allow scientists to do further research to determine how to prevent the biological factor that impacts a person's chance of developing an eating disorder.

Impact on the Individual, Family and Community

The impact of disordered eating is far-reaching and potentially fatal. For the individual, the risks include malnutrition, heart problems, lack of menstruation among girls and women, death or suicide. A person with an eating disorder often cannot get through this basic need level to further learn, grow and develop. The very traits that may have led them to an eating disorder, such as depression, anxiety and compulsive behavior, may grow worse. Treatment is essential for a person with an eating disorder. Although there is no "cure," a person suffering with an eating disorder can be in remission and learn to live a healthy and productive life.

The effect on the family and community as they deal with a person struggling with an eating disorder can be significant. Families can focus all of their energies on trying to help or manage the person with the eating disorder and lose sight of the issues and needs or other family members. Family members may try to focus on the eating patterns and manage those without looking at the underlying mental health issues. Within the college community, students become a family of friends who help and support one another. When a person has an eating disorder, this new "family" may not know how to help and may try to over-manage the friend or avoid the person so they can ignore the problem. Often a student with an eating disorder may find it is difficult to find a roommate as their eating habits and subsequent behaviors may have caused friends to become frustrated with them or withdraw. There may be a high level of disagreement among community members regarding whether or not to seek help or ask college officials to intercede. Nevertheless, it is always beneficial for anyone, whether it is a peer, family, faculty or staff or community member, to reach out and assist someone who is impacting her/his health through an eating disorder.

Signs of Hope through Treatment and Cultural Changes

As more and more research is done on those struggling with eating disorders, studies will indicate underlying causes and what can be done to prevent eating disorders and treat those who have them. Recent research shows that people with anorexia nervosa decide what they eat by engaging part of their brain associated with habitual behavior (*People with anorexia nervosa*, 2015). Brain research looking at self-esteem, impulsive behaviors, depression, habit formation and obsessive-compulsive disorder may offer much-needed promise and hope.

A variety of therapies may also prove successful in helping individuals get their eating disorders in remission. The first step would be for a medical practitioner, nutritionist or psychologist to do an assessment on the person to ensure proper treatment, diagnosis and/or referral. From there, a number of options may be identified, including counseling, cognitive therapy and cognitive behavioral therapy and interpersonal psychotherapy. Counseling may take the form of individual counseling or group counseling. Cognitive therapy involves helping patients realize connections between their dysfunctional thoughts and behaviors, examine their attitudes about eating and weight and substitute more reasonable thoughts over dysfunctional ones. Cognitive behavioral therapy adds the use of modifying behavior, such as limited times for weighing oneself, to the therapeutic process (Pearson & Rivers, 2006).

A number of prevention programs have been developed in the past ten years with promising results. Intervention programs using cognitive dissonance that help participants shift beliefs through arguing against the thin ideal have proven effective in changing attitudes and behaviors. Interventions that decreased attitudinal risk factors and promoted healthy weight control behaviors were particularly effective (Shaw, Stice, & Becker, 2009). One promising program, The Body Project, an intervention program done for high school and college women to help combat body image ideals and change behaviors, has research showing positive effects for participants with positive changes in attitudes towards their bodies as well as decrease in disordered eating behaviors.

Although the entertainment industry is often criticized for the emphasis on thinness, there are some hopeful signs there, too. Popular actresses such as Melissa McCarthy are advancing the efforts of fashion for larger women and are shifting the emphasis from body size to artistic talent. Media mogul Oprah Winfrey has been public throughout the years with her struggles with weight. In 1988, she went public on her television show revealing rapid weight loss through her use of a liquid diet. Although Winfrey was unable to retain the weight loss, she educated thousands by candidly talking about her weight challenges and emphasizing body acceptance. Musicians are writing songs and singing about beauty in all body sizes. "Baby Got Back" recorded by Sir Mix A Lot in 1992 glorified big butts and brought attention to the beauty of more rounded bodies. Celebrities such as Jennifer Lopez and Beyoncé regularly show off their rounded posteriors. Singer Meghan Trainor proclaimed, "Don't worry about your size" because "Every inch of you is worthy from the bottom to the top" in her 2015 hit song "All about That Bass."

The French government recently responded to concerns over fashion models in their country that were alarmingly thin by passing a law that bans excessively thin fashion models from the runways. Agencies could be punished by fine or prison time for employing models whose Body Mass Index (BMI) is lower than levels proposed by local health authorities (Persad, 2015). France follows Spain, Italy and Israel in instituting laws that ensure models will meet a healthy standard before being allowed to model in their countries.

The proliferation of online resources has aided many individuals struggling with disordered eating. Due to the private nature of eating disorders, online support groups and websites with online assessments and resource information can be valuable tools for those struggling with disordered eating. Online versions of intervention programs can reach thousands and have a significant impact. Unfortunately, the online world also includes websites that are pro-anorexia, such as "pro-ana," and pro-bulimia, such as "pro-mia," and provide details on how people can follow rules for fasting or purging and maintaining the anorectic or bulimic lifestyle. Some reports show, however, that many participants on "pro-ana" and "pro-mia" sites offer support to one another. Since participants are typically anonymous, this support, with privacy and secrecy, may result in participants offering advice for getting proper treatment.

The internationalization of U.S. colleges and universities may help American students see different perspectives regarding body image ideals. As American colleges and universities further diversify with more and more students attending from countries all over the world, it should be noted that many cultures around the world do not view thinness as a positive attribute or one that signifies higher economic status. In many undeveloped countries, those with wealth eat plentifully and are not afraid to boast of their hearty appetites through resulting rounded bodies while those who are poor often show signs of malnutrition. Perhaps as American students increasingly interact with international students, opinions will shift, and they will expand their notion of what represents the ideal body image.

In 2014 Cynthia Bulik, Professor of Eating Disorders in the University of North Carolina at Chapel Hill School of Medicine talked at the National Institutes of Health (NIH). She noted several facts about eating disorders that were summarized as "9 Eating Disorders Myths Busted" (*Nine Truths*, 2014). Bulik reported that eating disorders can affect anyone and that genes and environment play important roles in their development. Although eating disorders impact family and personal functioning, families are not to blame and can help in the recovery process. She added that eating disorders are a serious illness and can carry an increased risk for medical complications as well as suicide. Early detection and intervention are crucial and may allow those impacted to make a full recovery.

Recommendations

Student affairs professionals, faculty members and other college personnel can have a high degree of influence over the health and welfare of the students they advise. Shaping the community to be well-educated, supportive and caring will prove valuable as students conquer disordered eating and help peers develop and sustain healthy eating patterns. The following are a variety of recommendations and ideas on how these concerned college professionals can support, influence and educate students. The most imperative message is that, while college professionals can influence the environment and educate the college community, some individuals will require clinical diagnosis and help from a trained professional. Serious eating disorders cannot be resolved only by love or friendship. Persons with diagnosed disorders need help from a psychologist and/or trained professional who is experienced treating students with eating disorders and will work diligently to help them get the treatment they need.

Personal Interactions

- If suspecting that a student has an eating disorder, simply inquiring about how the student is doing may help. Speak up. Ask the student how the academic term is going and how he or she is dealing with stress. Offer counseling or other health resources.
- Listen to any concerns shared about atypical eating habits or patterns either from students or their peers. Investigate further when possible.
- Confront students who inappropriately remark, either by jokes or taunting, about weight or eating behaviors of themselves or others. Seek to educate and help others understand the serious nature of disordered eating and that joking about it or mocking it is not the way to help.

Referrals

- Realize that some individuals with eating disorders may need very specialized clinical help. Offer appropriate university and community referrals.
- Create a support group for students with disordered eating that is led by a licensed psychologist and which offers private and confidential support for students.
- Develop a website that students can access that includes resources, awareness and referral information.

Educational

- Work with the health promotions office and/or a nutritionist to develop educational programs that address eating disorder problems. Make students aware of warning signs and how to seek help. Present programs in the residence halls and at student organization meetings.

- Acknowledge National Eating Disorders Week each year. It occurs in late February and can be a meaningful time to hold seminars, provide additional publicity about resources and increase awareness. Collaborate with international students from countries where the ideal body image is not thin and work with them to host a discussion group to consider the differences and rationale for what constitutes beauty in different cultures.
- Engage organizations that may have significant outreach and influence on student behaviors. This should include the fraternity and sorority councils, athletic student clubs and residence hall organizations. Have them co-sponsor educational sessions, promote resources to their members and be advocates for resources that address disordered eating.
- Work closely with athletic coaches to educate them on how to recognize eating disorder behaviors and address them. Also, educate coaches on effective coaching language and other ways they can guide student-athletes to maintain healthy eating behaviors. Consider them as partners in advocating for students and for offering appropriate referrals.
- Enlist offices, such as the women's center or offices representing gay, lesbian, bisexual or transgender students, who may work with populations more typically affected by eating disorders to be partners for educational programming and awareness. Ensure that staff members are aware of college and community resources and can refer students as needed.

Environmental

- Review promotional items, bulletin boards and publicity to ensure that a wide variety of body images are pictured and include more than thin-sized models.
- Review television shows watched by students as a group such as *The Biggest Loser* that glorify extreme weight loss and non-stop exercising to lose weight. Although students should have freedom to watch what they choose, use this example as a talking point to discuss drastic measures for losing weight.
- In a residence hall setting, refuse to allow diet challenges or promotions. Post information about university-sponsored and researched efforts such as Overeaters Anonymous or clinically endorsed programs through the college health service.
- Consider policy implications regarding food plan requirements. A student required to purchase an all-you-can-eat meal plan may need a medical exemption if struggling with binge eating or other eating disorder issues.
- Take note of any plumbing issues arising in the residence halls. Clogged pipes may result from purging or the overuse of laxatives.
- Set limits on time allowed on exercise equipment. Most gyms allow 30 minutes at a time. Post the time limits and monitor use, when possible.
- Emphasize the variety of fitness class offerings and ensure that these include yoga and other classes that emphasize stretching or fitness over calorie burning.
- Remove scales from residential halls to avoid constant weigh-ins.
- List resources available on a bulletin board or in a bathroom for students to see and use when necessary.

Conclusion

College students are at a vulnerable age and time for developing eating disorders. The research shows that adolescents are at a high risk due to their current life stages. They are experiencing puberty with many body changes causing them to re-evaluate their physical presence and consider ways to shape it. Their brains are continuing to develop, which may cause them to test limits and take dangerous risks with their bodies. They are exposed everywhere to media images of toned, fit bodies and the impression that "if you are in good shape, your life is great." The pressure to fit in with their peers is stronger than ever.

Students exhibiting disordered eating are at risk of not succeeding in college, as well as jeopardizing their lives. The college years can be a critical time for developing healthy eating habits, and college professionals can have an important impact on helping students make healthy choices. Through ongoing educational efforts, students can realize the health dangers of disordered eating and, hopefully, seek the advice and guidance they need to approach eating in a healthy and reasonable way.

It is also important for college professionals to note that educational efforts, counseling and intervention efforts take time to influence behaviors. Just as dangerous eating patterns did not develop overnight, nor will the changes happen right away. Individuals must show ongoing care for their students regardless of their eating behaviors. Since many students' eating disorders are shrouded in secrecy, professionals must continue to talk about healthy habits and challenge and support students as they deal with their individualized health issues. The numbers are staggering, but getting the proper assistance can help students struggling with this problem. The efforts must continue and college communities can have a significant impact on this crucial public health issue.

References

Bidwell, A. (2013). *Researchers Find Genes Linked to High Risk of Eating Disorders.* Retrieved November 11, 2015, from http://www.usnews.com/news/articles/2013/10/08/researchers-find-genes-linked-to-high-risk-of-eating-disorders

The Body Project. (2015). Retrieved November 21, 2015, from http://www.bodyprojectsupport.org/

Burton, N. (2012). *Our Hierarchy of Needs: Why True Freedom Is a Luxury of the Mind.* Retrieved September 10, 2015, from https://www.psychologytoday.com/blog/hide-and-seek/201205/our-hierarchy-needs

Collins, M. E. (1991). Body figure perceptions and preferences among pre-adolescent children. *International Journal of Eating Disorders, 10*(2), 199–208.

Diagnostic and Statistical Manual of Mental Disorders (DSM-5). Retrieved December 9, 2015, from http://www.dsm5.org/Documents/Eating%20Disorders%20Fact%20Sheet.pdf

Feldman, M., & Meyer, I. (2007). Eating disorders in diverse, lesbian, gay, and bisexual populations. *International Journal of Eating Disorders, 40*(3), 218–226.

Gottlieb, C. (2014, February 23). *Disordered Eating or Eating Disorder: What's the Difference?* Retrieved November 11, 2015, from https://www.psychologytoday.com/blog/contemporary-psychoanalysis-in-action/201402/disordered-eating-or-eating-disorder-what-s-the

Hornbacher, M. (2006). *Wasted: A Memoir of Anorexia and Bulimia.* New York: HarperCollins.

Keeling, R. P., & Hersh, R. H. (2011). *We're Losing Our Minds: Rethinking American Higher Education.* New York: Palgrave Macmillan.

Latson, J. (2015). *How Karen Carpenter's Death Changed the Way We Talk about Anorexia.* Retrieved February 4, 2015, from http://time.com/3685894/karen-carpenter-anorexia-death/

McConville, S. (2014, June 5). *More Ethnic Minorities Are Suffering From Eating Disorders*. Retrieved November 11, 2015, from http://www.eatingdisorderhope.com/information/eating-disorder/ethnic-minorities

Miller, M. C. (2013). *Nighttime Overeating Can Throw Weight and Health Out of Sync*. Retrieved October 1, 2015, from http://www.health.harvard.edu/blog/nighttime-overeating-can-throw-weight-and-health-out-of-sync-201309136658

National Collegiate Athletic Association (NCAA). (2013, June 6). *Disordered Eating and Eating Disorders*. Retrieved December 3, 2015, from http://www.ncaa.org/health-and-safety/medical-conditions/disordered-eating-and-eating-disorders

NEDA (National Eating Disorders Association). (2015). *Eating Disorder Statistics and Research*. Retrieved December 3, 2015, from https://www.nationaleatingdisorders.org/get-facts-eating-disorders

Nine Truths about Eating Disorders. (2014). Retrieved December 8, 2015 from http://www.aedweb.org/index.php/25-press-releases/171-9-truths-about-eating-disorders

Novotney, A. (2009). Psychologists are developing promising new treatments and conducting novel research to combat eating disorders. *Monitor on Psychology, 40*(4), 46.

Pearson, F. C., & Rivers, T. C. (2006, Fall). *Eating Disorders in Female College Athletes: Risk Factors, Prevention, and Treatment*. Retrieved November 11, 2015, from https://www.questia.com/library/journal/1P3-1222012961/eating-disorders-in-female-college-athletes-risk

People with anorexia nervosa have different brain activity. Retrieved December 9, 2015, from http://www.stonehearthnewsletters.com/people-with-anorexia-nervosa-have-different-brain-activity/anorexia/#sthash.8qeD3sAE.vIv8vnRV.dpbs

Persad, M. (2015, April 3). M. France votes to ban models under a certain body mass index. Retrieved November 11, 2015, from http://www.huffingtonpost.com/2015/04/03/france-models-body-mass-index_n_6999244.html

Shaw, H., Stice, E., & Becker, C. B. (2009). Preventing eating disorders. *Child Adolescent Psychiatric Clinics of North America, 18*(1), 199–207.

Smolak, L. (2011). Body image development in childhood. In T. Cash, & L. Smolak (Eds.), *Body Image: A Handbook of Science, Practice, and Prevention* (2nd edition, pp. 67–75). New York: Guilford.

Striegel-Moore, R. H., & Bulik, C. M. (2007). Risk factors for eating disorders. *American Psychologist, 62*(3), 181–198.

White, M. A., & Grilo, C. M. (2005). Ethnic differences in the prediction of eating and body image disturbances among female adolescent psychiatric inpatients. *International Journal of Eating Disorders, 38*(1), 78–84. doi:10.1002/eat.20142

8

Tobacco

Creating a Tobacco-Free Campus

JAN L. GASCOIGNE AND AARON MAUNER

Introduction

Prescription drugs, heroin, cocaine and marijuana are often highlighted in the media as drugs of abuse on college campuses. Yet, the two substances that have the most potential to cause short-term and long-term issues for college students are alcohol and tobacco. This chapter focuses on tobacco, which is often overlooked by campuses as an issue, due to the immediate impacts of these other substances. However, tobacco use is more deadly (over 480,000 deaths annually in the United States) and more insidious, more cunning, more deceptive, less examined and less addressed on the nation's college campuses. This chapter takes a closer look at tobacco use on college campuses, including some typically unknown facts about tobacco, some common myths and misperceptions, things that are changing within the world of tobacco usage and what both individuals and campuses can do to promote a tobacco-free generation.

Tobacco Use

Since 1999, rates of tobacco use among young adults have seen steady and consistent declines (Johnston et al., 2015; Kann et al., 2013). The rate of smoking among college students has declined significantly over the last 15 years with similar trends being seen in the use of all forms of tobacco whether it is cigars, cigarillos, snus, dissolvable tobacco or hookah (Johnston et al., 2015). Despite these improvements, approximately 1 in 6 high school students nationwide admits to smoking cigarettes at least once in the last month and 2 out of 5 students report having tried smoking at least once (Kann et al., 2013). The issue with these data is that, due to the highly addictive nature of nicotine, it is estimated that approximately 80% of high school smokers will continue smoking into adulthood (U.S. Department of Health and Human Services, 2012). "Even with considerable declines in smoking among U.S. adolescents since the late 1990s, about one in seven (14%) of 12th graders in 2014 currently smoke *cigarettes*, and one in fifteen (7%) is already a *daily smoker*" (Johnston et al., 2015). Notwithstanding decreases in use of cigarettes, in recent years, the use of smokeless tobacco products has been on the rise among adolescents (Johnston et al., 2015). In addition to this, use of tobacco has been known to precede and increase the risk of becoming an illicit drug user in the future (U.S. Department of Health and Human Services, 2012). Compounding this with the fact that 99% of all adults that have ever tried a cigarette have done so by age 26, the need for targeted intervention in the young adult age group is critical for addressing this issue (Center for Behavioral Health Statistics and Quality, 2010).

Smoking Trends among College Students

Smoking trends within college age students has shown some interesting but predictable trends over the years. It has been well documented that the rate of tobacco use of all kinds increases substantially from the 12 to 17 age group to the 18–25 age group (Johnston et al., 2015). Most recent data illustrates tobacco usage rates were 21% higher in the 18–25 age group as compared to the younger cohort (Center for Behavioral Health Statistics and Quality, 2015). According to the National College Health Assessment, 10.6% of undergraduate students and 10.3% of graduate students report having smoked cigarettes within the last 30 days (American College Health Association, 2015). The percentage of young adults using smokeless tobacco products (dip, chew, snuff) and cigars (including cigarillos and little cigars) was reported as 6.4% and 11.2%, respectively, in the National Survey on Drug Use and Health (U.S. Department of Health and Human Services, 2012). In addition, the CDC reports that rates of e-cigarette usage tripled from 2013 to 2014 among high school students and noted that e-cigarettes were the most commonly used tobacco product in 2014 among high school students (Centers for Disease Control and Prevention, 2015b). Given that many of these students may soon be entering colleges across the U.S., efforts to address these new products will be important for campus professionals in building a comprehensive tobacco control strategy (Centers for Disease Control and Prevention, 2015b).

Not surprisingly, tobacco use exists in varying rates across gender, gender identity and race. With regard to gender, rates of tobacco use have typically been higher in males as compared to females; however, rates of cigarette smoking have been shown to vary over the years. Conducted annually since 1975, the Monitoring the Future Survey has been conducted nationwide and represents a helpful source of long-term data and trends over time. Over the course of this study, there have been years in which rates of smoking have been higher in females than in males, and these trends have been highly sensitive and correlated to direct marketing campaigns focused on either males or females (Johnston et al., 2015; U.S. Department of Health and Human Services, 2012). Since 2011, rates of smoking within the last 30 days in general have declined significantly among females; however, males have shown little change in smoking rates over that same time period (Center for Behavioral Health Statistics and Quality, 2015; Johnston et al., 2015). In addition to the use of cigarettes, males were consistently more likely to have smoked little cigars, flavored little cigars and regular little cigars (Johnston et al., 2015). Males were also much more likely to use smokeless tobacco products as well, showing higher use of snus and dissolvable tobacco in 2014 (Johnston et al., 2015).

It has also been well documented that the rates of smoking differ dramatically between the heterosexual population and the LGBT community (Lee, 2009). A meta-analysis found that smoking rates among lesbians, gays and bisexuals ranged from being 10% to 24% higher among adolescents as compared with their heterosexual counterparts (Ryan, 2001). According to a study done surveying over 31,000 11th grade students across the state of Oregon, gay and bisexual males reported having 10–15% higher prevalence of monthly tobacco use than heterosexual males, with lesbian and bisexual women reporting 11–27% higher prevalence of monthly use than their heterosexual counterparts (Hatzenbeuhler, 2001). Researchers have proposed that this differential in tobacco use is likely due to the increased stress experienced by youth in the LGBT community stemming from lack of acceptance and feelings of isolation (Sheahan, 1992; Shiffman, 1985). On a positive note, research has indicated that the presence of a more supportive social environment for LGBT youth resulted in the reduction of this disparity with tobacco use in the LGBT community (Hatzenbeuhler, 2001).

The use of tobacco products has been shown to have differential usage across race as well. Overall rates of tobacco use were incredibly high among American Indian and Alaska Native populations (40.1%) and those reporting two or more races (31.2%) with lower rates observed among Whites, Blacks, Native Hawaiians/Pacific Islanders, Hispanics and Asians listed in order of decreasing prevalence (Center for Behavioral Health Statistics and Quality, 2015). Rate of cigarette use in the last 30 days mirrored this trend with American Indians or Alaska Natives having the highest prevalence and Asians having the lowest (Center for Behavioral Health Statistics and Quality, 2015). Similar trends were seen among adolescents and young adults. According to the Youth Risk Behavior Surveillance Survey, tobacco use was "higher among white male (33.2%), black male (17.8%) and Hispanic male (20.7%) than white female (20.7%), black female (11.1%) and Hispanic female (15.3%) students, respectively" (Kann et al., 2013). The rates of smokeless tobacco and cigar usage differed between races as well. White males are consistently the most dominant users of smokeless tobacco with other race and gender having very little (less than 2%) usage (U.S. Department of Health and Human Services, 2012). Although cigar usage is most popular among White males, Black and Hispanic males have lower but very similar usage rates (U.S. Department of Health and Human Services, 2012).

Emerging/Re-Emerging Products and Reasoning

According to the numerous tobacco use surveys conducted across the United States, despite an overall decrease in the use of cigarettes and cigars, hookah and e-cigarette use has been on the rise among youth and young adults. Seeing these trends engenders the question of why they are rising in popularity. The short answer to this question is the emergence of flavored tobacco products and, with the exception of cigars, an increase in prevalence of the thinking that e-cigarettes and hookah are safer alternatives to cigarette smoking. Recent studies show that of the youth who currently use tobacco products at least once a month, 70% of these youth have used a flavored tobacco product (Centers for Disease Control and Prevention, 2015a). Among these students, the most prevalent methods for consuming these flavored tobacco products were e-cigarettes (63.3%), hookah

(60.6%) and cigars (63.5%) (Centers for Disease Control and Prevention, 2015a). The popularity of these flavored products is mirrored in the fact that 3 times the number of high school students use at least one flavored tobacco product as compared with those who use only non-flavored products (Centers for Disease Control and Prevention, 2015a).

In recent years, the usage of hookah has been on the rise among young adults as well. A recent longitudinal study found that almost 1 in 4 young adults has ever used hookah to smoke flavored tobacco and that 8% of those who had never used hookah at the start of the study did so within the 6 months that study was conducted (Villanti, 2015). As a major source of flavored tobacco use, the rising usage data is compounded by the fact that many perceive hookah use as less harmful than smoking cigarettes. This perception could not be further from the truth. Research has shown that, depending on which toxic compound is being measured, one hookah session can expose an individual to the equivalent of between 1 and 50 cigarettes worth of one of these toxic compounds (Cobb, 2010). The bottom line is that hookah use, like all other tobacco usage, exposes the user to nicotine and contains the same, if not higher, amount of the harmful compounds found in cigarettes that may lead to lethal diseases.

As it has grown in popularity in recent years, e-cigarette use, or vaping as it has become popularly referred to, has been viewed as a safer alternative to smoking cigarettes. Electronic cigarettes were introduced in the United States in 2007 and have begun to increase in popularity in recent years. E-cigarettes are electronic devices designed to aerosolize nicotine for the purpose of inhalation by its user (Caponetto, 2014). They are designed to provide the same physical and visual stimulation that one would get from smoking a real cigarette without producing any smoke or requiring any kind of combustion (i.e., burning) (Caponetto, 2014). "Users report buying them to help quit smoking, to reduce cigarette consumption, to relieve tobacco withdrawal symptoms due to workplace smoking restrictions and to continue to have a 'smoking' experience but with reduced health risks" (Caponetto, 2014). Recent studies have shown that the amount of nicotine consumed varies greatly based on the device and "e-liquid" cartridge used. However, assuming a typical cigarette can be consumed in approximately 15 puffs, taking 15 puffs on a typical e-cigarette resulted in the user consuming less than half (sometimes significantly less than half) of the amount of nicotine found in one cigarette (Goniewicz, 2013).

E-cigarettes have been marketed as a way to consume nicotine by just breathing in harmless "water-vapor," although this statement is highly misleading (Grana, 2014). The main components of most "e-liquid" are in fact propylene glycol and glycerin, not water (Grana, 2014). Although not much data is available about the health risks associated with e-cigarette use, it is known that exposure to these two chemicals in particular in the industrial setting has been correlated to cancer, behavioral changes and central nervous systems issues (Dow Chemical Co., 2013; Grana, 2014). As of now, the potential harm that may come from prolonged "vaping" sessions and chronic use of e-cigarettes is unknown. They are currently unregulated by the Food and Drug Administration for human consumption, although laws around the sale and use of them are currently in development.

The good news is that, currently, e-cigarette usage is very low among young adults (18–25 year olds) (Delnevo, 2015). In a recent survey of almost 37,000 adults, only about 5% of 18–25 year olds used e-cigarettes periodically or on a daily basis (Delnevo, 2015). However, these rates are likely to increase. Recent data reveals that the use of e-cigarettes among high school students is now the highest usage rate of all tobacco products (Johnston et al., 2015). Prevalence among e-cigarette use among 10th and 12th graders in the United States was 16% and 17%, respectively, in 2104 (Johnston et al., 2015). Vaping is the most common delivery system used for flavored tobacco products, and their rise in popularity is mirrored in the popularity of flavored products.

In addition to this, e-cigarettes have seen dramatic increases in use as a cigarette smoking cessation aid. Recent studies show that people who have quit cigarette smoking within the last calendar year were four times more likely than current smokers to use e-cigarettes (Delnevo, 2015). This fact is a double-edged sword. Knowing that e-cigarettes can potentially help some users quit smoking is good news, but given the uncertainty of the health risks, coupled with the fact that they still contain nicotine and could sustain addiction and lead to relapse, leaves this method of cessation in question.

Cigars in general have not seen the increases in use that e-cigarettes and hookah have in youth and young adult age groups. Whether it be large or small cigars, the flavored products are more popular than there unflavored counterparts, and most gains in popularity of these products mirror the popularity of flavored products (Johnston et al., 2015). The important thing to note about these trends in popularity of tobacco products is to realize the changing landscape of the tobacco industry. As the tobacco industry develops new products, it is vital that cessation programs, anti-tobacco campaigning and research adapt rapidly to address these new products and misinformation in order to effectively combat the industry's new tactics.

Consequences of Tobacco Use on the Health of Young Adults

Due to the efforts of many targeted anti-smoking advertisement campaigns, the long-term effects of cigarette smoking and tobacco use in general have in recent years become common knowledge. Knowledge about the prevalence of lung cancer and heart disease, the most prominent of the group, among users have led to reductions in people beginning to smoke and has inspired some to quit. Despite the relative lack of public knowledge on the subject, the short-term health effects are numerous and starting smoking at a young age is a "critical period" for the development of nicotine addiction and potential long-term health impact (U.S. Department of Health and Human Services, 2012). The relevance of this information becomes all the more pertinent in light of recent projections from the U.S. Surgeon General that suggest that should trends continue in the direction they are presently, 5.6 million young adults alive today will die prematurely as a direct result of tobacco use (U.S. Department of Health and Human Services, 2014).

The most immediate effect of tobacco use is the development of addiction as well as nausea and lightheadedness. Although what exactly leads to nicotine addiction and the speed at which addiction can occur differs based on an individual's genetic makeup coupled with usage patterns, the hallmarks of nicotine dependence are highly controlled or compulsive use of tobacco products, psychoactive effects and drug-reinforced behavior (U.S. Department of Health and Human Services, 2010). Once addiction is established in a person, they can begin to feel symptoms of withdrawal within 4 to 6 hours of the last use of nicotine (U.S. Department of Health and Human Services, 2012). Symptoms of withdrawal include "depressed mood, insomnia, irritability, anxiety, difficulty concentrating, restlessness, increased appetite and cravings for tobacco/nicotine" (U.S. Department of Health and Human Services, 2012). These adverse reactions to nicotine withdrawal are often what make quitting so difficult; however, these pale in comparison to the short-term effects that tobacco use can have on an individual's health.

The short-term health effects of tobacco use differ based on the delivery method by which the tobacco is consumed. Smoking has been linked with "cough and phlegm production, an increased number and severity of respiratory illnesses, decreased physical fitness, an unfavorable lipid profile and potential retardation in the rate of lung growth and the level of maximum lung function" (U.S. Department of Health and Human Services, 2012). Smoking has also been linked with increased blood pressure, vasoconstriction and increased carbon monoxide levels in the body, thus hampering the body's ability to obtain oxygen from the air (U.S. Department of Health and Human Services, 2012). Smokeless tobacco on the other hand has been linked with early indications of gum degeneration; lesions on oral tissue; leukoplakia (a precursor to oral cancers, tooth decay, tooth loss and gum disease) and irreversible gum recession (U.S. Department of Health and Human Services, 2012; World Health Organization, 2007).

The U.S. Surgeon General has suggested that there may be a "critical period" at which beginning tobacco use can affect the onset and severity of tobacco-related morbidities (U.S. Department of Health and Human Services, 2012). With the average age at which a person has tried a first cigarette being 16 in the United States, many of their body systems are still in development at this age (U.S. Department of Health and Human Services, 2012). Exposure to the incredibly high amounts of harmful chemicals found in tobacco products while bodily systems are still in development may enhance the damaging effects these chemicals have (U.S. Department of Health and Human Services, 2012). Research has shown that the risk for some diseases commonly associated with smoking, like lung cancer, rises steeply with the duration of use and not as much with the amount of usage (U.S. Department of Health and Human Services, 2012). Thus, the younger someone starts to use tobacco products, the more likely they are to develop one of the diseases just based on the duration of usage alone. The fact of the matter is, "people who begin to smoke at an early age are more likely to develop severe levels of nicotine addiction than those who start at a later age." This fact, and the fact that addiction leads to prolonged usage and increased difficulty with stopping tobacco use, are what are of the outmost interest for health professionals (U.S. Department of Health and Human Services, 2012).

Secondhand Smoke (Passive Smoking, Involuntary Smoking)

Within the past decade, the scientific community has made a real push to eluci- date the dangers of secondhand smoke to the general public. Sometimes referred to as passive smoking, involuntary smoking or environmental tobacco smoke, secondhand smoke is exposure to either smoke from the burning end of the cigarette or smoke being exhaled by the smoker. Tobacco smoke is a compos- ite of over 4,000 different chemicals, and studies have shown that secondhand smoke contains many of these same chemicals (U.S. Department of Health and Human Services, 2006). In fact, the 2006 U.S. Surgeon Report on secondhand smoke suggests that those exposed, particularly to the smoke from the burning end of the cigarette, may be inhaling some of the chemicals at even higher con- centrations than the person who is smoking that cigarette (U.S. Department of Health and Human Services, 2006). According to this same report, the National Toxicology Program approximates that at least 250 of the chemicals found in secondhand smoke are known to be toxic or carcinogenic (U.S. Department of Health and Human Services, 2006). The bottom line is that chronic exposure to secondhand smoke has been directly linked to premature death in both children and adults (U.S. Department of Health and Human Services, 2006). "Exposure of adults to secondhand smoke has immediate adverse effects on the cardiovascular system and causes coronary heart disease and lung cancer" (U.S. Department of Health and Human Services, 2006). Based on their findings, the Surgeon Gen- eral came to two conclusions regarding secondhand smoke. First, there is no "risk-free level of exposure" (U.S. Department of Health and Human Services, 2006). Even small amounts of the chemicals present in secondhand smoke can be toxic or carcinogenic to some, and chronic exposure can be just as harmful. Second, the Surgeon General proposes that the only way to fully protect people from secondhand smoke is to have a smoke-free environment (U.S. Department of Health and Human Services, 2006).

Why Do College Students Use Tobacco?

It is hard to imagine that most college students do not know the harm associated with tobacco use. Given the data and health consequences associated with tobacco use, why do college students continue to use tobacco, particularly in a society that has been increasingly less tolerant of tobacco? This next section provides an overview of tobacco company marketing of cigarettes and strategies used to target young adults and addiction as well as social and physiological factors that may motivate a student to use tobacco.

Tobacco Industry Marketing

The 1998 Master Settlement Agreement (MSA) was the result of a lawsuit from 46 state attorneys general and the U.S. Department of Justice against five major tobacco companies with a focus to recoup tobacco-related illness Medicaid costs. The MSA resulted in exposure of the tobacco industry's internal documents, which included marketing practices, addiction research and strategies to increase tobacco use. The tactics and strategies of the industry to find new customers by targeting the young adult market became better understood and can be utilized to help educators address tobacco use on campus.

A Time of Transition

Leaving home, starting a new job, beginning college or entering the military, making new friends and the ability to legally purchase tobacco are all part of a life transition from adolescence to young adulthood. This time period plays a critical role in the adoption and solidification of adult behaviors.

In fact, the tobacco industry documents outlined a strategy to introduce tobacco during these times of transition. Ling and Glantz reviewed 200 tobacco industry documents and concluded that the industry has a strategy to transition a smoker from their first cigarette to becoming a confirmed pack-a-day smoker. This strategy has three stages. Stage 1 starts with exposing teens to tobacco products. Stage 2, then, utilizes marketing to solidify use or increase use by focusing on transitions points when young adults begin new behaviors such as joining a workplace, entering college or the military (Ling & Glantz, 2002). This marketing is focused around leisure and social activities. Finally, Stage 3 is focused on the analysis of values, lifestyles, role models and aspirations of young adults. This analysis was used to create marketing and events that were meaningful to young adults in transition. Documents exposed marketing efforts focused on nightclub promotions in college communities that included giving away free cigarettes or smokeless tobacco, tobacco-branded clothing and other free items, music and event sponsorship and fraternity chew-and-spit contests as well as deep discounting of products. According to the Campaign for Tobacco Free Kids, e-cigarettes are being marketed in similar ways as cigarettes with magazine ads, sponsorships of concerts, auto races, celebrity endorsements and flavors (Campaign for Tobacco Free Kids, 2015). These marketing tactics are used to entice young adults to adopt smoking or the use of smokeless tobacco and to increase consumption with the intent of forging a life-long habit.

Given the data that shows that, of adults who are smoking, most of them started smoking before they turned 18 years old, public health prevention efforts have been focused on preventing youth from starting to use tobacco. These prevention efforts start as early as elementary school in an attempt to inoculate youth against the pressure to try cigarettes or smokeless tobacco. Because the data was so compelling that most people who reach the age of 18 without smoking do not start, prevention efforts were very limited past the age of 18, and most tobacco control efforts for young adults shifted to focus on cessation programs. New research has exposed this life transition from youth to young adulthood as an important gap in efforts to eliminate tobacco use and opportunity for interventions (Mermelstein, 2015).

Nicotine Dependence: "I Will Quit before I Become Addicted"

Dr. Stanton Glantz was quoted at the Wisconsin College Summit (2002) as saying, "Public health has always been fixated on 12 year olds, but the truth of the matter is the tobacco companies have always been focused on the 18–25 year olds, that is where long term addiction starts" (Breathe California, 2016).

Nicotine dependence is a key factor in why some students smoke. Current research has demonstrated that symptoms of nicotine dependence (such as craving and anxiety) can develop quickly even after occasional smoking. Although there is no minimum threshold documented to establish dependence, for some smokers it can begin as early as their first few cigarettes (DiFranz, 2007). Nichter (2015) interviewed students who shared that they transitioned from trying their first cigarette socially to becoming a one-to-two a day cigarette user in about two months.

Smoking has been shown to interact with the neurotransmitters in the brain and in particular, dopamine. Dopamine is one of the neurotransmitters in the brain that controls the reward and pleasure center. Research has demonstrated that smoking can deliver nicotine to the brain within 10 seconds and thus provides the smoker an immediate sense of pleasure (Center for Behavioral Health Statistics and Quality, 2015). As an individual smokes, the brain adapts itself and creates more receptors for the nicotine, thus increasing the need for more and more intake of nicotine to satisfy the cravings (Center for Behavioral Health Statistics and Quality, 2015). Withdrawal from nicotine can create cravings, depression, agitation and moodiness.

"I Only Smoke When I . . ."

In addition to physiological response to nicotine, there is also evidence of the use of tobacco being paired with events or actions that are happening when nicotine enters the body. For example, if a person smokes while drinking coffee, the brain pairs the two, so when a person drinks coffee the brain also craves a cigarette. This neuropsychological pairing is known as a trigger, and a smoker may have numerous events throughout the day that trigger the desire for a cigarette. For example, smoking behavior may be paired with driving, coffee drinking, after meals, drinking alcohol and being around others who are smoking. Understanding why a student smokes is helpful for the cessation process. Helping smokers understanding their specific triggers can ensure individuals will develop a quit plan that provides alternatives to smoking when these events occur.

Smoking Identity: "I Smoke but I Am Not Really a Smoker"

In trying to understand the complexity of smoking behaviors, researchers uncovered the importance of labels in working with collegiate smokers. Identity has been found to be an important concept in collegiate smoking. Levinson et al. (2007) and Berg et al. (2009) asked students who reported currently using cigarettes if they considered themselves a smoker, and in both studies, over half denied being a smoker. These studies highlight the complexity of classification of smoking behaviors and an individual's self-acknowledgement of being a smoker. Nichter (2015) notes the importance of this dissonance in identity and through conversations with college students uncovered that not defining oneself as a smoker has the potential for missing important opportunities to address smoking behavior in the college population. Being aware of this dissonance can have implications on how we can address tobacco on college campuses.

College professionals may need to rethink what has been done to understand the depth of the problem and how to best develop messages to promote prevention of use and encourage cessation for those who may not identify as a smoker. For example, data collected by the CDC and other youth health risk assessment agencies across the U.S. rely on surveys to estimate the prevalence of tobacco use among young adults; the social smoking phenomenon brings into question survey data that asks respondents to report whether or not they are a smoker.

Social smoking is certainly not something new in the United States. Defined as those who smoke in social situations as a result of perceived peer pressure or social constructs, recent studies have estimated the prevalence of social smoking to be between 51–80% of college students (Mermelstein, 2015). Social smokers self-report that they almost never smoke alone or only smoke while drinking alcohol or when others are already smoking. The concerns with this behavior are threefold. First, the potential for a progression of tobacco use through continued exposure to cigarettes makes light smokers progress into heavy cigarette use. Second, any usage, no matter how infrequent, could lead to stable usage over time. Finally, social smoking hampers cessation efforts. Because social smokers do not view themselves as smokers, they are significantly less likely to feel the need to participate in cessation efforts (Mermelstein, 2015). Nichter's (2015) conversations with social smokers echo these concerns. She highlights the following potential consequences that may affect social smokers since the "smoker" label does not resonate with them. They may:

- end up smoking on a non-daily basis for many years (*I will quit once I graduate*);
- not be aware of their intermittent smoking as something that could lead to dependence (*I will quit before I get addicted*);
- develop paired dependence (*I always smoke when I drink*);
- dismiss potential health consequences (*I don't smoke that much or I smoke a healthier brand*);
- dismiss quit messages targeting smokers (*I am not a smoker*); or
- underestimate ability to quit (*I only smoke during certain times, I can quit when I want to*).

Stress: "Smoking Helps Me Relax . . ."

In a 2012 survey, more than half of college students reported above-average or tremendous stress levels (American College Health Association, 2012). Nichter, Nichter and Carkoglu (2007) found that college students smoke for stress relief, in anticipation of stress or to focus thoughts during stress. Nicotine is often seen as a stress reliever for college students. Although students often connect smoking with relaxation, the opposite is true in terms of physiology. When a person smokes, the nicotine is actually a stimulant and causes the body to release adrenaline, which can lead to increased heart rate and blood pressure. The feeling of stress relief may be due to psychological addiction and relief from physical withdrawal symptoms.

Campus Strategies to Address Tobacco

Tobacco control work has come a long way since the first Surgeon General's report in 1964 (Centers for Disease Control and Prevention, 2006). The Centers for Disease Control and Prevention released the CDC's "Best Practices for Comprehensive Tobacco Control Programs" in 2014 (Centers For Disease Control and Prevention, 2014). This document outlines the best evidence-based practices for states to develop comprehensive tobacco control programs to establish smoke-free policies, establish social norms around tobacco use, promote and assist tobacco users to quit and to prevent the initiation of use. The document notes that having multilayered interventions is necessary to have an impact on tobacco use. Evidence-based practices that can translate from this document to college campuses are policy interventions, education and media and cessation programs. These are large efforts that will need the support and contribution from numerous departments on campus such as:

- Administration (president, deans, faculty, governance groups)—can provide leadership in addressing this issue on campus through the development of policies to restrict tobacco on campus, to be supportive of prevention and media campaigns and to ensure that cessation opportunities are available on campus at low cost or free.
- Student health organizations (health centers, counseling centers, student health promotion, peer education)—can lead campuswide policy development and implementation. Additionally, they can lead the development of culturally appropriate prevention programming and ensure that cessation support efforts are aligned to meet and support young adults where they are in the process.
- Student activities committees (programming board, fraternities and sororities, athletics)—can develop a campus culture that supports tobacco-free lifestyles. Fraternities and sororities could promote and host smoke-free events. Athletic departments could provide leadership around smokeless tobacco prevention and break the association between certain sports such as baseball and chewing tobacco.
- Facilities and grounds—can provide documentation of the campus cost associated with smoking and tobacco use. Costs such as maintenance, litter and even fire damage could help build support for policy change. Additionally, facilities and grounds could help with campus signage when policies are developed.
- Community partners (American Cancer Society, American Lung Association, state or local health departments)—can be tapped into for resources in all three areas (policy, education and cessation).

Additionally, the Truth Initiative has a goal of creating the first tobacco-free generation. In order to achieve that goal, they need help and college campuses can make valuable contributions, not only by supporting individual students in examining their health behaviors, but also by:

- creating the campus as a tobacco-free workplace for faculty, staff and visitors;
- leading the way for the communities around campuses to make tobacco-free laws and ordinances; and
- engaging the academic community to be a forceful civic partner in tackling tobacco issues through the wide array of disciplines and intellectual ingenuity on campus.

In combination, the Best Practices document coupled with the Truth Initiative goals provide college and university campuses with the core elements needed to build a comprehensive campus program.

Elements of Comprehensive Campus Program: Policy

The American College Health Association's document, *Position Statement on Tobacco on College and University Campuses*, notes that efforts to promote tobacco-free environments have

> led to substantial reductions in the number of people who smoke, the amount of tobacco consumed and the number of people exposed to environmental tobacco hazards.
>
> (p. 1)

In 2012, the Department of Health and Human Services launched the Tobacco Free College Campus Initiative (TFCCI) website in collaboration with The University of Michigan Tobacco Research Network. This website serves as a clearinghouse for college and universities to understand the impact of tobacco on a campus and to provide resources and guidance for the development of tobacco-free policies. Changing policy on campus is typically not a simple or straightforward process and rarely can be accomplished by one person or unit. Each campus needs to garner an understanding of the campus climate with regard to tobacco use and readiness for policy change, procedures for policy change, best routes or channels to communicate need, proposed policy, process for development of policy and various other factors that may impact proposed policy (Connecticut Department of Public Health, 2014).

As of January 2016, over 1,400 campuses in the U.S. are smoke free, with about two-thirds of these campuses being tobacco free and over 802 of these campuses prohibiting e-cigarette use or vaping on campus. Since 2010, the number of campuses reporting having smoke-free policies has almost tripled (American Nonsmokers' Rights Foundation, 2016). Because of this momentum, national organizations, state health departments and individual campuses have developed guides and toolkits to help campuses assess the current tobacco use, policies and cessation programs on campus and, based on these findings, to develop a comprehensive approach to tobacco control that includes the adoption of policies to reduce or eliminate tobacco use on campus. These toolkits provide step-by-step instructions as well as best practices for implementing new policies. TFCCI's website provides numerous examples, toolkits, strategies and technical assistance to support college campuses in creating a tobacco-free campus.

Elements of Comprehensive Campus Program: Prevention (Education and Media)

Prevention efforts can help develop awareness of tobacco issues that impact the campus and surrounding community, promote tobacco-free policies and highlight cessation resources. In order to develop the most appropriate programs, an understanding of campus data (use and attitude survey, environmental scan) can serve as a starting point for understanding the current campus in terms of tobacco use, policies and cessation efforts.

For example, Cronk et al. (2011) found that most college students smoke more during the beginning of the semester and on weekends, so understanding patterns of use on campus may provide opportunities to link smoking prevention and cessation programs to peak use times such as orientation or weekend programming. In addition to formal data collection instruments, the campus prevention specialist, health educators, peer educators or research methods classes could hold focus groups with smokers to learn more about their motivation to smoke, motivation to quit and thoughts on how the college could help them quit. Engaging students or classes in the data collection, analysis and message development are also ways to further deepen the tie between the educational and wellness mission of the institution.

Social Norms Marketing

One way that colleges can use the data they collect about tobacco is through social norms marketing. Social norms marketing is based on the concept that most students misperceive the number of their peers that engage in high-risk health behaviors such as social smoking. Because of this misperception, many students may accept social smoking as the norm for college students and may actually begin or continue to smoke because of this misperception. The truth is that most students choose not to smoke, even socially, so social norms marketing using campus-specific data can erode misperceptions by using current, local data. Social norms marketing has been used for tobacco prevention, tobacco cessation and tobacco policy on college campuses. The Social Norms National Research and Resource website provide examples of collegiate campaigns and resources on utilizing this process.

Programming

Many campuses develop programs throughout the calendar year to address high-risk health behaviors. These programming times may follow health-related dates such as the Great American Smokeout held the third Thursday of November;

health programing may also be woven into other campus events such as women's history month, where programming could focus on how tobacco companies target women. The following are a few suggestions for programs that address tobacco:

- As part of orientation, add tobacco education to the wellness sessions.
- During alcohol awareness week, discuss the relationship between alcohol and tobacco and offer cessation tips.
- Host a Great American Smokeout during the national event on the third Thursday of November.
- Provide healthy stress management opportunities during mid-terms and finals.
- Conduct a New Year's resolution campaign to help tobacco users stay quit after the holiday break.
- Collaborate with the Career Center to host a Start Your Career Tobacco Free event.
- Collaborate with the Greek community to host quit challenges or smoke-free events.
- Collaborate with the athletic department to sponsor quit chew events.

For more programming ideas, check out the BACCHUS Network, an initiative of the National Association of Student Personnel Administrators (NASPA).

Elements of Comprehensive Campus Program: Cessation

Nonsmokers often wonder, why don't smokers just quit? Quitting tobacco use is hard. Researchers have suggested that nicotine is as addictive as heroin, cocaine and alcohol. Physical dependence on nicotine can cause withdrawal symptoms such as irritability, craving, depression, anxiety, cognitive and attention deficits, sleep disturbances and increased appetite. In addition, behavioral factors such as the sight, smell, feel of a cigarette as well as the rituals associated with smoking may increase the withdrawal symptoms. The combinations of these symptoms make it difficult for a smoker to quit. It is estimated that it takes between 8–11 quit attempts for the average smoker to quit.

Despite the difficulty, quitting tobacco use is well worth the effort. Quitting tobacco has many health benefits and the earlier a person quits, the greater the benefits. Reductions of lung cancer, lung disease, heart disease and infertility in women childbearing age are all benefits associated with quitting. Respecting the withdrawal process and appreciating the difficulty facing those who choose to quit is a must in supporting students toward a tobacco-free future. The gift of a tobacco-free future is immeasurable in terms of health and quality of life.

It is valuable to be ready to provide resources for quitting, especially if the campus is planning prevention and policy campaigns. The BACCHUS Network suggests a range of action items to consider for campus cessation programs (BACCHUS Peer Education Network, 2002).

Garnering an understanding of what services are offered on campus is a great first step. Many environmental scan tools include a section on cessation services.

In addition to the campus scan, talking with campus cessation providers can help understand the following about campus services:

- Who provides cessation services for the campus?
- How are the providers trained?
- Are the cessation services used?
- Are the cessation services advertised?
- How effective are the services? Are they evaluated?
- Do the cessation services include cessation with all types of tobacco products (i.e., smokeless tobacco, snus, e-cigarettes)?

This type of scan may provide valuable insight on potential gaps in services provided and how well these services are being utilized and if they are effective in helping students with quitting.

The campus assessment may reveal that the campus does not offer cessation services. If this is the case, a starting point maybe to connect with the local or state health department. They can provide linkages to community-based resources that students (and faculty and staff) are able to access. Additionally, support for anyone who wants to quit using tobacco can be found nationally at the Quitline (1-800-Quit-Now).

College student smokers possess many traits that make it challenging to address their smoking behavior. These include not seeing themselves as smokers, low motivation to quit and infrequent use of cessation support. These characteristics may lead some professionals on campus to have misperceptions about the utility in providing smoking cessation services for students. Strategies can be developed to help faculty members, student affairs professionals and other staff on campus understand that most college students express a desire to quit sometime in the future and that successful quitting may take many attempts; this understanding is a first step in opening up a dialogue about opportunities to provide students with support for quitting and with creating an environment that understands students' motivations to quit.

Tools such as the stages of change model and motivational interviewing techniques are useful to understand in order to create a safe and welcoming space for students to explore their current use of tobacco, the benefits they get when they use versus their desires to quit and the development of a plan if they are ready to quit. Motivational interviewing is a technique that helps the smoker explore and resolve their ambivalence about behavior change. This technique is often coupled with the stages of change model (Campaign for Tobacco Free Kids, 2015).

James O. Prochaska and Carol C. DiClemente developed the Stages of Change or Transtheoretical Model in 1979. This identifies six stages a person goes through when making any behavior change. These stages, as illustrated with tobacco cessation, include:

- Stage 1, Pre-Contemplation: In this stage, the tobacco user is not thinking about quitting and is not motivated to quit; the user may not be aware of the health consequences of use nor aware of the need to change (Prochaska, 1994).

- Stage 2, Contemplation: In this stage, the tobacco user has started to think about their tobacco use. They are more open to learning more about tobacco use, the impacts it may have on their lives and available resources to quit (Prochaska, 1994).
- Stage 3, Preparation: In this stage, the user has decided to quit. They have made a plan, researched and decided about types of cessation support they will utilize including potential medications, lined up friends and family for support and set a quit date (Prochaska, 1994).
- Stage 4, Action: In this stage, the user has stopped using tobacco. They may need consistent social reinforcement and support. Additionally, they may choose to use pharmacological support such as nicotine replacement products or approved medications (e.g., patches, gum, nasal spray) to decrease symptoms of withdrawal (Prochaska, 1994).
- Stage 5, Maintenance: This is the stage where the former tobacco user learns to find alternative behaviors for those events that used to signal smoking or chewing such as a party or when having a cup of coffee. Long-term strategies are developed to remain tobacco free (Prochaska, 1994).
- Stage 6, Relapse: For some, this stage may not occur, but it is normal for many people as it is estimated that it take the average person 8–11 quit attempts before they are successful. Relapse typically happens in action and maintenance stages. If this happens, it is important to let the individual provide support for the individual and help them make a fresh start in quitting (Prochaska, 1994).

This model can be utilized by peer educators, residence hall staff and health and counseling center personnel to build comprehensive programming and cessation services that address the motivation of tobacco users. By understanding this model, campus professionals can meet the user at the appropriate place along the continuum and connect them with appropriate interventions and support. For example, a person in the pre-contemplation stage would not be receptive to making a quit plan; rather, providing education to raise awareness about tobacco and its immediate impacts may support the person into moving into the contemplation stage.

Conclusion

The case for comprehensive tobacco programs on college campuses is clear. Tobacco use is an addictive behavior that leads to short-term and long-term health consequences. Most people who use tobacco begin as youth or young adults and too often continue to smoke for years.

A great deal of progress has been made in the last 50 years in decreasing tobacco use and the associated consequences. But, there is more to be done. The introduction of new tobacco products such as hookahs and e-cigarettes and the marketing associated with them has the potential to increase tobacco use and associated harms. Social smoking blurs the lines for some students in identifying their risks and taking action to quit. Young adulthood is a transition period in which individuals solidify health behaviors.

Colleges and universities have the opportunity to clearly outline campus strategies for student wellness including supporting and promoting tobacco-free living. Partnerships across campus units such as student affairs, faculty, academic support or administration, can collaborate with community partners and student peer leaders to promote lifelong health habits. Leadership that advocates and implements prevention education, tobacco-free policies and cessation services can ensure students who came to campus tobacco free graduate from college tobacco free and to support any student who came to campus using any form of tobacco product with the resources and support necessary to graduate tobacco free.

References

American College Health Association. (2011). *Position Statement on Tobacco on College and University Campuses*. American College Health Association. Hanover, MD: American College Health Association.

American College Health Association. (2012). *Reference Group Dat Report: Spring 2012*. American College Health Association, National College Health Assessment II. Hanover, MD: American College Health Association.

American College Health Association. (2015). *National College Health Assessment Executive Summary: Graduate Students Reference Group Spring 2015*. American College Health Association. Hanover, MD: American College Health Association.

American Nonsmokers' Rights Foundation. (2016). *Smokefree and Tobacco-Free U.S. and Tribal Colleges and Universities*. American Nonsmokers' Rights Foundation. Berkeley, CA: American Nonsmokers' Rights Foundation.

BACCHUS Peer Education Network. (2002). *Journey of a Lifetime*. BACCHUS Peer Education Network. Retrieved from http://citeseerx.ist.psu.edu/viewdoc/download?doi=10.1.1.688. 6932&rep=rep1&type=pdf

Berg, C. J., Lust, K. A., Sanem, J. R., Kirch, M. A., Rudie, M., Ehlinger, E., Ahluwalia, J. S., & An, L. C. (2009). Smoker self-identification versus recent smoking among college students. *American Journal of Preventive Medicine, 36*, 333–336.

Breathe California. (2016). *Youth Tobacco Education*. Retrieved from http://www.ggbreathe.org/what-we-do-2/programs/tobacco-cessation/youth-tobacco-education/

Campaign for Tobacco Free Kids. (2015, June 17). *E-Cigarette Marketing Continues to Mirror Cigarette Marketing*. Retrieved from Tobacco Unfiltered. Retrieved from https://www.tobaccofreekids. org/tobacco_unfiltered/post/4974

Caponetto, P. C. (2014, January 9). The emerging phenomenon of electronic cigarettes. *Expert Review of Respiratory Medicine, 6*(1), 63–74.

Center for Behavioral Health Statistics and Quality. (2010). *Preventing Tobacco Use among Youth and Young Adult: The Epidemiology of Tobacco Use among Young People in the United States and Worldwide*. Substance Abuse and Mental Health Services Administration, National Survey on Drug Use and Health. HHS.

Center for Behavioral Health Statistics and Quality. (2015). *Behavioral Health Trends in the United States: Results from the 2014 National Survey on Drug Use and Health*. Substance Abuse and Mental Health Services Administration, National Survey on Drug Use and Health. HHS.

Centers for Disease Control and Prevention. (2006, December). *History of the Surgeon General's Reports on Smoking and Health*. Retrieved from Smoking & Tobacco Use. Retrieved from http://www. cdc.gov/tobacco/data_statistics/sgr/history/

Centers For Disease Control and Prevention. (2014). *Best Practices for Comprehensive Tobacco Control Programs—2014*. U.S. Department of Health and Human Services, Centers for Disease Control and Prevention, National Center for Chronic Disease Prevention and Health Promotion, Office on Smoking and Health. Atlanta, GA: U.S. Department of Health and Human Services.

Centers for Disease Control and Prevention. (2015a). *7 in 10 Students Who Currently Use Tobacco Used a Flavored Product*. Department of Health and Human Services, Centers for Disease Control and Prevention. Atlanta: Department of Health and Human Services.

Centers for Disease Control and Prevention. (2015b). *E-Cigarette Use Triples among Middle and High School Students in Just One Year*. U.S. Department fo Health and Human Services.

Cobb, C. W. (2010). Waterpipe tobacco smoking: An emerging health crisis in the United States. *American Journal of Behavioral Health, 34*(3), 275–285.

Connecticut Department of Public Health. (2014, March). *Living and Learning Tobacco Free: Creating a Tobacco Free Campus*. (C. D. Health, Producer). Retrieved from Connecticut Department of Public Health: www.ct.gov/dph/lib/dph/hems/tobacco/pdf/tf_campuses.pdf

Cronk, N. J., Harris, K. J., Harrar, S. W., Conway, K., Catley, D., & Good, G. E. (2011). Analysis of smoking patterns and contexts among college students smokers. *Substanc Use and Misuse, 46*(8), 1015–1022.

Delnevo, C. G. (2015). Patterns of electronic cigarette use among adults in the United States. *Nicotine & Tobacco Research, 18*(5), 1–5.

DiFranza, J. S. (2007, July). Symptoms of tobacco dependence after brief intermittent use: The development and assessment of nicotine dependence in youth-2 study. *Achives of Pediatric Adolescent Medicine, 161*(7), 704–710.

Dow Chemical Co. (2013). *Product Safety Assessment (PSA): Propylene Glycol*. Dow Chemical Company. Retrieved from http://msdssearch.dow.com/PublishedLiteratureDOWCOM/dh_08ea/0901b803808eabba.pdf?filepath=productsafety/pdfs/noreg/233-00248&fromPage=GetDoc

Goniewicz, M. K. (2013, January). Nicotine levels in electronic cigarettes. *Nicotine & Tobacco Research, 15*(1), 158–166.

Grana, R. B. (2014). E-cigarettes: A scientific review. *Circulation, 129*, 1972–1986.

Hatzenbeuhler, M. L. (2001, June 6). Community-level determinants of tobacco use disparities in lesbian, gay, and bisexual youth results from a population-based study. *Archives of Pediatrics and Adolescent Medicine, 165*(6), 527–532.

Johnston, L., O'Malley, P., Bachman, J., & Schulenberg, J. (2015). *Monitoring the Future National Survey Results on Drug Use, 1975–2014*, Volume 2. Ann Arbor, MI: Institute for Social Research, The University of Michigan.

Kann, L., Kinchen, S., Shanklin, S. L., Flint, K. H., Kawkins, J., Harris, W. A., et al. (2013). Youth risk behavior surveillance—United States, 2013. *MMWR, 63*(4), 1–172.

Lee, J. G. (2009, August). Tobacco use among sexual minorities in the USA, 1987 to May 2007: A systematic review. *Tobacco Control, 18*(4), 275–282.

Levinson, A. C. Campo, S., Gascoigne, J., Jolly, O., & Zakharyan, A. (2007, August). Smoking, but not smokers: Identity among college students who smoke cigarettes. *Nicotine & Tobacco Research, 9*(8), 845–852.

Ling, P. G., & Glantz, S. A. (2002, June). Why and how the tobacco industry sells ciggarettds to young adults: Evidence from industry documents. *American Journal of Public Health, 92*(6), 908–916.

Mermelstein, R. N. (2015). *The Truth about Social Smoking among Young Adults*. Webinar on Social Smoking Co-hosted by The Truth Initiative. Smoking Cessation Leadership.

Nichter, M. (2015). *Lighting Up: The Rise of Social Smoking on College Campuses*. New York: New York University Press.

Nichter, M., Nichter, M., Carkoglu, A. (2007). Reconsidering stress and smoking: A qualitative study among college students. *Tobacco Control, 16*, 211–214.

Prochaska, J. N. (1994). *Changing for Good: A Revolutionary Six Stage Program for Overcomign Bad Habits and Moving Your Life Postively Forward*. New York: Harper Collins Publishers Inc.

Ryan, H. W. (2001). Smoking among lesbians, gays, and bisexuals: A review of the literature. *American Journal of Preventative Medicine, 21*(2), 142–149.

Sheahan, S. L. (1992). Stress and tobacco addiction. *Journal of the American Academy of Nurse Practitioners, 4*, 111–116.

Shiffman, S. W. (1985). *Coping and Substance Abuse*. New York: Academic Press.

U.S. Department of Health and Human Services. (2006). *The Health Consequences of Involuntary Exposure to Tobacco Smoke: A Report of the Surgeon General*. U.S. Department of Health and

Human Services, Centers for Disease Control and Prevention, Coordinating Center for Health Promotion, National Center for Chronic Disease Prevention and Health Promotion, Office on Smoking and Health. Atlanta, GA: U.S. Department of Health and Human Services.

U.S. Department of Health and Human Services. (2010). *How Tobacco Smoke Causes Disease: The Biology and Behavioral Basis for Smoking-Attributable Disease: A Report of the Surgeon General.* U.S. Department of Health and Humans Services, Centers for Disease Control and Prevention. Atlanta: National Center for Chronic Disease Prevention and Health Promotion, Office on Smoking and Health.

U.S. Department of Health and Human Services. (2012). *Preventing Tobacco Use Among Youth and Young Adults: A Report of the Surgeon General.* U.S. Department of Health and Human Services, Centers for Disease Control and Prevention. Atlanta: National Center for Chronic Disease Prevention and Health Promotion, Office on Smoking and Health.

U.S. Department of Health and Human Services. (2014). *The Health Consequences of Smoking—50 Years of Progress: A Report of the Surgeon General.* U.S. Department of Health and Human Services, Centers for Disease Control and Prevention. Atlanta, GA: National Center for Chronic Disease Prevention and Health Promotion, Office on Smoking and Health.

Villanti, A. (2015). Correlates of hookah use and predictors of hookah trial in U.S. young adults. *American Journal of Preventive Medicine, 48*(6), 742–746.

World Health Organization. (2007). *Smokeless Tobacco and Some Tobacco-Specific N-Nitrosamines.* IARC Monographs on the Evaluation of Carcinogenic Risks to Humans. *89.* Lyon, France: World Health Organization.

9

Substance Dependence and Recovery
Trading Stigma for Success
THOMAS HALL AND BETH DERICCO

Introduction

Discussion about substance dependence and recovery is often highly charged. Because of the moral and social stigma associated with drug use, faculty and student affairs professionals may be tempted to adopt a "don't ask, don't tell" approach. It is unlikely campuses collude to discourage students in recovery to apply to attend their institutions; more likely, the scenario rests in the belief that "regular" or non-clinical college personnel are not qualified, unable or unwilling to talk about topics related to substance and process addictions. Public discourse on substance dependence and recovery is treated as a secret under the guise of "protecting" the student. For example, a student shared her experience of talking about her recovery in a graduate class of social work majors; after class, her professor advised her to be careful sharing too much information because "people might talk."

This chapter is about "talking." Student affairs professionals in particular and other campus personnel, such as faculty, administrators and staff, need to talk more, not less! Faculty, staff and students are trained to talk about an array of stigmatized subjects; many do it quite well. Suicide prevention programs such as Question, Persuade, Refer (QPR) are taught to undergraduate students. Conversations on campus abound regarding social justice, domestic violence, gender identity, privilege and micro-aggressions, all of which are in the public eye and stigmatized to varying degrees. Yet, talking about alcohol and drug addiction and stories of recovery are not widely reported on campuses. Times change, and so do attitudes and beliefs about stigma. Conversations about suicide prevention, domestic violence and gender were less prevalent or non-existent in the (not too) distant past. Perhaps the same will be true about substance dependence, abuse and recovery in years to come.

A meaningful discussion of substance dependence, abuse and recovery starts with a simple premise; sometimes students arrive on campus with a substance abuse problem, and sometimes students develop a problem after they arrive on campus. Despite this chapter being about "treatment," prevention of drug and alcohol dependence is always within reach of campus strategies and efforts. Student affairs professionals are often the first professionals in the academy to respond to campus and community substance use norms. Prior to alcohol and other drug (AOD) use, especially when there is a "new" substance on the scene, health education and awareness (what had been called "primary prevention") is vital. In addition to nurses, doctors and counselors, professional and paraprofessional staff members such as resident advisors, academic advisors, faculty and career counselors are in the position to alert students to the dangers of substances and recognize the signs and symptoms of use/abuse. Recently, the availability of synthetic drugs such as Flakka, research chemicals that are analogues of prescription drugs and "natural" opioids such as Kratom are found widely available. Many of these and other drugs are purchased online. By the time this chapter is read, new drugs will be available that pose new threats; this is a continuously evolving issue and a moving target. Primary prevention is vital when dangerous substances are introduced on campuses, as well as in the larger community. Student affairs professionals, in particular, and other campus professionals serve a vital role as gatekeepers to alert medical and counseling staffs to the latest drug trends.

An important contextual framework throughout this chapter is that substance abuse and dependence are progressive; the more concerned individuals know about the science of prevention and intervention, the better equipped they are to prevent or interrupt the development of a substance use disorder or a relapse back into addiction.

This chapter includes several anecdotes of students who are in treatment or recovery. "Jennifer's" story illustrates that students who experience trauma are at higher risk for developing a substance use disorder. A better understanding of dynamics related to substance abuse treatment and recovery benefits students like Jennifer who are ready to change. If the stigma of addiction is such that conversations about substance use disorders are avoided, then students like Jennifer—ready to change—may slip out of sight.

Jennifer's resident advisor referred her to the campus substance abuse treatment clinic. Her R.A. noticed Jennifer spent most of her time by herself. Jennifer completed a significant amount of college coursework online in high school. She attends classes with students older than her. Jennifer's R.A. initiated a conversation with Jennifer, and she reported class was OK but did she not have any friends. Jennifer started crying and told her RA she was drinking every night to help her sleep and afraid of being an "addict."

Jennifer agreed to meet with a substance abuse counselor. Her therapist found out Jennifer was not doing well. Jennifer started drinking at age 12. She started abusing drugs when she was 13. She smoked crack cocaine several days a week for two years. However, she denies any use of crack cocaine since age 16. Her alcohol use has been daily for the past year. She reported a history of blacking out and driving under the influence.

Jennifer experienced significant trauma throughout her childhood. Because of her mom and dad's problems with addiction, she often struggled to find food to eat as a child. Despite her history of trauma and ongoing substance abuse, Jennifer has 3.25 GPA and a part-time job. College campuses have students like Jennifer who struggle to hold on. They could live in your residence hall or attend your first-year seminar class or visit your office for any number of reasons.

The purpose of the discussions in this chapter is to provide a theoretical and contextual framework for student affairs professionals, faculty and other college personnel who may be at the beginning stages of exploring the ways in which alcohol and other drug use, dependence, addiction and recovery fit into the campus student life experience. For most of these professionals, this chapter will provide a background for understanding the student in front of them. For others, this overview may set a career trajectory for specialty work.

Overall, the aim of this chapter is to provide higher education professionals on campus an introduction to the benefits and challenges of providing students access to a continuum of substance abuse prevention and recovery support services. The content is organized around the following four themes. First, institutional receptivity and resistance to substance abuse programs are reviewed, and the risks and benefits of providing care are delineated. Second, common philosophical approaches to substance abuse prevention, intervention, treatment and recovery are compared. Third, a comprehensive continuum of campus support is discussed. Lastly, a guide for creating sustainable campus recovery support programs is provided.

The Societal Context

Substance use disorders, addiction and recovery seem to be hot topics in the news; celebrities and rock stars are more open about their personal stories of addiction and recovery. For higher education, recovery is also a hot topic. Groups like Active Minds, Young People in Recovery (YPR), Transforming Youth Recovery (TRY) and the Association of Recovery in Higher Education (ARHE) are working hard to normalize conversations about substance abuse and dependence and process addictions (e.g., alcohol and other drug dependence and abuse as contrasted with gambling, Internet, food dependence and abuse). That said, for the average American, these issues are still fraught with stigma and damaging associations that prevent help-seeking. The cost of substance abuse treatment remains a barrier for many, in spite of the Affordable Care Act, parity and more readily available health insurance options.

The Patient Protection and Affordable Care Act (PPACA)—also known as the Affordable Care Act or ACA and generally referred to as Obamacare—is the landmark health reform legislation passed by the 111th Congress and signed into law by President Barack Obama in March 2010.

The legislation includes a long list of health-related provisions that began taking effect in 2010. Key provisions are intended to extend coverage to millions of uninsured Americans, to implement measures that will lower health care costs and improve system efficiency and to eliminate industry practices that include rescission and denial of coverage due to pre-existing conditions.

Noted substance abuse researchers and public policy experts Tom McLellan and Abigail Woodworth (2014) cite the continued segregation of substance abuse and dependence issues from other health issues when it comes to treatment. Separation of bio-behavioral health issues like addiction and mental health conditions from medical conditions with a physical basis is often arbitrary. Stigma surrounding substance abuse increases when in reality many medical conditions that manifest physically have a bio-behavioral root.

Research on early intervention clearly indicates that professionals and para-professionals can catalyze the "aging out" process so that young people exhibiting risky substance use behavior are encouraged to reduce risk and act in a way more in line with their personal goals and values. On campus, substance use and abuse are still seen as a normal part of the experience and often allowed to progress to levels of dependence and addiction; sometimes one experience of use or excess creates a life-altering consequence.

Aging Out

For college and university students, environmental factors often play a supportive role in enabling risky alcohol or other drug use. Factors such as employment, marriage, parenthood and others that increase commitment and responsibility and reduce social time encourage less risky use.

Evidence-informed early interventions (e.g., BASICS) that challenge expectancies related to the benefits of alcohol and other drug use, clarify peer norms and explore motivations often assist with this aging out process.

An unflattering narrative about substance abuse on college and university campuses became popular during the 1990s after several tragic incidents. Scott Krueger's death in 1997 catalyzed the issue for society at large and campuses when major publications, including *Newsweek* and *The New York Times*, ran cover stories on the quantity and frequency of college student alcohol use that piqued the interest of lawmakers, researchers and parents. A narrative emerged that college student drinking was harmful. Pressure to address the "problem" of drinking led researchers to examine campus rituals and traditions that glorified substance abuse and other risky behaviors. Some concluded that campuses were unresponsive to rampant alcohol abuse and, worse yet, that campus norms promoted excess. Over the next 30 years, various prevention strategies were instituted at the local, campus, state and national levels. Yet even today, college campuses search for effective strategies to address substance abuse and dependency, although there is more clear evidence than ever before regarding what works to reduce harm. It is difficult to determine if substance abuse is a function of intrusive parenting strategies or a lack of economic mobility for new college graduates. Helicopter parenting and delayed emancipation may account for the narrative that students are largely uninterested or unable to constrain their impulses with regard to substance abuse and are contributing factors to the prolonged adolescent period referenced in popular and research literature. However, uncertainty about the etiology of a social problem does not alter the reality that young adults, especially college students—who abuse substances—put themselves and others at risk for accidents and injuries. In addition, student health and safety is intimately related to retention and progression to graduation, career success and alumni engagement (Eisenberg, Golberstein, Hunt, 2009). Lastly, contemporary substance abuse interferes with higher education's basic mission—preparing a well-rounded and knowledgeable citizenry.

The prevalence of substance abuse and dependency on campuses is difficult to estimate. However, estimates of substance use are readily available. The Monitoring the Future (MTF) study has tracked college student substance use annually since 1980 (Johnston, O'Malley, Bachman, & Schulenberg, 2015). The most recent survey found daily marijuana use tripled between 1991 and 2014. Past year cocaine use increased from 2.7% in 2013 to 4.4% in 2014. Anecdotal reports of rising opiate use on college campuses are not reflected in the 2014 MTF report. However, opiate-related deaths are rising among 18 to 30 year olds (Frank et al., 2015). In addition to illicit drugs, the Monitoring the Future Study found 63% of college students report drinking in the past 30 days, and 35% report binge drinking. Lastly, 43% report being drunk in the past 30 days, and 4% report daily alcohol use (Johnston et al., 2015).

Drinking alcohol has long been identified as risky for the health of young adults because of increased risk of drowning, injuries from falls, motor vehicle crashes, risky sexual behaviors, poor school performance and increased likelihood of suicide and homicide (Byrnes, Miller, & Schafer, 1999; Kenney & LaBrie, 2013; Lewis, Litt, Cronce, Blayney, & Gilmore, 2014). The 2003 Institute of Medicine report *Reducing Underage Drinking: A Collective Responsibility* also highlighted underage and high-risk alcohol use as a public health problem most effectively addressed through multiple solutions by multiple stakeholders.

When looking at the general population, most of the adults in the country do not use or abuse substances, and for those who do, different sorts of interventions and policies must be implemented to minimize harms. Tom McLellan (McLellan & Woodworth, 2014) of the Treatment Research Institute, and former deputy "drug czar" as well as others have shown that regardless of dependence and addiction, use may become harmful to the individual across many spectrums of their lives. For this large percentage of the population (65–70 million Americans!) health, productivity and relationships may be affected. Around 23 million have reached the dependence threshold where diagnosis is clear, while only about one-tenth of those get into treatment. Of the population seeking treatment, about 5% are in the 18–24 year old age range, while, according to McLellan, about 3% think that they should seek treatment (McLellan & Woodworth, 2014). Data indicate about 4% of students with alcohol-/drug-related problems may seek treatment or recovery services while they are in college (Clements, 1999; Knight et al., 2002). It is clear that, for higher education to successfully assist students and reduce substance abuse and dependence, many colleagues need to be knowledgeable and engaged in the effort. With the prominence of collegiate recovery, many are looking to experienced colleagues (e.g., Augsburg College, Rutgers University, and Texas Tech) for support and guidance.

> **Dependence** is characterized by a physical or psychological reliance on a substance. Psychological dependence often occurs prior to physical dependence. Dependence is characterized by increasingly seeking out the substance in recreational and social settings, tolerance causing increased quantity of use, craving or strong desire for the substance causing increased use and psychological and physical withdrawal when use stops.
>
> **Addiction** differs from dependency in that the individual seeks the substance in spite of social and behavioral negative consequences and with an urgency that grows over time. Addiction is characterized by loss—loss of control, conflicted relationships with significant others, inability to consistently meet family, parental and work-related role expectations. Addiction is also reported to affect neurotransmission and interactions within reward structures of the brain.

Despite estimates of substance use disorders, students in need of intervention and treatment services may not find support on campus. Their substance use may adversely impact academic success and social engagement. As noted, this chapter includes a review of selected best practices with regard to substance abuse intervention, treatment and relapse prevention programs. This includes a discussion of how policies, programs and services may support or detract from student success. This discussion is relatively new for many campus personnel. Often campus programs that support students in recovery are formative. Best practices are institutionalized on campuses that are early adopters; these are the few that recognized decades ago the potential of serving students in recovery. For most, best practices are not easily disseminated, consistent or well adopted. While the number of campuses that offer services for students in recovery increases every year, for the larger overall community of higher education institutions, recovery on campus is in the early stages of adoption or institutionalization.

> **Bio-behavioral health issues** include mental health issues that originate from a genetic component and are exacerbated by associated behaviors. Social and environmental factors influence the manifestation of genetic vulnerabilities with regard to addiction.
>
> **Continuum of care** refers to an integrated and coordinated approach to addressing the whole person when addressing substance use disorders, so

that a focus on the physical, psychological and spiritual health is addressed concurrently. The continuum of substance abuse care includes inpatient detoxification and treatment, short-term or long-term residential treatment, transitional living, intensive outpatient treatment, outpatient treatment, relapse prevention, recovery coaching and mutual aid support groups.

Evidence-informed practice refers to research-based approaches that are carefully and strategically adapted to the environment in which they are replicated.

Progression of use refers to the movement from experimental to recreational to dependent to addictive use.

Substance Abuse Prevention and Treatment in Higher Education

Both institutional receptivity and resistance to recognize and address substance abuse programs has evolved over the past 50 years. Campuses have been struggling to address the topic of alcohol abuse for decades. Straus and Bacon's (1953) research set the stage for the contemporary study of alcohol consumption and student life; their formative research on college drinking was the first of its kind, as they were the first to quantify risk associated with alcohol use.

The U.S. Congress has legislatively mandated how campuses address alcohol and other drug issues. For example, in 1989, as a condition of the reauthorization of Title 1 funding, the U.S. Congress passed The Drug-Free Schools and Campuses Act (DFSCA). The DFSCA required mandatory substance use education in primary, secondary and post-secondary institutions. The intent of this legislation was to increase accountability for campuses through regulating annual notifications to inform students about the risks of substance use and to provide information about getting assistance if they had a problem. In the 1990s, the U.S. Department of Education funded the Higher Education Center for Alcohol and Other Drug Use Prevention. As a result, the public health model became more prevalent. In 2002, the National Institute on Alcohol Abuse and Alcoholism (NIAAA) concluded alcohol use by students on campus and in the communities surrounding colleges and universities was a major public health problem and "clearly dangerous for the drinker and society." This also marked the publication of the typology for addressing alcohol use on campus, between this and the other approaches detailed by the NIAAA, campuses had clear action steps and guidelines for addressing alcohol and other drug use on campus and in the surrounding community.

Peter Lake describes the history of campus approaches for addressing substance abuse; institutional control efforts were first guided by paternalistic approaches, then disengagement or "hands off," more recently a combination of paternalism and consumerism now referred to as the "Facilitator" era (Lake, 2013). Contemporary approaches dealing with substance use are more intentional than were historical efforts. Prevailing research indicates that a prevention model based on a public health approach is best suited to address the individual as well as the environment and is the most appropriate and effective for campus. That said, many campuses continue to resist fully adopting a process focused approach in favor of less effective knowledge-based approaches that function in isolation rather than in concert with individual and community factors. In an update to the seminal "Call to Action," the National Institute of Alcohol Abuse and Alcoholism (NIAAA) produced a guide, "What Colleges Need to Know Now" that highlighted new data and research (NIAAA, 2007), and recently an online decision making tool, the Alcohol Intervention Matrix (CollegeAIM) was developed to assist campuses further.

The Drug-Free Schools and Communities Act changed how campuses respond to alcohol and other drug use. Persistent media reports of campus drinking problems defined college life as a high-risk enterprise; dangerous alcohol use and associated risky behavior was no longer seen as a rite of passage. Societal attitudes that had once tolerated alcohol use within the primary framework of campus life were no longer acceptable (Serdula, Brewer, Gillespie, Denny, & Mokdad, 2004). Subsequent health interventions integrated alcohol educational programs, social-norms marketing, brief motivational interventions, policy interventions and clinical interventions. These were some of the growing number of approaches being researched for effectiveness. Over time these efforts have become more sophisticated and generally adopted by many institutions of higher education. The growing body of research on brain development and plasticity, legalization or decriminalization of marijuana, availability of synthetic drugs, prescription drug analogues and abuse of prescription opiates has extended the conversation about substance abuse from alcohol to other substances, including a growing awareness of the nature and consequences of dependence and addiction. Despite ongoing efforts to prevent substance abuse, college and university students continue to be identified as a population with disproportionate incidence of motor vehicle accidents, as well as other intoxicated health, legal and social problems (Hingson, Heeren, Winter, & Wechsler, 2005).

Campus conversations about substance abuse and dependency were recently accelerated as a result of the 2015 White House Office of National Drug Control Policy. For the first time, the strategy included specific recommendations for colleges and universities related to substance abuse treatment and recovery.

Health promotion is a model of enhancing the health and wellness of a population by focusing on creating an environment that values well-being and promotes this through environmental and individual activities. Health promotion recognizes that "health" is a complex and multifaceted and encompasses emotional, intellectual, physical, occupational, social and spiritual aspects of the individual, is context driven, so that age, differing abilities and the like may influence operational definitions and outcomes of "health"; positive and holistic well-being may be promoted nevertheless.

> **Harm reduction** is a health promotion approach that seeks to minimize risky behavior through a recognized set of strategies, policies and programs that are implemented in a targeted manner towards those involved in substance abuse behaviors and that increase the health and safety of the entire community by targeting on a population that may increase community risks. For many this term has a negative connotation; some funding sources will not support harm reduction activities. It is critical to remember that reducing risk is a health-promoting concept, and tools to do so are within the parameters of a comprehensive health promotion effort.

Primary prevention employs harm reduction strategies. For example, educating students on the size of a single alcohol "pour" may seem counterintuitive, yet students who drink liquor may "free pour" the equivalent of several drinks. This example shows how primary prevention can lead to learning new skills that may prevent alcohol poisoning. Another example of primary prevention is making students aware of risks associated with "new" drugs. For example, synthetic drugs are relatively easy to obtain. Students may not realize that chemicals ordered online that appear similar to brand name prescription drugs are not the same. These chemicals are unregulated, and their dosages are unreliable. The National Drug Control Strategy (U.S. Office of National Drug Control Policy, 2015) recommends that Institutions of Higher Education (IHEs) strengthen efforts to prevent drug use in communities by supporting substance abuse prevention on campuses. Critical components of this effort are the inclusion of early intervention opportunities by expanding and evaluating screening for substance use in healthcare settings. Lastly, IHEs are encouraged to integrate treatment for substance use disorders into health care and augment support for recovery by offering campus-based recovery support programs and mutual self-help groups.

Despite these recommendations, integration of substance abuse or addiction treatment on college campuses is not widespread. Some campuses offer specialty care such as psychiatry, dental, physical therapy and substance abuse treatment, but many are unable to do so. Campus student health centers and counseling centers have limited resources, and prioritizing student access to services often limits the provision of specialty care. Perhaps, campuses have a responsibility to provide services to students who either need substance abuse intervention and treatment or recovery support. Students in recovery are an underserved, marginalized population on campus. On the basis of social justice, campuses should officially recognize and accommodate students struggling with a substance use disorder. Finally, pragmatism ought to guide campus access to recovery support. When a campus milieu promotes inclusiveness, all students benefit. New campus traditions provide attractive alternatives to stereotypical "rite of passage" behaviors. Students in recovery are often leaders in creating "sober" socials. Spontaneous sober parties generate sustained interest in creating new narratives about college life. Developing a Collegiate Recovery Program is not rocket science. However, it does take science. Specifically, it takes a public health approach.

> **Abstinence** refers to a deliberate lack of substance use.
>
> **Sobriety** refers to a deliberate lack of substance use as a result of a real or perceived concern about previous substance use.
>
> **Recovery** refers to a voluntarily maintained lifestyle characterized by sobriety, personal health and citizenship. A person in recovery seeks to live a life that is balanced and whole, so that the primary substance of previous use is no longer an issue, and other substances (e.g., alcohol, other drugs, food, gambling, sex) do not take the place of the primary substance of abuse.

Theoretical Models for Addressing Substance Abuse Prevention, Treatment and Recovery

Alcohol is the most abused drug both on and off campus. Babor, Higgins-Biddle, Dauser, Higgins and Burleson (2005) estimate that about 5% of the population is likely alcohol dependent (see Figure 9.1). The following diagram graphically

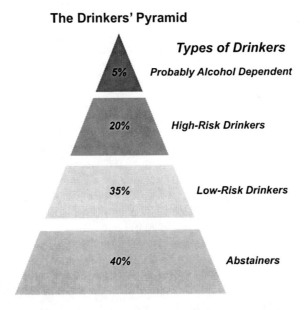

Figure 9.1 Historical Models of Prevention, Intervention, Treatment and Recovery

Source: Babor et al. 2005.

represents the distribution of drinkers. The number referenced by the Monitoring the Future study (Johnston et al., 2015) of students who drink is similar to Babor, Higgins-Biddle, Dauser, Higgins, and Burleson's (2005) estimates. On college campuses, much more attention is paid to the 20% identified as high-risk drinkers, as this group often comes to the attention of campus professionals through behavioral concerns or conduct-related issues. Alcohol-dependent drinkers often "learn the ropes" to avoid detection. Because of their physical tolerance, they do not appear drunk and often have "practiced" avoiding detection for a long time. It is counter-intuitive, but college students who are dependent often "fly under the radar" and may not come to others' attention until their academic performance forces them out of school or they experience significant personal loss. The assumptions made about who uses substances in a detrimental way, their character and characteristics play a role in the assumptions about the source of substance abuse problems and the solution. Historically, prevention, early intervention and treatment models are generated not only from research and science, but rather, also from these assumptions.

The field of substance abuse prevention has a long history, and the use of different models creates the framework or paradigm to conceptualize and address the alcohol or other drug problem. It is important to have an understanding of the *history* in addressing prevention, since the particular model used makes certain assumptions about the problem, its cause and the solution. Also vestiges of these models are imbedded within current paradigms, policies and practices.

1. *Early Temperance Model*: In the Early Temperance Model, distilled spirits were considered the chief source of alcohol problems. The strategy for solving this problem was to eliminate distilled spirits. Although this prevention model was articulated in the late 1700s, the belief that alcohol problems only result from the consumption of distilled spirits, rather than beer or wine, still persists.
2. *The Prohibition Model*: The Prohibition Model redefined the source of alcohol problems as the consumption of any amount of any type of alcoholic beverage, including beer and wine. The proposed solution was the elimination of all types of alcoholic beverages and the promotion of total abstinence through national prohibition. A strategy used by proponents of the Prohibition Model was to use any message that increased support for prohibition regardless of its accuracy. Another strategy was to foster contempt toward alcoholics in the hope that drinkers would be seen as "bad" people, leading people who wanted to be seen as "good" not to drink. This model, which fostered the stigmatization of alcoholics, still impedes prevention and treatment efforts today. Additionally, the view that consuming *any* amount of alcohol was problematic contributed to a lack of emphasis on the role of quantity and frequency of consumption in alcohol problems. Lastly, the spreading of inaccurate information to further the Prohibition agenda contributed to a public skepticism about alcohol control measures, a skepticism that persists today.
3. *Disease Model*: In the Disease Model, alcoholism is considered a disease and is defined as any drinking that leads to problems for the individual or society.

After the Prohibition era, little was done in the way of alcohol research until the 1940s. After the creation of Alcoholics Anonymous and the research of E. M. Jellinek and others, in 1951, the World Health Organization stated that alcoholism was disease. In 1966, the American Medical Association accepted alcoholism as a disease. An identifiable set of symptoms was outlined, and treatment activities were devised; however, no prevention strategy was articulated. Although this model has primarily been applied in the intervention and treatment of alcoholism, some have tried to apply the model to prevention by teaching about the Disease Model or intervention and treatment activities.

4. *Normative Model*: Prompted by the social consciousness and activism of the 1960s, socio-cultural research of alcohol was underway. Research findings demonstrated that some cultures had lower rates of alcoholism than others. Cultural norms, customs and attitudes regarding alcohol were seen as influencing drinking behavior and rates of alcoholism. Prevention activities were, therefore, aimed at educating individuals on "healthy" norms and encouraging adherence to norms similar to those held in cultures with low rates of alcoholism. The goal of the Normative Model was the responsible use of alcohol. One effect of this model on prevention efforts that persists today is the emphasis on outcomes of alcohol use as the measure of "responsible" use; that is, if no harmful or negative results occurred, then the use was responsible. Another effect has been the perception that, if people are using alcohol consistently with the norms of their culture, everything is fine. This belief interferes with prevention efforts, as students often rationalize their behavior by saying, "Everyone here drinks like I do."

5. *Information Model*: Up to this point, prevention models had focused solely on alcohol. The Information Model represents the first attempt to address other drugs in addition to alcohol. The assumption of this model is that people develop AOD problems due to a lack of information. Prevention activities are aimed at increasing peoples' factual knowledge of alcohol and other drugs. Research findings have shown that this type of education does not reduce AOD use and may lead to increased experimentation. One lasting impact of this model is that people are taught information at young ages and hold the belief that they know all there is to know about alcohol and other drugs. Many college students are resistant to the idea that they have anything new to learn.

6. *Development Model*: As the field moved more toward individual interpretations for drug and alcohol use and research was increasingly conducted by psychologists, the Development Model was articulated. This model states that people develop addictions to substances as a result of deficits in their developmental process, such as low self-esteem, poor coping skills or susceptibility to peer pressure. According to this paradigm, improving interpersonal competence decreases drug/alcohol use. This model of prevention has perpetuated the belief that substance problems only occur among those people who are troubled or lacking in life skills.

7. *Public Health Model*: The Public Health Model is based on research regarding the prevention of infectious disease and alcohol research indicating that

the percentage of heavy drinkers is proportional to per capita consumption of alcohol. In this model, drug/alcohol problems are seen as caused by the agent (alcohol or other drugs); the host (person, biological and psychological) and the environment (family, community, society). Activities are aimed at changing environmental factors, particularly controlling alcohol availability through policies that will reduce consumption.

Contemporary Models of Prevention, Intervention, Treatment and Recovery

BEHAVIORAL MODELS

Choice Theory holds behavior is influenced by acting, thinking, feeling and physiology (Glasser, 1999). Individuals are described as having a great deal of control or choice over acting and thinking and little control over feeling and physiology. Choices made in thinking and acting have a significant effect on feeling and physiology. Substance abuse is a relationship problem. Individuals attempt to manipulate their feelings by using substances. For example, if a student thinks drinking will change his/her mood, she/he may drink until feeling better. However, feeling better after several drinks is actually a placebo effect. In time, the pharmacological effects of alcohol will render the person physically impaired (which may adversely impact a relationship (e.g., drunk dialing). Ultimately, a feedback loop is developed that leads the student to drink more to feel better, despite the fact that heavy alcohol consumption makes the student feel worse. Finally, this behavior leads to a pattern of thinking that results in feeling a loss of control.

Similar to Choice Theory, Cognitive Behavioral Theory (CBT) explains substance dependence as a collection of various symptoms and behaviors related to the use of substances that result in harmful consequences. Cognitive Behavioral approaches also deal with the way people think and act. CBT holds individual thoughts, beliefs, attitudes and perceptual biases to learned behavior that influence how a person feels and the intensity of their emotions. The appearance of adverse symptoms associated with individuals who abuse substances is variable, does not support the existence of a specific biological process that predisposes a person toward alcoholism (Marlatt & Witkiewitz, 2002). Cognitive Behavioral theorists describe problematic behavior as reversible and reject labels such as addict.

THE DISEASE MODEL

Addiction, according to the *American Heritage Dictionary of the English Language, Third Edition*, is "a compulsive physiological need for a habit forming substance. . . ." In other words, addiction is defined as a physical disease. It is framed as a health problem, not a moral failing. According to this definition, the addicted individual does not choose to become an alcoholic or drug dependent, nor does the illness stem from a lack of willpower. Proponents of this model claim addiction is a biological and psychological disease that is incurable and progressive (Covey, 1996). The Disease Model posits addiction is a brain disease that affects brain systems responsible for motivation and reward. In addition, cognitive control, delayed gratification and cost benefit analyses of behavior are negatively impacted by addiction.

Currently, no conclusive medical tests exist to determine alcohol addiction or dependency. In the absence of a definitive test for addiction, the medical profession has developed a guide for physicians to define the likelihood of addiction. Definitions of addiction reported in clinical and research literatures are often criticized for being too subjective. The National Institutes of Health (NIH) and the *Diagnostic and Statistical Manual of Mental Disorders* (5th ed.; *DSM-5*, 2013) address critics by providing clear definitions of addiction. The DSM-5 definitions are very specific. Substance Use Disorders (SUD) are defined by 11 criteria that describe specific diagnostic features of dependence. Substance use disorders are nominally classified as mild, moderate and severe (*DSM-5*, 2013).

THE BIOLOGICAL MODEL

The Biological Model is a continuation of the Disease Model. Dependency is defined as having a physical beginning, stemming from an individual's physiological or genetic characteristics. Individuals are born with a genetic or bio-physiological predisposition that causes them to become chemically dependent. Because the effects of physical and environmental factors are difficult to distinguish from one another, a single biological explanation for addiction is elusive. Not all behavioral health professionals agree on the biological or disease models. There are some who reject these models in favor of a cognitive schema that emphasizes individual choice.

PUBLIC HEALTH MODELS

An examination of the varying models for addressing alcohol and other drugs and public health in general provides a helpful framework for analysis and action planning. The following section outlines selected models of substance abuse and addiction. Some of these models are complementary, while others are not. Some of the concepts discussed may seem "out of step" with assumptions typically associated with substance abuse. This section briefly introduces selected models with the hope of spurring readers to conduct their own more thorough review of the professional substance abuse, dependency and addiction literature.

A public health approach suggests that addiction is a symptom of social disintegration, disorder and inequity. Hopelessness and alienation ultimately lead to substance use and chemical dependency as a means of coping in a hostile environment (Bloom, 1996). Community models are helpful in acquiring a systemic understanding of addiction. Fellin (1995) defines three different types of communities: those based on geographical or physical location, non-place communities of identification (race, gender, sexual orientation) and personal communities that are an integration of the multiple communities in an individual's life. Cohen (1985) defines community as "the arena in which people acquire their most fundamental and most substantial experience of social life outside of the home." Pardeck,

Murphy and Choi (1994) suggest "Community is the domain where certain assumptions about reality are acknowledged to have validity."

Social Learning Theory (SLT) is aligned with public health model. SLT explains addiction as a learning process. Because humans are able to think about future consequences of behavior, they can plan and evaluate their behavior. Individual learning takes place in the social environment directly (by personal experience) and indirectly (by modeling of others). SLT identifies four general principles that explain behavior: differential reinforcement, vicarious learning, cognitive processes and reciprocal determinism (Bandura, 1977). SLT defines addiction as learned behavior acquired and sustained as a function of social learning. Learning occurs through imitation, trial and error and other cognitive mental processes in relationship to an individual's primary and secondary group affiliations. SLT proponents believe that the same principles of learning apply at all points on the continuum between substance use and chemical dependency. In addition to SLT, additional models describe substance abuse. Three additional models are briefly described in the following paragraphs. The difference between the aforementioned models and what follows is the locus of control for change. Each of the following models holds the individual accountable for change.

The Social Ecological Model is a widely used public health approach that recognizes the synergistic influences on the individual that influence values, beliefs and decision making. This model makes explicit the notion that to create a change in individual behavior, it is vital to also examine (and perhaps change) the environment in which the individual lives, works and plays. The Social Ecological Model has been adopted by international (e.g., Centers for Disease Control and Prevention, World Health Organization), national and local organizations as a foundational planning tool for disparate health issues from the management of chronically ill children, violence prevention and to campus alcohol prevention. Ecological models rest on specific assumptions about the intersection between individual and community health beliefs. First, health behavior is a convergence of individual, family and community factors. Second, symbols both influence and are influenced by individual, family, community and societal levels. Consideration is given to specific behavioral concerns. For example, alcohol abuse has specific implications across all levels or units within the social ecological model. Lastly, interventions are more effective when behavior change strategies are capable of accounting for dynamics that influence behavior across a broad environmental spectrum. Thus, comprehensive interventions replace piecemeal or narrow strategies that are considered in isolation: the individual, peers and family and the community in general.

The Social Ecological Model is the predominant approach in public health initiatives (see Figure 9.2). For example, the CDC used this approach as it developed a strategy to prevent child abuse and neglect (Keller, 2015). This model is influenced by several of the theoretical approaches previously described. Preventing child abuse and neglect is widely accepted as the "right" and "moral" thing to do. Yet for college students who are substance dependent, a model such as this is not likely to be embraced as an institutional priority.

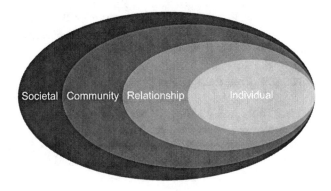

Figure 9.2 The Social Ecological Model

Creating a Campus Continuum of Substance Use Care: Examples of the Socio-Ecological Model on College Campuses

Individual Level Assessment, Intervention and Treatment

One of the signature campus-based alcohol abuse intervention programs is Brief Assessment and Intervention Strategies for College Students (BASICS) (Dimeff, Baer, Kivlahan, & Marlatt, 1999). The BASICS intervention suggests, but does not require, that underage college students abstain from illegally obtaining and drinking alcohol. Support for teaching underage students how to reduce harm related to drinking is widely accepted (Baer, Kivlahan, Blume, McKnight, & Marlatt, 2001; Murphy et al., 2001). A similar program for marijuana is available (Lee, Neighbors, Kilmer, & Larimer, 2010). However, harm reduction strategies for marijuana use are currently not as widely accepted as BASICS. As public policy changes mediate stigma around marijuana use, intervention prevalence might change as well. Campus support for teaching students protective behaviors with regard to prescription or illicit drug abuse are rare.

> **Early intervention** is a research-based strategy to assist students in aging out of risky substance use behavior upon examination of expectations and motivations for use; consequences of use and academic, personal and social goals. On campus, one of the most common early intervention tools is Brief Alcohol Screening and Intervention for College Students (BASICS).

Another widely used approach is Screening, Brief Intervention, and Referral to Treatment (SBIRT); this is an early intervention risk reduction tool that has shown great success when implemented appropriately (Robertson-Boersma, Butt, & Dell, 2015). The purpose of SBIRT (similar to BASICS) is to identify those who exhibit the most risky substance use behavior through assessment and to quickly provide appropriate level of care intervention. SBIRT began as a tool for hospital and primary care medical personnel, but it has been adapted for use on college campuses.

There are several instruments that can be used to determine if a referral to treatment is indicated. The Alcohol Use Disorder Identification Test (AUDIT) and the Cannabis Use Disorder Identification Test (CUDIT) and the lesser-known Drug Use Disorder Identification Test (DUDIT) are examples of screening measures that can provide non-medical personnel guidelines or cut points for when to refer students for treatment. Students who present signs and symptoms that indicate treatment is necessary have a few common themes. First, heavy drug use in high school is an indicator of risk-taking behavior. Sensation seeking is associated with increased risk of substance abuse. It is likely that some students enrolling as freshman already have an addiction. These students are more likely to come to the attention of campus administrators because they are unfamiliar with campus life and not savvy. A professional counselor can offer confidentiality and may learn about an addiction at a time the student feels more vulnerable. As students get more familiar with campus life, they feel less vulnerable and are not as likely to be open.

Some students begin abusing substances after they arrive on campus. These students have not yet learned how to abuse drugs and stay "under the radar." These students present to counseling staff, doctors in health services and academic advisors with time management problems, poor sleep habits, anxiety and academic concerns. Resident assistants may pick up on some of these difficulties by observing how residents cope with the first six weeks of classes. It is important for campuses to prepare staff members to recognize symptoms of poor coping and intervene. Substance abuse screening can be done by an array of staff. Another group of students who present with substance abuse/dependence concerns are graduate students. This makes sense because some of these students have developed addictions during their undergraduate years. The stress of doctoral programs sometimes triggers an increase in substance abuse that becomes very problematic for the student. In general, substance dependence is not easily defined. However, being mindful of academic performance and interpersonal relationships can help facilitate a substance abuse assessment that may result in an episode of treatment.

Some campus mental health professionals perceive mandated assessment, intervention and treatment as problematic. Mandated assessment is viewed as a dual relationship—a relationship with the student and a relationship with the referring agency or campus department. There are merits to this line of thinking; however, unlike less stigmatized mental health care, students' first episode of care for substance related problems is often mandated. Sometimes mandated students are ready to change and their arrest, DUI or student conduct violation provides an opportunity to assess for substance use disorders and to provide intervention or treatment. These students are not concerned with the complications of a dual relationship; they are ready to let someone know they are out of control and want help.

Treatment services are typically provided by community agencies rather than college health or counseling centers; one primary reason has to do with cost-effectiveness and expertise, since most campuses just won't have the specialized personnel to accommodate on-site treatment services. Thus, it is important for student affairs and other college professionals to reach out to community providers and create a referral list of agencies to distribute to various campus departments. For this reason it is important for college professionals to be engaged with community public health agencies. Mental health and substance abuse treatment providers are often willing to partner with campuses to assist students. In addition, academic departments may be engaged with external treatment providers.

Treatment services are appropriate for students who can be managed in an outpatient setting and continue to attend classes and fulfill major role responsibilities. For some students, outpatient treatment is not possible; these students are unable to continue their education because of the severity of their substance abuse. Intensive outpatient programs, inpatient detoxification programs and residential treatment programs would be appropriate for this group of students. Some campuses have "care management" teams that work with students who present with severe mental health/substance abuse disorders. Care managers coordinate student referrals to community agencies. Several national substance abuse treatment centers have liaisons that work specifically with college students. It is important for college professionals to be aware of these resources before a student needs to be referred for intensive outpatient or inpatient care. If campuses are prepared to support students managing an addiction, treatment need not derail a higher education career; it can be seen as a "pause" in academic life.

Intensive Outpatient Program (IOP) is a substance abuse treatment program that may combine medical management, such as detoxification, with nine or more hours of individual or group psychotherapy. The aim of therapy is to identify underlying causes for substance abuse and to learn and practice recovery-related skills. IOP care may be a less restrictive component of inpatient care or may occur in a private therapy practice. IOP is designed to provide treatment and support for individuals who work full time of who are re-integrating into their communities after inpatient or residential care.

Partial Hospitalization Program (POP) is a substance abuse treatment program that is typically more intensive and often shorter in duration than IOP.

Social Justice and Inclusiveness—Do We Want "THOSE" Students on Campus?

The *Oxford English Dictionary* defines "social justice" in terms of the distribution of wealth, opportunities and privileges within a society. The aim of social justice is to create and maintain a campus culture that promotes inclusivity. Creating an inclusive campus promotes scholarship and community well-being. Students in recovery often navigate a system that is not consistently supportive. Current campus traditions may not promote and support recovery from addiction. The relationship between students in recovery and the institution can be conflicted. However, campus administrators and student advocates are increasingly becoming aware that making provisions for support of students in recovery is a social justice issue.

Nonetheless, students in recovery are not always welcomed on college campuses. Sometimes campus personnel fear students in recovery will be a "bad" influence on other students, and some parents do not want their children living in campus housing with recovering "addicts." Previous treatment for substance abuse or legal charges associated with substance abuse may disqualify some applicants. Additionally, students in recovery interact with campus personnel and students who know a friend, family member or celebrity who is an "addict." Judgmental attitudes about the character of students in recovery may be conscious for some and unconscious for others. Generalizations about the character of "addicts" are often determined by past experiences (frequently negative). Derogatory terms such as "addict" or "junkie" are not unknown to students who share their recovery stories.

Establishing Campus Recovery Services

Core components of campus recovery programs include top administrative buy-in. College Presidents, Provosts and Vice Presidents must be persuaded that programs and services for students in recovery are a good fit for the institution. The alternative to administrative buy-in is a grassroots effort led by students. This is a good place to start; however, students who get into recovery while they are in college tend to be older. It is difficult to sustain recovery services because students leave campus after they graduate. With each new class of interested students, a leader emerges and then graduates. Grassroots activism for recovery is difficult to sustain over time.

Dedicated full-time staffs are important for sustaining recovery services and programs. Students need an advocate who they know and trust. The program needs at least one person who is high energy and can coordinate opportunities for students to socialize on and off campus. The coordinator is a liaison to campus departments, community treatment providers and advocates for students leaving campus to get treatment and those returning after treatment. A staff member who is familiar with 12-step meetings, Smart Recovery and other support groups is important. Dedicated space for students to meet, study and play is another key element of successful recovery communities. This includes space for support group meetings, at least one office for recovery coaching and academic advising.

Support groups are an important component of campus recovery programs. Support groups provide students with coping skills to succeed in their academic pursuits. The opportunity to hear the successes and setbacks of others who are dependent instills confidence. Recovery becomes a real experience, separate from the prescribed therapeutic factors of professionally led treatment programs.

Twelve-step support groups are the most widely recognized peer-facilitated support groups. Twelve-step groups include but are not limited to Alcoholics Anonymous (AA); Al-Anon supports family members and friends of alcoholics. Narcotics Anonymous is a 12-step fellowship open to anyone trying to overcome any type of drug or process addiction.

Alternatives to 12-step programs are also successful. For instance, SMART Recovery is a non-faith–based alternative to AA. SMART Recovery uses "steps" based on Cognitive Behavioral Therapy and provides a "toolkit" of CBT worksheets designed to address pre-existing maladaptive coping mechanisms. Harm Reduction, Alcohol Abstinence and Management Support (HAMS) also relies heavily on Cognitive Behavioral Therapy (Anderson, 2010). HAMS is not an abstinence-based support group. Harm reduction–inspired support groups are often criticized because it is assumed they cannot be successful. It is assumed that moderation is not possible for anyone who is actually dependent.

> **Collegiate Recovery Communities (CRCs)** is designed to provide broad-based support to students in recovery and often includes friends and allies of those students. The CRC is a hub for efforts that support the student in recovery. CRCs may include allies and friends of the student in recovery, as well as general supporters from off campus. The CRC encompasses programs and policies that target academic achievement, health and wellness by providing students in recovery with natural opportunities to participate in campus life while also influencing the campus environment to be supportive of those students who determine that no- or low-risk substance options are most appropriate for them.
>
> **Collegiate Recovery Programs** (CRPs) differ from CRCs in that they provide direct services for students in recovery. While CRC and CRP initiatives often overlap, CRPs may require an application for admission. CRPs often offer academic advising, tutoring, career planning, coaching and mentoring, as well as self-help and other support groups. Sober housing may be a component of these programs. Some of these services require partnering with community agencies or practitioners.

Dedicated funding is important to the success of recovery programs and services. Funding demonstrates administrative buy-in and sustainability. Funding may come from internal or external sources; another opportunity to demonstrate administrative support is for the college or university foundation to create a dedicated fund for a recovery center and designate a foundation staff member to solicit funds for the center.

Campus-sponsored Collegiate Recovery Communities provide students an opportunity to thrive in a larger campus environment that is sometimes inhospitable. Those who have not experienced the shame of addiction may not understand how a campus could be "unsympathetic" to the "Catch-22" of anonymous people. Sharing one's recovery story risks rejection or, even worse, sympathy. "Sheila" and "Josh" are examples of the power of a second chance. They were fortunate; both attended institutions that understood the difference between sympathy and empathy. Sympathy is reserved for past loss, empathy for the present and optimism for the future.

> Sheila is addicted to heroin; she started with prescription opiates in high school. While she was in her first year of college, law enforcement shut down the "pill mills." Sheila could not find prescription opiates, and when she did, they were expensive. She eventually paid for drugs with sex. Eventually Sheila left school due to failing all her classes. After she got sober, a friend Sheila met in rehab told her about a program that would help her get back into school. She found the courage to return to college. Sheila is now an orientation leader and involved in the student government.
>
> Josh is 21 years old, and he is in recovery and has abstained from any drug use for 12 months. Two years ago, Josh was suspended from his previous institution because of a DUI that resulted in a serious injury to his best friend. When he tried to return to college, Josh was required to have an alcohol and drug assessment prior to clearance for admission. Josh was frustrated about the admission process and feared his previous DUI would disqualify him from being admitted into a pre-dental program. When Josh returned to campus, he felt out of place and wondered if he made the right choice. However, Josh heard about a campus group that sponsored sober football tailgates. Josh was surprised to find a 12-step community on campus. As a result he joined the Collegiate Recovery Program. A faculty member introduced Josh to a local physician who was in recovery. Josh recently graduated and was offered a scholarship to medical school.

Both Sheila and Josh felt intense shame and guilt because of their substance abuse. For Josh, it was a DUI that broke his friend's ribs and jaw. For Sheila, it was the pain she caused those close to her. Fortunately for both Sheila and Josh, they were resolute to realize their goals, and they had campus support. Both students experienced hard times; both questioned if they deserved to succeed, and both were part of a community that provided emotional, social and academic support when they needed it most. It was too easy for Sheila and Josh to give into their guilt and shame, to believe the noise of self-doubt and panic. Yet the symbolic and real support they received from the respective campuses carried them through times of self-doubt, guilt and fear. Two different campuses provided another chance for Shelia and Josh to succeed. Their success epitomizes why creating an inclusive environment is important. Given these success stories and many others, it is puzzling that so many campuses remain ambivalent about providing treatment and recovery support.

Lastly, it is important to understand the relapse rates for substance dependence are similar to other chronic illnesses such as hypertension or type 1 diabetes (Chew, 2011); thus, administrators, faculty members and student affairs professionals must be aware of appropriate ways of responding. There is a major difference between a lapse and a relapse. Changing behavior is a process; starts and stops along the way to sobriety are typical. First, a lapse entails a short-lived return to conduct inconsistent with change. A lapse is differentiated from a relapse by the frequency and duration of a "slip up" or a return to behavior that is inconsistent with recovery. Relapse is an extended return to behavior at odds with goals of abstinence (Marlatt & Donovan, 2005). A lapse might lead to a night of drinking. If, however, a night of drinking turns into days of drinking, relapse is a likely scenario. Lapses can be managed without much attention from administrators. For example, Student Health Centers can assess and intervene as needed. Self-help groups and recovery coaching is an option. Lapses need not lead to a medical leave of absence or withdrawal from classes. Relapse on the other hand may require institutional or administrative intervention. Students who relapse should to be given the opportunity to develop a plan to get "back on track" and demonstrate in addition to self-help groups, they are actively seeking medical, psychiatric or psychological care.

Treatment for dependence and addiction need not derail a higher education career and can be seen as a "pause" in academic life. There are several myths about relapse that are concerning. First, a relapse does not indicate a treatment failure, nor does relapse undo previous progress. The change process is dynamic, and gains may be followed by losses; not unlike the stock market, recovery is a long-term investment that requires persistence. Second, relapse does not automatically indicate a lack of will or motivation—it provides an opportunity for a student to strengthen their resolve.

When a student does return to campus, existing recovery support provides opportunities for cognitive, intellectual, social and career guidance. For example, career support may include connecting with faculty, staff or alumni who are in recovery and can help students network in their chosen career path. Academic advising is important because sometimes students who return to college after treatment try to "prove" they belong and may sign up for 7:30 am classes in organic chemistry, Russian and calculus. Students may need an academic advisor to give them permission to design a schedule that does not set them up for failure. It is important to keep in mind that there is not a prototypical student in recovery. Substance dependence cuts across all demographic sectors of modern society, yet students in recovery do share common bonds: hope and opportunity as well as shame and apprehension.

> **Relapse** includes a return to substance use after a declared period of non-use, regardless of the length of either the period of non-use or the period of a return to use. Additionally, relapse refers to a return to substance use whether or not the individual returns to the original substance or to another illegal substance.

Campus/Community Efforts—Health Promotion/Harm Reduction

Harm reduction is a public health approach (overlapping with health promotion) to enact policies intended to diminish the harmful consequences linked with numerous legal and illegal behaviors. On campus, harm reduction strategies include providing students with free condoms; teaching underage students alcohol "protective" strategies and offering safe rides, blood alcohol content (BAC) reference cards and medical amnesty programs. The enthusiasm for harm reduction has varied levels of support, based on the specific strategy. For example, there are few critics of equipping cars with air bags, having seat belt laws or posting speed limits. However, the harm reduction approach of needle-exchange programs has many critics, when in fact needle-exchange programs reduce the likelihood of IV drug users sharing syringes, thus reducing the risk related to blood-borne pathogens such as HIV or hepatitis C. The overarching concern regarding harm reduction is that it sends a message to the community that risky or illegal behaviors are acceptable. Early intervention, as described in this chapter, is used as a harm reduction tool that can interrupt the progression of use and assist those with behaviors of concern in getting the help that they need.

Student affairs professionals, faculty and other professional staff are all instrumental in setting the "tone" of campus harm reduction efforts. It is important for campuses to stay abreast of continually changing drug use trends and to be familiar with the continuum of harm reduction strategies from abstinence to less conventional risk reduction. Often, the campus climate changes after a crisis involving health and safety. Within the framework of the Socio-Ecological Model, campus/community interventions generate the greatest impact on campus. Academic departments defer to student affairs departments for guidance regarding how to manage critical incidents. Professional staff members can make a difference on campus by understanding how to define and communicate ways in which harm reduction can be implemented on the campus. This can further include advice on best practices and helping ensure that certain programs and policies developed during a crisis do not fade away after campus returns to "normal."

Societal Efforts

Harm reduction efforts also apply at a macro level. However, the stigma of substance abuse, dependency and recovery may inhibit those who have not experienced personal tragedy related to alcohol or other drug use from getting involved in activism efforts. Professionals from different parts of the campus, particularly when working together, can well represent the interests of college students and advocate for sensible public policy. Consider the positioning of detailed insights of student affairs professionals coupled with perspectives from law enforcement personnel, strategies and experience of marketing and governmental affairs professors and experiences of college students.

For example, laws have been recently enacted to reduce harm related to opiate overdose, thus illustrating the importance of advocacy at the state and national level. Presently opioid overdose deaths among the college-age cohort are of great concern for public health agencies. Several states have responded by making an opiate overdose antidote (Naloxone) available to family members without a prescription. In addition, laws have been or are being enacted to shield first responders from civil liability if they administer Naloxone. In selected states, police officers are trained how to administer this antidote without the fear of civil liability. Some colleges have even trained their police officers to administer Naloxone. The use of Naloxone is an example of the impact that college professionals can have on statewide policy. By openly discussing the availability and abuse of opiates on college campuses, the narrative changes from "heroin use is a problem of disenfranchised inner city populations" to "heroin use is a problem in the suburbs and on college campuses."

There are numerous opportunities for advocacy to benefit student access to substance abuse care. Many states have enacted medical amnesty laws that shield individuals from prosecution for simple drug possession if the police or 911 operators are called to respond to a potential drug or alcohol overdose. It may seem that campus substance abuse efforts are limited to "days" (Alcohol Screening Day, Great American Smokeout) or even weeks (Drug Awareness Week), yet changes at the campus, community, state and national level impact students every day of every week. As an added bonus, after these laws are enacted, they require no additional staffing or budget expenses for the college or university. The laws and policies even work on days the campus is closed and after normal business hours. The benefit of advocacy far outweighs the cost in time and effort.

Applications for Campus

The most difficult step in developing a comprehensive substance abuse prevention, intervention, treatment and recovery services is the first one. A comprehensive campus approach benefits from a focus on the individual and the environment aided by a helpful template for campus action (DeJong & Langford, 2002). After the first step is taken, many resources are available to sustain steps that follow. The College AIM resource provides an important summary of the research to date on addressing substance abuse and dependency on campus across the spectrum from prevention to intervention (U.S. Department of Health and Human Services, 2015). However, the first priority for sustaining campus and community efforts is to engage key stakeholders. Prevention efforts that are the responsibility of one office or person are limited in both scope and growth potential.

"Turf wars" or "kingdom building" often found on campus can have deleterious effects on implementing social ecological strategies. To avoid the pitfalls of too much specialization, a "Hub and Spoke Model" is recommended. This model is process focused, as opposed to content based. The model is the most effective structure to offer opportunities for group involvement, while protecting individual members' time and level of commitment. This structure is ideal for a campus-based task force or community coalition as it offers opportunities for involvement while protecting individual members' time and levels of commitment. The model relies on comprehensive, evidence-informed and research-based data from community trials, community mobilization models and change models that are critical to effective, efficient and sustained action. The team providing leadership is limited in terms of number of members (small enough to meet regularly with ease) and the members are knowledgeable and well-connected.

This Hub and Spoke Model ensures that no one person plays a dominant leadership role, strives to have the interests and concerns of many addressed and helps to prevent burn out. The model ensures that a charismatic leader will not drive the group but will be a helpful and enthusiastic role model. This guarantees that, when leadership changes, many of the group participants will find meaningful and useful roles and opportunities. Additionally, this approach recognizes that the skills of those managing and implementing programs related to health on campus have skills that are adaptable to a variety of issues regardless of content. While content knowledge will always be helpful, skills related to creating and sustaining environmental change are critical to creating a change in the culture of health in higher education.

Conclusion

The discussion in this chapter of the benefits and challenges of providing students access to a continuum of substance abuse prevention and recovery support services has concluded. One of the main results sought among readers of this chapter is better preparation to articulate benefits of caring for a unique student population. Professionals' understanding of philosophical approaches to substance abuse prevention, intervention, treatment and recovery provides a platform to provide leadership on your campus. Hopefully a takeaway from this chapter is the importance of campus faculty, staff and students being aware of opportunities to intervene. It may be as simple as listening to a student's story or conducting a brief screening or referring a student to treatment. Student health and safety is a community effort. Lastly, a guide for creating sustainable campus recovery support programs was provided. It is vital that campus professionals, from all parts of the campus, not be deterred by the magnitude of the recommendations; developing a sustainable program is a lot like recovery itself—there are highs and lows, starts and stops, sorrows and joys. It is important that concerned campus personnel not be dissuaded by a lapse; as persistence is the most important element of a successful program. It is also important to remind colleagues that risk takers and sensation seekers are the innovators and creative minds who solve big problems. Substance abuse and dependency results in a loss of intellectual capital that college campuses, and society as a whole, cannot afford.

References

Anderson, K. (2010). *How to change your drinking: A harm reduction guide to alcohol* (2nd ed.) New York: The HAMS Harm Reduction Network.

Babor, T. P., Higgins-Biddle, J., Dauser, D., Higgins, P., & Burleson, J. A. (2005). Alcohol screening and brief intervention in primary care settings: Implementation models and predictors. *Journal of Studies On Alcohol, 66*(3), 361–368.

Baer, J. S., Kivlahan, D. R., Blume, A. W., McKnight, P., & Marlatt, G. A. (2001). Brief intervention for heavy-drinking college students: 4-year follow-up and natural history. *American Journal of Public Health, 91*(8), 1310–1316.

Bandura, A. (1977). *Social Learning Theory*. Englewood Cliffs, NJ: Prentice-Hall.

Bloom, M. (1996). *Primary Prevention Practices*. Thousand Oaks, CA: Sage Publications.

Byrnes, J. P., Miller, D. C., & Schafer, W. D. (1999). Gender differences in risk taking: A meta analysis. *Psychological Bulletin, 125*, 367–383.

Chew, S. (2011). *Why Obama's Deputy Drug Czar Ditch DC*. Retrieved from https://www.thefix.com/content/interview-mclellan?page=all

Clements, R. (1999). Prevalence of alcohol-use disorders and alcohol-related problems in a college student sample. *Journal of American College Health, 48*, 111–118.

Cohen, A. P. (1985). *The Symbolic Construction of Community*. London: Tavistock.

Covey, G. (1996). *Theory and Practice of Counseling and Psychotherapy*. Pacific Grove, CA: Brooks/Cole.

DeJong, W., & Langford, L. M. (2002). A typology for campus-based alcohol prevention: Moving toward environmental management strategies. *Journal of Studies on Alcohol, Supplement, 14*, 140–147.

Diagnostic and Statistical Manual of Mental Disorders (DSM-5). (2013). Washington, D.C.: American Psychiatric Association.

Dimeff, L. A., Baer, J. S., Kivlahan, D. R., & Marlatt, G. A. (1999). *Brief Alcohol Screening and Intervention for College Students (BASICS): A Harm Reduction Approach*. New York: Guilford Press.

Eisenberg, D., Golberstein, E., & Hunt, J. B. (2009). Mental health and academic success in college. *B.E. Journal of Economic Analysis & Policy: Contributions to Economic Analysis & Policy, 9*(1), 1.

Fellin, P. (1995). *The Community and the Social Worker*. Itasca, IL: Peacock Publishers, Inc.

Frank, D., Mateu-Gelabert, P., Guarino, H., Bennett, A., Wendel, T., Jessell, L., & Teper, A. (2015). High risk and little knowledge: Overdose experiences and knowledge among young adult nonmedical prescription opioid users. *International Journal of Drug Policy, 26*(1), 84–91.

Glasser, W. (1999). *Choice Theory: A New Psychology of Personal Freedom*. New York: HarperPerennial.

Hingson, R., Heeren, T., Winter, M., & Wechsler, H. (2005). Magnitude of alcohol-related mortality and morbidity among U.S. college students ages 18–24: Changes from 1998–2001. *Annual Review of Public Health, 26*, 259–279.

Johnston, L., O'Malley, P., Bachman, J., & Schulenberg, J. (2015). *Monitoring the Future National Survey Results on Drug Use: 1976–2014: Volume II, College Students and Adults*. Ann Arbor, MI: Institute for Social Research.

Keller, H. (2015). Ecological research promoting positive youth development. In S. Barnes (Ed.), *Academics in Action! A Model for Community-Engaged Research, Teaching, and Service* (pp. 98–123). New York: Fordham University Press.

Kenney, S. R., & LaBrie, J. W. (2013). Use of protective behavioral strategies and reduced alcohol risk: Examining the moderating effects of mental health, gender, and race. *Psychology of Addictive Behaviors, 27*(4), 997–1009.

Knight, J. R., Wechsler, H., Kuo, M., Seibring, M., Weitzman, E. R., & Schuckit, M. (2002). Alcohol abuse and dependence among U.S. college students. *Journal of Studies on Alcohol, 63*, 263–270.

Lake, P. F. (2013). *The Rights and Responsibility of the Modern University: Who Assumes the Risks of College Life?* Durham: Carolina Academic Press.

Lee, C. M., Neighbors, C., Kilmer, J. R., & Larimer, M. E. (2010). A brief, web-based personalized feedback selective intervention for college student marijuana use: A randomized clinical trial. *Psychology of Addictive Behaviors, 24*(2), 265.

Lewis, M. A., Litt, D. M., Cronce, J. M., Blayney, J. A., & Gilmore, A. K. (2014). Underestimating protection and overestimating risk: Examining descriptive normative perceptions and their association with drinking and sexual behaviors. *Journal of Sex Research, 51*(1), 86.

Marlatt, G. A., & Donovan, D. M. (Eds.). (2005). *Relapse Prevention: Maintenance Strategies in the Treatment of Addictive Behaviors*. New York: Guilford Press.

Marlatt, G. A., & Witkiewitz, K. (2002). Harm reduction approaches to alcohol use: Health promotion, prevention, and treatment. *Addictive Behaviors, 27*(6), 867–886.

Murphy, J. G., Duchnick, J. J., Vuchinich, R. E., Davison, J. W., Karg, R. S., Olson, A. M., Smith, A.F., & Coffey, T. T. (2001). Relative efficacy of a brief motivational intervention for college student drinkers. *Psychology of Addictive Behaviors, 15*(4), 373–379. doi:10.1037/0893-164X.15.4.373

McLellan, A. T., & Woodworth, A. M. (2014). The Affordable Care Act and treatment for "substance use disorders": Implications of ending segregated behavioral healthcare. *Journal of Substance Abuse Treatment, 46*(5), 541–545.

National Institute on Alcohol Abuse and Alcoholism (NIAA). (2002). *A Call to Action: Changing the Culture of Drinking at US Colleges.* Task Force Report. Retrieved from http://www.collegedrinkingprevention.gov/media/taskforcereport.pdf

National Institute on Alcohol Abuse and Alcoholism (NIAA). (2007). *What Colleges Need to Know Now: An Update on College Drinking Research.* Retrieved from http://collegedrinkingprevention.gov/1College_Bulletin-508_361C4E.pdf

Pardeck, J. T., Murphy, J. W., & Choi, J. M. (1994). Some implications of postmodernism for social work practice. *Social Work, 39*(4), 243–246.

Robertson-Boersma, D., Butt, P., & Dell, C. A. (2015). Focus: Addiction: Reflections on how a university binge drinking prevention initiative supports alcohol screening, brief intervention, and referral for student alcohol use. *The Yale Journal of Biology and Medicine, 88*(3), 339.

Serdula, M. K., Brewer, R. D., Gillespie, C., Denny, C. H., & Mokdad, A. (2004). Trends in alcohol use and binge drinking, 1985–1999: Results of a multi-state survey. *American Journal of Preventive Medicine, 26*(4), 294–298.

Straus, R., & Bacon, S. (1953). *Drinking in College.* New Haven, CT: Yale University Press.

U.S. Department of Health and Human Services. (2015) *Planning Alcohol Interventions Using NIAAA's CollegeAIM (Alcohol Intervention Matrix).* Washington, D.C.: National Institute on Alcohol Abuse and Alcoholism.

U.S. Office of National Drug Control Policy. (2015). *National Drug Control Strategy.* Washington, D.C: Office of National Drug Control Policy, Executive Office of the President.

Part V
Occupational Wellness

10

Career Wellness

From Great Depression, through Great Recession, to Great Ascension

FRANCES LUCAS AND R. BRITTON KATZ

Introduction

Remember the Great Depression (1928–1939) depicted in the black-and-white photographs, the long lines of mostly White men at soup kitchens conveying a sense of economic desperation? Many of those persons photographed were current students' grandparents or great-grandparents. Contrast those grainy images against the recent Great Recession (2007–2014) in which Facebook, LinkedIn and YouTube sites offer thousands of job search methods for students who may still be living under their parents' roof. While it may seem that so much has changed, the stress of uncertain futures for some students is as dramatic as it was 80 years ago.

The career aspirations of Americans seeking employment two and three generations ago were not assisted with technology networking. In fact, few had access to a telephone. In contrast, contemporary college undergraduates have a trove of high-technology options for overcoming the vicissitudes of an evolving job market.

Locating and securing a job was then culturally biased to favor the male gender, Caucasian race, absence of physical disability and Christian affiliations. While those preferences are still alive and tolerated in some companies, more employers are moving toward diversifying the demographics of their employees. Federal actions including the Civil Rights Act of 1964, the Americans with Disabilities Act of 1990 and Affirmative Action under Title VII expanded employment possibilities for historically marginalized populations.

Despite the opportunities availed in new career development technologies and in recent federal and state actions to support all citizens, the stress impacting budding unemployed professionals remains persistent and pervasive. Students today are worried about finding jobs that they will enjoy, how to repay rising college debt and how to make ends meet in a fluctuating economy. And, if left unabated over time, stress can manifest itself in the loss of physical, mental, financial and spiritual wellness.

Undergraduates and their parents, who are mostly Boomers born between the Great Depression and the Great Recession, seek a tangible connection between their offspring's baccalaureate degrees and their vocational possibilities. When describing college seniors and their job searches, Coburn and Treeger (2009) report, "At just the time that students may be feeling vulnerable and looking to their parents for reassurance, many parents become anxious as well. Instead of providing a calming perspective, they often inadvertently add their own worries to those of their children" (pp. 391–392).

As a result of so much attention being given to finding the "right" job for today's college graduates, many higher education professionals are emphasizing the influence of career services, career development and career education in the recruitment, retention, persistence and graduation of future generations of students.

To assist current and future career development administrators and other higher education professionals when supporting college students of all ages, an analysis and synthesis of various issues is needed. A definition of career wellness, a summary history of career services in American higher education, the identification of key factors affecting career wellness and the positing of potential recommendations for administrators' and faculty actions will complete the chapter.

What Is Career Wellness?

Career wellness is attained when one's talents, joy and meaning are well matched with a job that takes place in a healthy work climate. Since most people spend more waking hours at work than anywhere else, work defines a huge part of individual identity and quality of life.

Great thinkers of all times have advised people to spend their time alive in fulfilling ways. "Let yourself be silently drawn by the strange pull of what you really love. It will not lead you astray" says Rumi, a thirteenth-century Persian poet and theologian (Goodreads.com).

One of the largest studies regarding good managers and healthy workplace conditions was completed by the Gallup organization, which extensively interviewed over 80,000 leaders in 400 companies. The research was analyzed and organized by Marcus Buckingham and Curt Coffman (1999). They reported the most pertinent aspects of a job where the employee will prefer to work and prefer to stay and report that most career wellness can be simplified by how the employee answers the following 12 questions:

1. Do I know what is expected of me at work?
2. Do I have the materials and equipment I need to do my work right?
3. At work, do I have the opportunity to do what I do best every day?
4. In the last seven days, have I received recognition or praise for doing good work?
5. Does my supervisor, or someone at work, seem to care about me as a person?
6. Is there someone at work who encourages my development?
7. At work, do my opinions seem to count?
8. Does the mission/purpose of my company make me feel my job is important?
9. Are my co-workers committed to doing quality work?
10. Do I have a best friend at work?
11. In the last six months, has someone at work talked to me about my progress?
12. This last year, have I had opportunities to learn and grow? (p. 28)

When a person can answer "yes" to most of these questions, they are experiencing career wellness. When answering "no" to most of the questions, individuals probably have low job satisfaction and will not experience career wellness.

Summarized History of Career Services in Student Affairs

Career counseling existed in the United States in 1890, according to Mark Pope. At that time, it was in vogue to use *vocational guidance* as the initial term at the birth of the guidance movement (Pope, 2000, p. 195).

Prior to World War II, the number of students in higher education was smaller. For the most part, faculty provided students with some career assistance. After the war, the GI Bill led to huge numbers of students enrolling in higher education, including demographic diversity. The message conveyed by the placement offices from 1945–1960 was "get a job." And, the offices' staff was often comprised of former military members and lower ranking faculty (Carney, personal communication, 2003).

The career counseling field evolved again in 1960 with the increasingly popular notion that work provided meaning in a person's existence (Pope, 2000). Career and life planning matched a student's values to interests and then to skills.

Within this same period of 1975–1990, cooperative education and internships became popular. A student gained career-related work experiences prior to commencement exercises in co-ops and internships. And, in 1980 career counseling and outplacement counseling blossomed as information sharing occupied the profession. From 1990, the "Technology Era," involving an era of incredible innovations in the Internet, technology and social media; marked expansion of intercultural diversity in demographics (including the arrival of larger numbers of international students and scholars); students' financially motivated expectations of securing employment following a baccalaureate degree program and emphasized commitment to networking (Carney, personal communication, 2003).

Career counseling colleagues are cautious to avoid the anachronistic title, "placement center and services." Instead, they lead "career centers," "career development" or "career education." And, while career counselors educate students to immerse themselves in career exploration, counselors also teach parents and families that they are no longer placement centers. With Skype interviews, online professional networks including LinkedIn and cloud-generated information among the advancements, the future of Career Services promises to evolve. And, increasing numbers of institutions feature their career centers as key offices contributing to student recruitment and student success.

As the twenty-first century continues, technology will continue to create exciting new tools. Think of counseling sessions offered through long-distance Skype interviews or a hand-held device in an airborne fuselage. But career counseling at its best will continue to feature carefully educated, trained and passionate administrators with honed listening talents; sincere empathy for youthful uncertainty and passion for generating career outcomes.

Various Forms of Career-Related Stress

Career Wellness is impaired if other student health issues are unaddressed. Research confirms the connection between mental health and academic successes during college (Eisenberg, Golberstein, & Hunt, 2009). Unsurprisingly, student mental health affects the resulting capacity for employment, career success, income and future good fitness (Douce & Keeling, 2014).

The statistics are sobering and discouraging. In 2015, the American College Health Association analyzed the data collected from 93,034 college or university students; of those students responding, 13.8% experienced depression and 21.9% reported anxiety (American College Health Association, 2015) such that these factors affected their academic performance. Further, 63.9% felt very sad at least once during the previous year, with 26.5% in the previous two weeks; 47.7% felt hopeless over the past year, and 18%, in the last two weeks; 85.6% felt overwhelmed by all they had to do and 34.5% reported feeling so depressed that functioning was difficult.

With 8.9% of students seriously considering suicide during the previous year, it is understandable that student affairs professionals remain concerned. A decade ago it was known that undergraduates struggle with symptoms and problems that impair functioning in their work (Soet & Sevig, 2006). Ask any veteran career center or counseling center administrator to proffer an anecdote regarding the work needed to support a mentally, emotionally or physically unwell student.

Upon reading these distressing statistics, it is no irony that the Millennial generation is the most stressed generation of adults since formal studies on college student stress were conducted (Dahl, 2013). The American Psychological Association issued its 2012 report titled "Stress in America," further registering that Millennials endured higher stress levels than their parents or grandparents. Moreover, these young adults are more prone to irritability or anger due to their distress, suggesting that they cannot cope with the increased stress levels as well as older Americans. The impacts upon students include substance abuse, violent behavior, eating disorders, personality or sleep disorders, family problems and impulsive behavior (Grayson & Meilman, 2006; Kadison & DiGeronimo, 2004).

> All that stress can be grueling, and it adds to emotional and mental health problems. A 2012 study by the American College Counseling Association found that 37.4 percent of college students seeking help have severe psychological problems, up from 16 percent in 2000. Of the 228 counselors surveyed, more than three out of four reported an increase in crises in the past five years requiring immediate response, 42 percent noted an increase in self-injury, and 24 percent have seen an increase in eating disorders.
>
> (Di Meglio, 2012)

To ameliorate the impacts of these issues, as reported by Soet and Sevig (2006), almost 30% of students currently meet or previously met with therapeutic counselors. College and university counseling centers reported greatly increased student demands for their services. Hence, student affairs vice presidents and deans have requested larger budgets and larger staffs in health care functional areas; they expect these demands to increase and to morph as students escort new mental health worries into their offices. And, despite the myriad of serious and complex health issues, students hope to earn degrees, enroll in graduate or professional schools, create productive lives and start families.

Without intervention, therapies and remedies, research confirms the career impediments generated by college students' fascination with illegal alcohol and drugs. For example, the U.S. Centers for Disease Control and Prevention calls the current level of heroin addiction among adults as an epidemic (Centers for Disease Control and Prevention, 2015). Perhaps more commonly, researchers and scholars have struggled, and continue to struggle, to create and implement effective strategies for curtailing alcohol abuse among college youth.

Interestingly, while the constant barrage of messages against tobacco use has met greatly reduced rates of consumption, more young adults are ingesting marijuana than ever. The Director of the National Institute on Drug Abuse reports,

> And the science of marijuana's long-term effects is increasingly clear. Besides being addictive, marijuana is cognitively impairing even beyond the phase of acute intoxication and regular use during adolescence may cause a significant, possibly permanent IQ loss. Brain scans in users who started when they were young show impaired neural development, probably because cannabis interferes with normal brain maturation.
>
> (Volkow, 2014)

For instance, the nexus of student health issues and career education is complicated by the current generation's drive toward perfection, yet paradoxically leaving them miserable (Twenge, 2006). While holding a core belief in being unique, special and capable of great achievements, they lack an inner resolve for confronting failures when those achievements do not materialize on schedule. Some call this absent factor resilience. Students know their social networking skills and online connections better than comprehending the value of real-time relationships (Hutchinson, 2014) and the positive impact meaningful family and friendship connections have upon overall college success. Higher education career education veteran Tonya Nations (personal communication, 2015) concurs, reporting that a lack of networking skills, combined with a dependency upon parents' decision making, can inhibit a young adults' career development focus. From a different perspective, Hutchinson (2014) notes that the "intense emphasis on career preparation," combined with increasing student debt-loads to finance higher education, contribute to the mental and emotional distress registered in the aforementioned studies (Smith & Snell, 2009).

With a current emphasis on initiating career education and development early in the college career, the centrality of addressing mental and physical health problems and stressors is clear. Administrators will counsel students to unearth the underlying issues while attempting to match them to career opportunities.

Student affairs practitioners with an ambition for career counseling will likely build stronger relationships with counseling centers, health centers, student affairs social workers and academic advisors to build strategies for supporting students. A growing number of case managers, often licensed clinical social workers, are joining student affairs staffs to address and monitor the myriad of simultaneous health issues brought by students to current campuses.

Until these negative health aspects change, student affairs professionals, academic advisors, faculty members and other college professionals will continue to fret over students' career progress. There are many deeply seated psychological and physiological issues that short-term service intervention cannot heal. And, student affairs offices and faculty members are not designed to proffer significant health care remedies. Colleges and universities are citadels of advanced learning, not long-term residential healthcare facilities.

Technological Advancements As Factors Affecting Career Wellness

Veteran college professionals, whether in student affairs or faculty roles, will note the rapid advancement of technology, even since 1997. The most prominent tools for student use to find jobs were books and printed directories. The Internet was young; the telephone was still a staple instrument for communication.

Some career development offices purchased an online version of DISCOVER (ACT) or ClarisWorks for resume writing. Students purchased disks that had an embedded resume program/template. If resources were available, then television was used to provide an orientation to career services, and a camcorder was used when conducting mock interviews (Nations, personal communication, 2015).

Today's student has many choices of technology, not only to assist them with narrowing their career interests, but also to assist them in marketing their skills. The challenge is that so does every other student; the market is flooded, complicated and it is much harder to be noticed.

Students need to be developing demonstrated skills as they experience college in order to stand out in a crowded marketplace. Internships and practicums in various work venues will jump out to future employers as places where certain skills were learned and practiced. One of the greatest advantages of today's students is the ability to communicate while using sophisticated forms of technology.

In cover letters, resumes and interviews, students can translate work, internship and practicum experiences into what they know and how they can make contributions. For example, students might cite a project in which they worked to demonstrate various achievements and how they used technology well.

When asked good interview questions, students can tell work stories demonstrating their use of the most current communication venues to complete a project. Several years ago, a good committee presentation simply meant strong public speaking skills. Today's students can use dynamic power points, videos, YouTube, music and many other ways to make a presentation come to life. They can enhance and develop those important skills by working onsite with organizations. Moreover, the students can use stories of events at work where they identified problems, researched for various solutions using the latest technology, tested options and clarified outcomes. All of these experiences will assist the student in showing potential employers how they have developed rational thought processes.

Sadly some students have been marketing themselves on social media for years, which can include silly antics and unflattering material that is still available for employers to surf and find. It might be one thing to explain limited job experience. But it is quite another to explain why as a teen someone thought it would be cool to snap chat a "selfie" of themselves participating in drinking games only to have it saved by someone and posted in Facebook. In short, there can be a lot more damaging material for employers to see than ever before.

Boomers are often heard remarking that they certainly are glad Facebook wasn't around when they were in college. Facebook was not founded until 2004, but a Pew Internet Project Survey found that 74% of adults who are online do use social networking (Pew Research Center, January, 2014, para. 1). Pew reports, "As of September 2014, 71% of online adults use Facebook, 23% of online adults use Twitter, 26% use Instagram, 28% use Pinterest, and 28% use LinkedIn" (Pew Research Center, Social Media Update, para. 1, September 2014).

Of course, social media is also an outstanding way to narrow the market for employers who want to market positions. When a company is looking for a certain type of employee, social media advertising can be find and broadcast to target markets.

But as fun and often frivolous as social media is for college students, it can be just as beneficial for businesses, and the key for any business targeting the college demographic is understanding (and adapting to) students' social media habits. From the time of day and frequency that one should post on social media to what platform will allow one to score the most interaction from this coveted group, there's much to be learned by analyzing students' usage of Facebook, Twitter, Instagram, Pinterest and more. When one's desired audience and customer base consists of college students, skillfully integrating social media into one's marketing strategy isn't just recommended—it's essential.

(Viner, 2014, para 2)

On the positive side for graduating seniors, there are many more avenues to connect with employers. These include such resources as LinkedIn, Facebook, Twitter and many other interactive options. Career centers on some college campuses are quite elaborate and have a full menu of activities for students at all levels—from first-year undergraduate students to doctoral students—to assist them in the career exploration journey.

Nations (personal communication, 2015) reports that the use of the Internet plays large in the plethora of career education functions, plus online versions of career assessments, online videos, social media, Microsoft Office, College Central Network, Skype, podcasts and CareerShift. One can quickly surf the Internet to find hundreds of job boards and job search websites with most having options for selecting a geographical range. As technological advancements emerge, e-portfolios will become standard when applying to graduate/professional school or employment.

More videotelephony products are also expected. And, the programs and products are utilized in sequence, beginning during the freshman year. "Many career centers have developed a four-year career plan, which guides students step by step from self-exploration to job hunting skills" (Coburn & Treeger, 2009, p. 77). The challenge with using the Internet and online products is that millions of people can be looking at the same job at the same time.

Financial Factors Affecting Career Wellness

"Money makes the world go round, the world go round," so goes the refrain in a *Cabaret* musical number (Kander & Masteroff, 1968). However, students increasingly believe their world is grinding to a halt because of higher education costs. Student loan debt surpassed $1 trillion in the second quarter of 2014, thus becoming the second highest category of household debt in the country (National Center for Economic Statistics, 2012). About half of all students borrowed money for tuition and other expenses using loans during 2013–2014, an increase from 30% in the mid-1990s. About 70% of U.S. graduates in 2012 incurred an average of $29,400 in loans, an increase from $26,000 in 2011 (Nawagunal, 2014).

While student loan defaults appear concentrated among borrowers who do not graduate or who attend for-profit institutions (Deming, Yutchman, Abulofi, Golding, & Katz, 2014), the issue is prevalent and growing because many colleges and universities raise tuition and fees in most years. Wyman (2015b) warns that the increased student loan debt adversely impacts all Americans. Wyman notes "young adults burdened by monthly debt payments are delaying home ownership and other big-ticket purchases, and cutting back on restaurant meals, vacation travel, and other forms of consumption that fuel a third of the national economy."

Therein lies one paradox; namely, how can students or graduates pay the loans if they cannot secure employment with high wages? Jennifer Silva (2013) commented on the challenges of 18-to-34 year olds that limit securing meaningful work in the present economy. A significant percentage return to their parents' homes with degrees because they are unable to afford their own residence while repaying student loans. In many instances, these loan debts are crushingly large, and if they are federal loans, then they cannot be forgiven in bankruptcy action. To guarantee some income, Silva (2013) reports that young graduates are willing to accept minimum-wage employment when nothing else appears.

A critical juncture seems to have been reached. In recent months, students initiated protests, marches and social media storms in direct response to their inability to pay tuition, fees and incidental costs for a higher education. Politicians seek votes with attractive promises of free community college and public university degrees.

Silva's work was underscored by a recent report from the Federal Reserve of New York (Nawagunal, 2014). In the Reserve's analysis, recent United States graduates encounter a challenging job market. The reality of remaining unemployed or in low-wage positions confront this generation to a degree not confronted by graduates in the previous 20 years. The Reserve noted that the latest trend for higher unemployment began in the recent 2011 recession and was exacerbated by the student debt crisis driven by spiraling higher education costs. In *A Crucible Moment: College Learning and Democracy's Future*, the National Task Force on Civic Learning and Democratic Engagement (2012, p. 20) reported that graduates enter a world with "intensified global competition" and "dangerous economic inequalities."

Unemployment for 2001 graduates was an astonishing 34%, but in the Reserve's data for 2012, the rate rose to 44% unemployment for recent graduates! It must feel discouraging for these graduates that available jobs did not require a college degree, including bartending and retail clerking (Nawagunal, 2014). It is no wonder that students revolt to these circumstances.

There are some scholars who redirect higher education from a narrowed focus upon an individual student's "return on investment," because it fails to address societal issues of inequality (Campaign for College Opportunity, 2013); instead, administrators must develop students' "cultural, civic, and political capital" (Calderon & Pollack, 2015) as well as their economic capital. Civic engagement and service-learning are among their remedies, as highlighted later in this chapter. But these remedies don't bring relief from the burden of educational debt.

The good news is that there are some financial factors that can benefit today's students. One benefit from the recently adopted Affordable Care Act, "Obamacare," is that it affords today's undergraduates with health insurance options that were unavailable to previous generations. As an example, students became eligible to remain on their parents' health insurance plans until the age of 26 (Cohen & Martinez, 2014). During 2014, the uninsured rates for persons 19–25 years of age fell 13.2%, an overall 40% decrease. The National Health Interview Survey recorded 20.9% of young adults without health insurance, the lowest percentage noted since the survey's creation in 1997 (Cohen & Martinez, 2014). Students also benefit from the reduced growth in health benefit costs, an average of 1.1% growth in 2012–2013 (Council of Economic Advisers, 2014). Conversely, according to Gruber and Krueger (1991) and Baicker and Chandra (2006), employees bear higher health benefits costs in the form of lower salaries and wages. So, if health benefit cost increases are limited, the effect propels faster wage growth and salaries for workers. In the annual report from the White House Council of Economic Advisers (2014), the unemployment rate for 25–34 year old college graduates was 3.7% in 2013, compared to 13.5% among those persons with less than a high school diploma.

College professionals should be encouraged by information originating with the U.S. Bureau of Labor Statistics. The Bureau projects faster job growth for positions that require a post-secondary level of education by 2022. In 2012, workers with a post-secondary education earned a median income of $57,770 compared to $27,670 for workers with high school diplomas (Nawagunal, 2014). The Lumina Foundation reports the OECD data (2015), which confirms that career options are broader if a person has a college education. Adults age 25–64 who have a bachelor's degree or equivalent are 80% employed, while 84% of those with a masters or equivalent are employed and 86% with a doctorate or equivalent are employed (p. 105).

If a lack of skills for particular forms of work is at the crux of unemployment (Wyman, 2015a), then colleges and universities must ensure that skills are accrued during the undergraduate and graduate degree programs. Or, unemployed or underemployed students may be singing, "Brother, can you spare a dime?" (Kapilow, 2012).

Gender Factors Affecting Career Wellness

As the percentage of United States citizens going to college has grown, so has the proportion of women who attend those colleges. In 1900, 2.8% of females between ages 18 and 21 went to college, however fewer people went to college, making the women 36.8% of the college population. During 1920, 47% of college students were women. "By the mid-1980s more women than men were attending colleges and universities as undergraduates, and half of all students obtaining master's degrees were women"(Pearson, Shavlik, & Touchton, 1989, pp. 16–17).

The current female to male ratio in college is weighted numerically highly with women:

On a national scale, public universities had the most even division between male-female students, with a male-female ratio of 43.6–56.4. While that difference is substantial, it is still smaller than private not-for profit institutions (42.5–57.5) or all private schools (40.7–59.3).

(Borzelleca, 2012, para. 4)

With more women attending college than men, one might expect that women would have the same chances of upward mobility as men in the workplace. Likewise, many of today's female college graduates are hoping for a level playing field in the world of work where their talents and work will be just as appreciated as the men. While that will be true for some women, many more will likely be surprised by sexism, which might still be a block for advancement.

In her book, *Lean In*, Sheryl Sandberg, who is the CEO of Facebook, laments:

The blunt truth is that men still run the world. Of the 195 independent countries in the world, only 17 are led by women. Women hold just 20 percent of seats in parliaments globally. In the United States, where we pride ourselves on liberty and justice for all, the gender division of leadership roles is not much better. Women became 50 percent of the college graduates in the United States in the early 1980's. Since then, women have slowly and steadily advanced, earning more and more of the college degrees, taking more of the entry-level jobs, and entering more fields previously dominated by men. Despite these gains, the percentage of women at the top of corporate America has barely budged over the past decade. A meager twenty-one of the Fortune 500 CEO's are women. Women hold about 14 percent of executive officer positions, 17 percent of board seats, and constitute 18 percent of our elected congressional officials.

(Sandberg, 2013, p. 5)

Female students need to understand these work dynamics in order to prepare for them and to overcome them. In their book, *Women Don't Ask*, Babcock and Laschever talk about the many ways women do not negotiate for higher salaries or promotions like men do. In addition, more and more women are single mothers with no one to share to financial burden of children or to help them at home with the responsibilities (Babcock & Laschever, 2007, p. xii).

Arianna Huffington in her book, *Thrive*, posits that women in this country are coming up on a third revolution. She describes the way women today are paying a much higher price than their male counterparts in highly stressful jobs.

The first women's revolution was led by the suffragettes more than a hundred years ago, when courageous women such a Susan B. Anthony, Emmeline Pankhurst and Elizabeth Cady Stanton fought to get the right to vote. The second was led by Betty Friedan and Gloria Steinem, who fought—and Gloria continues to fight—to expand the role of women in our society and give them full access to the rooms and corridors of power where decisions are made.

(Huffington, 2014, p. 23)

Huffington goes on to devote her book to the third revolution women need to have in the workplace, which is the right to have career wellness and take far better care of themselves.

That's because women are paying an even higher price than men for their participation in a work culture fueled by stress, sleep deprivation, and burnout. That is one reason why so many talented women, with impressive degrees working in high-powered jobs are unsustainable: as mentioned in the introduction—but it is so important it bears repeating—women in highly stressful jobs have a nearly 40 percent increased risk of heart disease and heart attacks compared with their less-stressed colleagues and a 60 percent greater risk for type 2 diabetes (a link that does not exist for men, by the way). Women who have heart attacks are almost twice as likely as men to die within a year of the attack, and women in high-stress jobs are more likely to become alcoholics than women in low-stress jobs. Stress and pressure from high-powered careers can also be a factor in the resurgence of eating disorders in women ages thirty-five to sixty.

(Huffington, 2014, p. 24)

Indeed, colleges and universities need to educate both young women and men about the extra stresses placed on women in the workplace and join in the cause to reduce those stresses.

Generational Values Differences as Factors Affecting Career Wellness

One of the hottest topics in the work force is how the twenty-somethings have such different values and attitudes from various generations who preceded them. In his prescient volume, *1984*, George Orwell (1949) said, "Every generation imagines itself to be more intelligent than the one that went before it, and wiser than the one that comes after it."

While youth has always baffled older generations, it seems that recent value shifts have stumped even the most astute talent developers. Not only are the older managers supervising a more demographically diverse work force than ever before, they are at a loss to determine how to best communicate with the new digital natives entering their doors.

In 2012, Judy Scott-Clayton reported a decline in the national labor market among 16–24 year olds. Although 90% of these young adults were enrolled in college or were employed, the labor market had a declining percentage among students who were likely to focus upon school alone; students did not want to combine work and school. Unlike previous generations, employment in the short-term likely brings shorter job tenure and more employer switches and career transitions (Taylor & Keeter, 2010).

According to the book *Generations at Work*,

> [T]wo-thirds of them used computers before the age of five. They are connected 24/7 to friends, parents, information and entertainment. The global economic downturn has affected them worse than any other generation, yet they remain optimistic and energetic. Accustomed to being the center of attention, they have high expectations and clear goals. They are willing to work and expect to have the support they need to achieve. They have older parents and were brought up in smaller families. One in three is a product of divorce. One in four has at least one college-educated parent.
>
> (Filipczak, Raines, & Zemke, 2013, p. 120)

The 40-hour work week seems antique to the Millennials (born 1980–2000) who are accustomed to accessing the information they need at anytime from anywhere on their phones, which seemingly are glued to their hands. Why should they waste fossil fuel and time driving to an office to do the work they can do just about anywhere? After all, aren't people supposed to be saving the earth and going green? And what does it matter when they do the work as long as it gets done on time?

Many of these workers are the children of the Baby Boomers (born 1943–1960) who valued long work hours and financial success, resulting in limited time with their children. The Boomer's children, now with children of their own, do not want to be absent from soccer games, recitals or other activities. Besides, with a computer, iPad or phone, they can finish what they were working on as soon as the child goes to bed.

One of the big differences in these workers is that they are not accustomed to a trial-and-error approach to work. They have been coached, taught and been in lessons after school much of their lives. Having branded themselves on Facebook and living in a real-time communication culture, they want to get it right the first time. They will look for employers with training programs that will show them and tell them what to do. Many will look for networks of people to pool their talent, because they are used to large networks of people communicating with one another.

One confounding attribute for the Millennials is the researched lack of coping strategy in the wake of failure or worry. But Career Coach Beverly Jones says that coping is a key quality in today's interglobal economy (Hannon, 2015). Jones endorses six tips for developing resilience that administrators can apply to students: (1) get connected in networks of positive relationships; (2) choose optimism, focus upon what goes right in your life and work; (3) learn something new and adapt to the rapidly changing work-world; (4) think like an entrepreneur or operate your career as if you were a one-person business; (5) look at the big picture and think of where the career needs to be in five or ten years; (6) get in shape physically, emotionally and spiritually, so that energy and fitness will shape the best work possible (Hannon, 2015, pp. 56–57). College professionals in student affairs, as well as faculty members and other college staff, will be challenged to motivate students to confront their multiple internal issues and then to tackle these tips.

Implications for Higher Education Professionals

Every functional area of contemporary student affairs is rapidly changing with service-driven, technologically stimulated society—in the United States and worldwide—and with the students who are growing up in this environment. It is an exciting era in which student affairs administrators and other college professionals can impact students' career futures. As previous statements in this article attest, college students today face many wellness issues. But, every generation of college undergraduates is tested by societal, financial or personal challenges. Careful strategic planning, with concomitant tactics, applies to successful approaches.

Implication 1: Asking Students the Right Questions

- What activities bring you the most joy?
- What are your strongest talents?
- What world needs should you address?

The intersection of those questions if demonstrated in three overlapping circles is the place to start looking for career wellness (see Figure 10.1).

Figure 10.1 The Right Questions to Ask Students

Implication 2: Helping Students Understand That Employers Increasingly Want to Hire Healthy, Happy Employees

Companies are starting more wellness incentives to reduce health insurance costs and increase productivity.

The research confirms that students will continue to enroll with increased incidences of mental health disorders. Kingkade (2016) reports,

> An increasing number of college students are seeking help for mental health issues, at a rate outpacing the growth in enrollment by five-fold, a new report shows. Data collected at 139 college and university counseling centers, from 2009–2010 through 2014–2015, reflects "slow, but consistent" growth in student reporting depression, anxiety, and social anxiety.
>
> (para. 2)

Senior-level administrators will endorse greater budgets and staffing in counseling centers and in health care centers. In certain areas, pressure will prompt the addition of contracted psychiatric care. This is not cheap; health care providers with advanced degrees and requisite experiences are expensive. And, while it is most important to treat the illnesses of students, more and more emphasis must be placed upon teaching students how to take care of themselves in all ways in order to become successful employees for others. It is also important for college professionals to engage with students in a more proactive way: to be "early responders'" with the students.

Implication 3: Seeing the Advent of Online Education as a Threat to the Future of Residential Institutions

The pledge of residential campuses to feature career education, career exploration and career development as a part of the student experience is a powerful marketing instrument for blunting the appeal of online classes. Thus, strategic leaders will note the need to expand the staffing, resources and programs for campus career centers. Plus, campus leaders may seek to incorporate career services in innovative ways, such as career-oriented courses, academically or student union-housed career services offices or residence hall-based career planning centers. Additionally, market savvy leaders will understand that appeal from the parents' point of view.

Implication 4: Comprehending That Internships and Experiential Learning Are Essential

In previous pages, the impacts of internships and part-time employment were noted. Involvement in internships, mentoring and work-related learning better prepares students for the workplace. White (2015) says,

> Internships are a great way to get experience on your resume before you graduate, which can make the post-grad job search easier and give you an edge against the competition. And interns—both past and present—agree, with nearly 71% of students stating that internships should be mandatory, according to a 2015 report on the State of College Hiring from Look Sharp.
>
> (para. 1)

Yet much work is to be achieved in concert with teaching faculty towards the establishment of academic and non-academic internships, volunteering and other opportunities. Certain institutions are building endowments for the provision of paid internships to students, and schools like the University of Richmond prove that donors will contribute to these endowments. The University of Richmond announced that it built a $9 million endowment solely for the provision of stipends for student internships, all under the leadership of the Division of Student Affairs.

Implication 5: Creating a Culture of Praise, Rewards and Recognition on Campus

Public praise and recognition for the students are important to any generation, but especially those of Generation Y (Millennials) and Generation Z. A culture of praise, recognition and rewards programs need not incur costs. But, the goodwill generated by recognizing students' positive contributions benefits students' young resumes and their job-seeking prospects. And, the general impact of a higher education should accelerate a student's maturation and character development because of deadlines, consequences, conflicts, time management and social interactions reflected in honors that pay tribute to students demonstrating these talents.

Implication 6: Instilling Confidence in Students' Self-Reliance Rather Than Dependency upon Parents or Other Authority Figures

The acronym HOVER is a helpful tool for career wellness. As created by Kerry Hannon in her book *Love Your Job* (2015), HOVER represents five core ingredients student affairs professionals can stoke in students regarding their career wellness: (1) hope, (2) optimism, (3) value (e.g., your self-worth), (4) enthusiasm and (5) resilience. With hope, students gain confidence. Optimism creates a positive, forward outlook despite the inevitable employment setbacks. If college educators reinforce a work ethic, then students, and soon-to-be graduates, value the skills, knowledge and talent they display through assertive effort. Enthusiasm is a charismatic energy field emanating from excited young professionals. And, resilience is that internal coping tactic for conquering life's adversities.

A more mature (e. g., lengthy) timetable for capturing employment or life-goals will be introduced via career counseling sessions, webinars or academic advisement appointments. And, the immediate introduction of first-year students to leadership positions allows them to broaden their own self-awareness; in other words, if they only perceived themselves in pre-medicine, then leadership roles can allow them to see a potential opportunity in other career areas as well. Most student affairs divisions offer undergraduate student leadership education and training. Further, higher education administrators are well situated to provide leadership development that conforms to societal expectations.

Career-building soft skills are enhanced in these programs. Johnson (2014) reports,

> According to the National Careers Service, soft skills are personal qualities and attitudes that help employees work well with others and encourage productivity within the workplace. And these types of skills may be more important than people realize. A recent study conducted by Millennial Branding and American Express showed that 61% of managers surveyed felt that soft skills were more important in new hires than hard skills or even technical skills.
>
> (para. 1)

Implication 7: Continuing or Expanding Professional Development Modules for Administrators

If student affairs administrators are to guide future practices, isn't it vital that they have experience themselves in their area of expertise? And, isn't it critical that they continue to learn about their area of expertise? A good guide would be to know the general lay of the land, yet an excellent guide would keep abreast of specific changes and shifts. A superior guide has an eye firmly planted on the future of college student needs. Richard Nelson Bolles recommends regular training of counselors. By helping career counselors improve, they improve their ability to serve current and future students (Bolles, 2012; Figler & Bolles, 2007). Career education concepts that are not likely to change in theory but may change in delivery include:

• Active learning and training that shapes student learning objectives
• Career development: consideration of personality, values, interests, abilities, education and experience

- Self-analysis
- Using institutional and community resources to effectively to achieve career goals
- Developing a supportive and inclusive career network or community
- Maintaining professionals' motivation and freshness as a higher education professional over a longer period of years
- Prepping career center professionals for the increased intercultural plurality in their future student bodies
- Developing mentoring skills. As defined by Wyman and Hannon, mentoring is a powerful way for administrators to personally impact the confidence and competence of young adults.

*Implication 8: Involving Students in Civic Engagement
and Service-Learning Opportunities for Personal Skill
Development and for Career Preparation*

This is a growing arena for faculty and student affairs educators to collaborate. A number of institutions are combining academic courses with civic engagement exercises to "produce workforce-ready professionals, but who are also socially responsible and social justice-centered professionals" (Calderon & Pollack, 2015). At California State University at Monterey Bay, students may be assigned internships at expensive hotels and golf resorts; these same students build friendships with hotel workers' families through a volunteer income tax assistance program, filing tax returns for low-income workers. At Pitzer College in 2012, students partnered with faculty and community leaders in a civically engaged effort to protect government representation for Pomona, California's disenfranchised populations (Calderon & Pollack, 2015). In the Millsaps College's "One Campus, One Community" program, students volunteer regularly in an adjacent socio-economically disadvantaged neighborhood, but the neighborhood leaders select the work performed. Education and training will better empower career counselors to comprehend the needs of students in historically or politically marginalized populations. Students work as they also achieve social, political and lasting change!

Conclusion

There is much to address, to study and to overcome while supporting students' career wellness. Administrators are increasingly aware of the aforementioned and evolving issues, and they will persevere. While there are significant challenges confronting contemporary students, every generation coped with some physical or emotional issues while developing career options. Finding meaningful work for others is the passion of Richard Nelson Bolles, author of the *What Color Is Your Parachute?* series of books. Bolles extols us to see "every career is an artist at work. It [a career] expresses who we are; it acts out our personalities" (Bolles, 2012). As student generations evolve, the world of career education must evolve with them to match them with meaningful work. The key to that goal is ensuring that future career development administrators are properly equipped with the resources in staff, technologies and space for flexibility in response. And, leaders of student affairs divisions, academic deans and other high-level college administrators must avoid irony by ensuring that the career development administrators are well-suited for this detail-laden work; if the administrators are passionate about career exploration and development, their own love of their profession can infect their students! Career education administrators are often the bridge that stressed students utilize to connect to happy, healthy career wellness.

In an interview with veteran career education administrator Tonya C. Nations (personal communication, 2015), career wellness is summarily described,

> I agree that much of what is in practice today among career counselors stems from Frank Parsons' theory of vocational guidance. He developed a talent matching theory that later became the Trait and Factor Theory of Occupational Choice. Like Frank Parsons, I believe that people perform best when their work suits their personality, values, interests, abilities, education and experience; and, the purposeful search for this suitability is career development. If an individual can express themselves through work that touches upon all six factors, then, I believe, they are more likely to achieve a greater degree of career satisfaction. Thus, purposeful career development can lead to personal career satisfaction that will likely yield balance, meaning and identity in and out of the worker role. To me, that is how Career Development is a form of Wellness.

Remember the words of financial icon Warren Buffett,

> There comes a time when you ought to start doing what you want. Take a job that you love. You will jump out of bed in the morning. I think you are out of your mind if you keep taking jobs that you don't like because you think it will look good on your resume. Isn't that a little like saving up sex for your old age?

References

American College Health Association. (2015). *National College Health Assessment II: Reference Group Executive Summary, Spring 2015*. Hanover, MD: Author. Retrieved from http://www.acha-ncha.org/reports_ACHA-NCHAII.html

Babcock, L., & Laschever, S. (2007). *Women Don't Ask*. New York: Random House.

Babor, T. F., & Higgins-Biddle, J. C. (2001). Brief intervention for hazardous and harmful drinking a manual for use in primary care. World Health Organization, Department of Mental Health and Substance Dependence. (WHO/MSD/MSB/01.6b).

Baicker, K., & Chandra, A. (2006). The labor market effects of rising health insurance premiums. *Journal of Labor Economics, 24*(3), 609–634.

Bolles, R. N. (2012). *Video Interview with Jenni Proctor*. Retrieved from https://www.youtube.com/watch?v=hcduo9esQT8

Borzelleca, D. (2012, February 16). The male-female ratio in college. *Forbes Magazine*. Retrieved from http://www.forbes.com/sites/ccap/2012/02/16/the-male-female-ratio-in-college/#7124387b1525

Buckingham, M., & Coffman, C. (1999). *First, Break All the Rules*. New York: The Gallop Organization, Simon and Schuster.

Calderon, J. Z., & Pollack, S. S. (2015, Summer). Weaving together career and civic commitments for social change. *Peer Review, 17*(3). Retrieved from https://www.aacu.org/peerreview/2015/summer/Calder%C3%B3n

Campaign for College Opportunity. (2013, December). *The State of Higher Education in California: The Gender and Racial Gap Analysis*. Retrieved from http://collegecampaign.org/portfolio/december-2013-the-state-of-higher-education-in-california-the-gender-and-racial-gap-analysis/

Centers for Disease Control and Prevention. (2015, July 7). *Today's Heroin Epidemic*. Retrieved from http://www.cdc.gov/vitalsigns/heroin

Coburn, K. L., & Treeger, M. L. (2009). *Letting Go: A Parent's Guide to Understanding the College Years*, 5th edition. New York: Harper Collins.

Cohen, R. A., & Martinez, M. E. (2014, January–September). *Health Insurance Coverage: Early Release of Estimates from the National Health Interview Survey*. Centers for Disease Control. Retrieved from http://www.cdc.gov/nchs/data/nhis/earlyrelease/Insur201303.pdf

Council of Economic Advisers, Rep. No. 978-0-16-092301-2 (2014). Retrieved from https://www.whitehouse.gov/administration/eop/cea/economic-report-of-the-President/2014

Dahl, M. (2013, February 7). *Millennials Are the Most Stressed-Out Generation, New Survey Says*. [Video Newscast]. Retrieved from http://www.honeycolony.com/article/millennials-are-the-most-stressed-generation/

Deming, D. J., Yutchman, Y., Abulofi, A., Golding, C., & Katz, L. F. (2014, September). *The Value of Postsecondary Credentials in the Labor Market: An Experimental Study*. National Bureau of Economic Research. NBER Working Paper 20528.

Di Meglio, F. (2012, May 10). Stress takes its toll on college students. *Bloomberg Business*. Retrieved from http://www.bloomberg.com/bw/articles/2012–05–15/stress-takes-its-toll-on-college-students

Douce, L. A., & Keeling, R. P. (2014). *A Strategic Primer on College Student Mental Health*. Washington, DC: American Council on Education.

Eisenberg, D., Golberstein, E., & Hunt, J. B. (2009). Mental health & academic success in college. *B.E. Journal of Economic Analysis and Policy, 9*(1), 1–40.

Figler, H. E., & Bolles, R. N. (2007). *The Career Counselor's Handbook*, 2nd edition. Berkeley and Toronto: Ten Speed Press.

Filipczak, B., Raines, C., & Zemke, R. (2013). *Generations at Work*. New York: American Management Association.

Grayson, P. A., & Meilman, R. W. (2006). *College Mental Health Practice*. New York: Taylor & Francis.

Gruber, J., & Krueger, A. B. (1991). The incidence of mandated employer-provided insurance: Lessons from workers' compensation insurance. In D. Bradford (Volume Ed.), *Tax Policy and the Economy* (Volume 5, pp. 111–144). Cambridge, MA: MIT Press.

Hannon, K. (2015). *Love Your Job, the New Rules for Career Happiness*. Hoboken, NJ: John Wiley & Sons Inc.

Huffington, A. (2014). *Thrive*. New York: Crown Publishing Group of Random House.

Hutchinson, D. S. (2014). Mental health: Creating and cultivating a campus community that supports mental health. In D. Anderson (Ed.), *Wellness Issues for Higher Education: A Guide for Student Affairs and Higher Education Professionals*. New York: Routledge.

Johnson, H. (2014, October 17). *6 Soft Skills Every Professional Needs*. Retrieved from http://advice.careerbuilder.com/posts/6-soft-skills-every-professional-needs

Kadison, R., & DiGeronimo, T. F. (2004). *College of the Overwhelmed*. San Francisco: Jossey-Bass.

Kander, J., & Masteroff, J. (1968). *Cabaret, the New Musical: Book by Joe Masteroff. Based on the Play by John van Druten and Stories by Christopher Isherwood. Lyrics by Fred Ebb. Piano reduction by Robert H. Noeltner*. New York: Sunbeam Music Corp.

Kapilow, R. (2012, February 8). *Brother Can You Spare a Dime?: American Song during the Great Depression*. Retrieved from http://www.npr.org/2008/11/15/96654742/a-depression-era-anthem-for-our-times

Kingkade, T. (2016, January 13). The number of college students seeking mental health treatment is growing rapidly. *Huffington Post*. Retrieved from http://www.huffingtonpost.com/news/college-mental-health/

Lumina Foundation. (2015). *Education at a Glance*. Retrieved from https://www.luminafoundation. org/files/resources/education-at-a-glance.pdf

National Center for Economic Statistics. (2012). *National Postsecondary Student Aid Study 2011–2012*. Retrieved from http://nces.ed.gov/pubs2013/2013165.pdf

National Task Force on Civic Learning and Democratic Engagement. (2012). *A Crucible Moment: College Learning and Democracy's Future*. Washington, DC: Association of American Colleges and Universities.

Nawagunal, E. (2014, January 6). Jobs become more elusive for recent U.S. college grads. *Reuters. com*. Retrieved from http://www.reuters.com/article/2014/01/06/usa-studentloans-jobs-idUSL2 NOKG1SW20140106

Orwell, G. (1949). *1984*. London: Secker & Warburg.

Pearson, C. S., Shavlik, D. L., & Touchton, J. G. (1989). *Educating the Majority: Women Challenge Tradition in Higher Education*. American Council on Education. New York: McMillan Publishing Company.

Pew Research Center: Internet, Science, and Tech. (2014). *Social Networking Fact Sheet*. Retrieved from http://www.pewinternet.org/fact-sheets/social-networking-fact-sheet/

Pope, M. (2000). A brief history of career counseling in the United States. *The Career Development Quarterly, 48*(3), 194–211.

Sandberg, S. (2013). *Lean In*. New York: Alfred A. Knopf Publisher.

Scott-Clayton, J. (2012). *What Explains Trends in Labor Supply amongst US Undergraduates, 1970–2009?* National Bureau of Economic Research. (NBER Working Paper 17744). Retrieved from http:// www.nber.org/papers/w17744

Silva, J. (2013). *Coming Up Short: Working Class Adulthood in an Age of Uncertainty*. New York: Oxford University Press.

Smith, C., & Snell, P. (2009). *Souls in Transition: The Religious and Spiritual Lives of Emerging Adults*. New York: Oxford University Press.

Soet, J., & Sevig, T. (2006). Mental health issues facing a diverse sample of college students: Results from the College Student Mental Health Survey. *NASPA Journal, 43*(3), 410–431.

Taylor, P., & Keeter, S. (2010, December 10). *Millennials: Confident Connected Open to Change*. Pew Research Center. Retrieved from http://www.pewsocialtrends.org/files/2010/10/millennials-confident-connected-open-to-change.pdf

Twenge, J. M. (2006). *Generation Me: Why Today's Young Americans are More Confident, Assertive, Entitled—and More Miserable than Ever Before*. New York: Free Press.

Viner, S. (2014, February 7). Social media statistics: How college students are using social networking. *Study Breaks Magazine*. Retrieved from http://studybreakscollegemedia.com/2014/social-media-statistics-how-college-students-are-using-social-networking/#sthash.sSGC7jv7.dpuf

Volkow, N. (2014, August 18). *Science Should Guide Marijuana Policy*. Retrieved from http://www. drugabuse.gov/about-nida/noras-blog/2014/08/science-should-guide-marijuana-policy

White, S. (2015, November 9). *7 Reasons Tech Internships Pay Off*. Retrieved from http://www.cio.com/ article/3003061/it-skills-training/7-reasons-tech-internships-pay-off.html

White House Council of Economic Advisers. (2014). Retrieved from https://www.whitehouse.gov/ administration/eop/cea/factsheets-reports

Wyman, N. (2015a). *Career Planning for College Graduates*. Retrieved from www.iseek.org/careers/ studentcareers.html

Wyman, N. (2015b). *Job U: How to Find Wealth and Success by Developing the Skills Companies Actually Need*. New York: Crown Business.

11

Civic Engagement

Connecting Social Responsibility, Well-Being and Academic Success

ASHLEY FINLEY, LINDA MAJOR AND NANCY MITCHELL

Introduction

The concept of wellness in higher education is multi-faceted as described in other chapters in this volume. The nexus of academic development, civic engagement and well-being provides insight into another aspect of wellness. It can be argued that being engaged in diverse communities helps students succeed in academic endeavors and promotes their own wellness. Civic engagement is a valued educational outcome that has the potential to address and solve critical local and global problems; it teaches students how to become socially responsible citizens. Higher education does more than give students the skills and capacities to be productive members of the workforce; it gives them the confidence, self-esteem and sense of purpose to enable them to find meaning in their lives and careers. It helps them realize that, through both independent and collective action, they can make a meaningful difference in the world. In short, civic engagement has the potential to help students flourish.

Being involved in civic-related issues is imperative for twenty-first–century learning and student development. The social problems that will face college graduates are complex, and resolving them demands that they develop the inclination and skills to participate actively to improve their communities. Across the country, racial conflicts and inequality continue to be witnessed. Extremists of different faiths and political ideologies have ignited tensions that play out to sometimes tragic conclusions. Furthermore, the success of a democracy is built on an assumption that constituents will engage in selecting their leaders, yet voting, one form of engaging in civic duty, indicates that only slightly more than half of the U.S. voting age population actually vote (American Presidency Project, n.d.). This is particularly disconcerting considering that more than 81% of the population of voting age turned out to elect Abraham Lincoln in 1860.

Poverty, health and environmental issues are only a few of the examples that illustrate the range and magnitude of the challenges today's college students face as citizen leaders. Confronting the issues that are challenging society demands that college students engage in real-world problem solving, both for problems they face today as well as those they will face following graduation. However, the enormity of these issues can be overwhelming and paralyzing. Therefore, giving students the skills to address even small aspects of the problems empowers them to act while giving them meaning and purpose.

The juxtaposition of educators' interest in increasing the commitment to civic engagement and a concern for students' wellness permits college professionals, whether student affairs administrators, faculty members, staff or others, to contemplate the symbiotic relationship between these two objectives. The wellness elements within this relationship can be conceived of as part of a broader cluster of psychosocial well-being outcomes that include optimism, self-esteem, happiness, meaning and purpose in life, social connectedness and social trust (Keyes, 2002). These outcomes rarely appear on a syllabus but are often most telling of student success—the ways in which learning helps students to have the confidence and perseverance to want to stay in school, to want to take on an internship, to tackle a previously unrecognized social injustice and to stay the path to graduation. The role of civic engagement in this relationship provides students with a sense of connectedness. It helps them realize that through both independent and collective action they can make a meaningful difference in the world.

What if college professionals—within student affairs as well as instructional faculty—started considering the connection of students' civic engagement with their psychosocial well-being as a central part of the path to graduation toward becoming qualified professionals who are also prepared for citizen leadership? What if colleges invested financial and human resources in those experiences and conditions that were most likely to increase student learning while improving their sense of personal well-being? What if the connection of learning to student development in well-being wasn't just the purview of student affairs but included other campus personnel such as faculty, advisors and others? What if campus leaders started considering that how learning helps students feel about themselves and others might be what matters *most*?

A central question among leaders in institutions of higher education becomes this: What can be done to best create an environment that fosters students' sense of social responsibility as an essential component of valuing student wellness and development? To examine this topic in this chapter, it is helpful to first define psychosocial well-being and civic engagement more fully and then explore current research on the intersection between the two. Finally, suggestions, including campus models, are offered for developing an environment that supports personal and social responsibility, including evidence of their effectiveness.

Making the Connection: Psychosocial Well-Being and Civic Engagement

Psychosocial Well-Being

The state of affairs on college campuses and around the country seems to point to a latent connection between civic unrest and collective well-being. That connection appears to be a result of civic action or engagement as an outcome of individuals *not* being well; civic action is a means for expressing grievances and anger about injustice. The focus of this chapter, however, is to better understand the way in which collective action might contribute to student's positive well-being: how being civic, in fact, helps individuals feel better.

What is psychosocial well-being? As Lynne Friedli notes, "There is widespread agreement that mental health is more than the absence of clinically defined mental illness" (2009, p. 10). In other words, professionals cannot fully assess the dimensions of psychosocial well-being by, for example, deploying a standardized scale to determine whether students are depressed. Psychosocial well-being is defined by many interlocking components drawn from elements of an individual's short-term and long-term affect, outlook and social functioning. Keyes (2002), for example, defines psychosocial well-being, or positive mental health, through the lens of "flourishing," a compilation of individual's hedonic tendencies (positive feelings) with their eudemonic behaviors (positive functioning). The concept of *flourishing* (see Keyes, 2002) combines aspects of positive emotions, positive daily functioning and positive social interactions as core dimensions of psychosocial well-being. Flourishing encompasses individual pleasure, but it is more than that. Eudemonia, like flourishing, includes personal happiness but also fulfillment that is about more than oneself. Thus, the psychosocial elements of learning reflect students' desire not just to feel joy but to share it with others by seeking or building a community of learners.

A significant body of evidence suggests that a growing number of college students struggle with mental health issues such as depression and anxiety. The American College Health Association (ACHA) data collected through its National College Health Assessment (NCHA) during the spring semester beginning 2009 through 2015 confirms that trend. Approximately 57% of the 2015 respondents felt overwhelming anxiety in the previous 12 months compared to 49.1% in 2009. A similar increase was observed in students who reported feeling so depressed it was difficult to function, 34.5% and 30.7%, respectively. In addition, college students' high-risk drinking and its primary and secondary effects remain a significant concern due to its adverse consequences including academic failure, personal health and acute risk. Regular access to and monitoring of datasets such as the NCHA, the National Association of Mental Illness (NAMI) and the Healthy Minds Study based at the University of Michigan may prove helpful in assessing the level of student psychosocial well-being, both individually and collectively.

Data from the Midlife in the United States Survey (MIDUS), funded by the MacArthur Foundation, suggests that several major chronic conditions (stomach problems, back problems, arthritis, high blood pressure and hay fever) are associated with mental health diagnosis. Those individuals identified as "flourishing" reported fewer chronic physical conditions even after controlling for sociodemographic variables, body mass index, diabetes status, smoking status and level of physical activity (Keyes, 2007).

In the same study, Keyes found that flourishing adults report less missed work, fewer half-days or less cutbacks of work; lower levels of health limitations of activities associated with daily living and the lowest utilization of health care. In addition, those diagnosed as completely mentally healthy reported lower levels of perceived helplessness and the highest levels of functioning goals, resiliency and intimacy.

Civic Engagement

Nearly 25 years ago, Ernest Boyer reminded college professionals of the complex mission of higher education in a diverse democracy and interdependent world, and today, evidence exists that a campus commitment to civic endeavors is needed more than ever (Saltmarsh & Zlotkowski, 2011). Business and government leaders urge institutions to produce learners who are not limited in their preparation for narrow workforce specialties but graduates who are competent thinkers in the liberal arts including ethics, global knowledge, intercultural literacy and strong communication and collaborative skills (National Leadership Council for Liberal Education and America's Promise, 2007). Civic and professional skills development are not mutually exclusive. Traditional learning outcomes, such as those described earlier, can be taught and discussed within the context of the public sphere allowing students to recognize their utility in both the public and private sectors. Engaging in campus- or community-based civic action then simultaneously reinforces the curriculum and provides an opportunity to practice the skills learned.

Many colleges and universities are answering that call for higher education to return to its original purpose of preparing graduates for a life of civic engagement through civic learning. Interest in increasing civic engagement is not new. In *Politics* (Aristotle, Jowett, & Davis, 1920), Aristotle argues that good citizens are necessary for good government and that education serves a useful purpose in advancing the civic virtues essential to citizenship. The curriculum developed by Thomas Jefferson for the University of Virginia departed from the traditional academic structure to include, in part, content that helped students understand their civic rights and obligations. More recently, the U.S. Department of Education, in cooperation with the White House, issued a national report seeking to reestablish "civic learning at the core rather than the periphery of primary, secondary and postsecondary education." The national report, entitled *A Crucible Moment: College Learning and Democracy's Future,* affirms that "a socially cohesive and economically vibrant U.S. democracy and a viable, just global community require informed, engaged, open-minded and socially responsible people committed to the common good and practiced in 'doing' democracy" (The National Task Force on Civic Learning and Democratic Engagement, 2012, p. 20). The 2012 report provides a framework for advancing the civic knowledge, attitudes and skills necessary to engage what Bernie Ronan describes as

> all aspects of the human person—the head, through thinking judging, deliberation, and advocacy; the heart, through empathy and care for the beneficiaries of one's civic action, as well as through friendship with those co-involved in the public work; and the hands, through voting, acts of service, and collaborative political action.
>
> (2011, p. 5)

This urgent call to revisit and revitalize the democratic purposes of higher education is also in reaction to the reported declines in civic behaviors such as voting in elections, participation in public meetings, volunteering and contacting or visiting with public officials especially among young adults. As reported in Robert Putnam's seminal book, *Bowling Alone: The Collapse and Revival of American Community* (2000), of special concern is the decline in social capital, in particular bridging capital, which is defined as the ability to work across differences. Congressional gridlock, racial tension (including campus-based micro-aggression) and the inability to advance meaningful immigration reform serve to reinforce the perception that American citizens have lost the ability to bridge their differences. It is argued that neither democracy nor society can operate effectively and efficiently without a healthy measure of social capital (Sander & Putnam, 2010).

The national trend reported by Putnam is verified at the state level by organizations dedicated to advancing civic engagement among its citizens. Data collected as part of the 2015 Nebraska Civic Health Index found that the youngest citizens have the lowest level of participation in most indicators of community engagement, including charitable giving and public meeting participation (Arends et al., 2015).

Making the Connection

In their review of the civic engagement and psychosocial well-being literature, Constance Flanagan and Matthew Bundick (2011) identified multiple studies suggesting a positive relationship to psychosocial well-being and various indicators of community engagement. The authors acknowledge a natural selection bias associated with volunteerism. For example, those with better mental health and higher levels of socioeconomic status and psychosocial well-being are more likely to opt into this type of civic engagement. However, research supports both that people with higher levels of well-being report volunteering more hours and that volunteering "enhances life satisfaction, self-esteem, sense of control over one's life, physical health, and happiness, and lowers depression" (2011, p. 22).

Academically based community service or service-learning is a teaching pedagogy within the sphere of civic engagement strategies that has grown in popularity since the 1980s. Service-learning integrates community service or community-based research with academic learning. Evidence-based best practices in higher education clearly demonstrate that academic service-learning enhances university–community partnerships; contributes to a discipline's scholarship of engagement and strengthens students' knowledge, skills and experiences in world issues. Research supported by the Higher Education Research Institute at UCLA found that course-based service showed significant positive effects in multiple outcomes including academic performance, values (commitment to activism and promoting racial understanding), self-efficacy, leadership, choice of a service career and plans to participate in service after college (Astin, Vogelgesang, Ikeda, & Yee, 2000).

A growing body of research related to social capital as a protective factor for high-risk behaviors provides insight regarding an underutilized construct for creating healthier environments at institutions of higher education (Bergen-Cico &

Vicomi, 2008; Reis & Trockel, 2003; Weitzman & Chen, 2005). Research supported as part of the Robert Wood Johnson Foundation (RWJF) initiative on high-risk drinking among college students found social capital to be a potential protection from high-risk alcohol consumption (Weitzman & Chen, 2005). Social capital was operationalized as the average amount of time students committed to volunteering over a 30-day period and then aggregated to the campus level. Reduced levels of high-risk drinking as well as primary and secondary harms were observed among students at colleges with higher levels of social capital.

Given the ongoing concern for the health and well-being of college students, their disengagement from democratic practices and the research evidence supporting that they are interrelated, higher education appears well positioned to address both through a thoughtfully constructed civic engagement initiative. The notion that civic engagement and well-being are linked is elemental to the meaning of a liberal education. College is not only a means by which students gain the intellectual skills to be successful in their careers; it also presents an opportunity for them to develop the personal and social capacities to flourish in their everyday lives. A liberal education should enable *all* students to understand their civic responsibilities and to connect to others on campus, as well as in their local, national and global communities (AAC&U, 1998), providing them with essential tools for engagement, belonging and self-discovery. This type of engagement should not be considered a "silver bullet," given the complexity of both issues, but a single strategy nested within a more comprehensive response.

National Support and Campus Models for Examining Student Well-Being and Civic Learning: The Bringing Theory to Practice Project

The connection between civic engagement and well-being has provided the impetus for multiple strands of research from which an empirical understanding of the relationship has begun to take shape. The national Bringing Theory to Practice (BTtoP) project provides one source of such focused research. For more than a decade, BTtoP has offered modest funding to campuses to implement and assess practices connecting students' learning and civic efforts in engaged-learning practices—such as learning communities, first-year seminars and service-learning courses—to outcomes related to their personal growth and well-being. A review of 80 grant reports from campuses over 10 years, across a diverse range of campus projects and programs aimed at aligning well-being, learning and civic engagement, found that a majority of campuses (approximately 57%) concluded that the program or intervention resulted entirely in positive outcomes related to students' well-being, such as an increase in students' trust in themselves, self-efficacy, sense of flourishing, increased sense of purpose and self-acceptance. More than a quarter of the campuses reported a combination of positive and negative results across various well-being outcomes. The remaining campuses (approximately 16%) found students' engagement had either no change in well-being outcomes or had the opposite of the intended positive effect at the conclusion of the program.

Specific findings from campus-based projects funded by BTtoP provide additional insights into the relationship between civic engagement and well-being. For example, Tufts University, in examining students' participation in curricular and non-curricular service experiences, found positive effects on students' sense of flourishing when service experiences were perceived to emphasize social change or political engagement. The element of social change within community engagement experiences was also shown to have the most persistent positive effect on students' sense of flourishing over time. Wagner College also discerned a connection between students' community engagement and flourishing through the study of their learning communities program. Project leaders at Wagner concluded that levels of student flourishing increased most significantly when students' learning community experiences involved a service-learning component where students engaged with a community partner, as compared with learning communities that involved only field trips into the community. St. Lawrence University used its required first-year program to evaluate the role of engaged-learning pedagogies on students' emotional well-being and flourishing. A multi-year study concluded that students who had participated in first-year seminars involving active learning, such as community-based research, had the highest levels of reported emotional well-being and sense of flourishing.

A multi-campus research study provided additional support for the link between students' civic engagement and their well-being. Preliminary research from a partnership between BTtoP and the Personal and Social Responsibility Inventory provided insights into how particular dimensions of students' engagement in personal and social responsibility, such as striving for excellence, contributing to a larger community and perspective-taking (see http://www.psri.hs.iastate.edu/) corresponded to levels of flourishing. Findings from an initial study with five campuses indicated students' sense of flourishing is more greatly influenced by their perceptions of being in a campus environment that supports personal and social responsibility than it is by a student's individual civic experiences, such as participating in service-learning (Mitchell, Reason, Hemer, & Finley, 2016). Specifically, students' perceptions of climates that support the development of moral reasoning and contributing to a larger community were most associated with higher levels of flourishing among student respondents. The research suggests the critical role campus climate can play in contributing to students' well-being. Thus, as campuses emphasize the value of a student's individual learning experiences, there is also a need to reinforce that a student's individual efforts are part of larger institutional ecology of thought and action that supports the civic meaning and purpose behind those experiences.

Finally, students' own words can often be the most compelling evidence behind the link between civic engagement and well-being. Another research study examining the attitudes of underserved students (i.e., racial minority, first-generation, low-income and transfer students) toward particular learning experiences revealed the important ways in which students' articulate the very personal effects of their engagement with community-based learning experiences (see Finley & McNair, 2013).

Comments reflected the ways in which, for example, community engagement inspires a different level of connection with course material that feels deeper and more meaningful than strictly class-based learning.

> I find that . . . being in a classroom is one thing, but being exposed to outside experiences and becoming involved with the community . . . has a different impact on you because learning in the classroom is just, you're just sitting there. You're not being exposed to as many experiences as you are if you're becoming involved with outside classroom activities as well.
>
> (Student in California)

Additionally, students' comments illuminated the personal value of community engagement in helping them to understand different viewpoints and lived experiences.

> [Y]ou have a better understanding when you do engage with the community. You understand more of what people are going through in general. You have more confidence to . . . interact and to be of some help in some way. . . . So I think [engaging in the community] probably brings that out in you more [than other kinds of learning].
>
> (Student in California)

> [T]here's (sic) so many people in the community. . .that you just kind of are pushed . . . into conversations with people that have a completely different background than you and completely different points of view. And I think [because of that] your maturity grows a little more because . . . you learn to accept it and kind of just let it sink in and not just . . . attack back. [E]veryone has different opinions. That's just how it is so I think that is worth a lot.
>
> (Student in Wisconsin)

Students also identified how community engagement experiences gave them a sense of self-efficacy to be part of something lasting and their own role in contributing to larger purpose.

> And my service learning was through conservation course, and we had to like cut down weeds and plant oak trees. I planted like a hundred oak trees. Even to this day, I mean it's still rewarding to know that those oak trees are right there, and that I helped plant them.
>
> (Student in Wisconsin)

> [In college] you have all [of] these resources available for you to go out into the community to help and do different things. . . . [Doing that] helps me to take a look at myself and see what I'm doing for myself as a person and what I'm contributing to the community that I'm also a part of.
>
> (Student in Wisconsin)

Finally, as the following quote captures, students also remarked on the power of community engagement in finding connection with peers, community members and faculty.

> [S]ervice-based learning is so underutilized because [by doing that] I had to learn . . .all [these] things, which then applied to the real world, which gave me the leadership experience, which gave me the experience that I can talk to an employer . . . [b]ut it [also] creates the network. It creates that community that you need. . . . I needed to know that I was making a differ-ence . . . and not that [my degree is] just . . . a piece of paper.
>
> (Student in Oregon)

Taking the Next Step: How Campuses Can Examine Connections between Civic Engagement and Wellness

There is much campuses can do to understand the role of civic engagement in fostering and promoting student wellness. *First, finding the right language to char-acterize what both civic engagement and well-being mean is critical.* For example, although the language of "flourishing" may resonate on one campus, it cannot be assumed this is the case everywhere. Campus leaders should look to the institu-tion's mission statement; strategic planning documents and conversations with faculty, staff and students to identify the language of well-being that captures interest from a wide spectrum of campus constituents. Similarly, the language used to articulate a campus' civic commitment should be thoughtfully articulated. Whether a campus uses the language of "social justice," "global citizens," "civic professionals," or something else—the words matter for building an inclusive environment for engagement.

Relatedly, campus leaders trying to generate conversations and interest in well-being and civic engagement will be aided by connecting these efforts with the core purposes of their institution. For example, Jesuit institutions, such as Georgetown University, have the Latin phrase *cura personalis*, or care for the entire person, as an essen-tial part of their mission. Other campuses may have well-being as an articulated learning outcome at the institutional level or within general education. Tidewater Community College, for example, has identified "personal development" among its stated institutional "core competencies." Articulations at the institutional level can provide foundational support to provoke conversations by asking, "How are we meeting this dimension of our institutional promise to students?" or "How can we be improving our efforts to make sure this promise is more widely realized?"

Third, course or program initiatives that seek to align student well-being with learning and civic engagement are often successful when flexibility is built into the development process. For example, within the University of Nebraska-Lincoln's Certificate for Civic Engagement program, students tie theory to practice, connect-ing what they learn in their general education program with a community-based civic action plan. Both their course selection and their civic experience are shaped by their academic discipline, personal passion or both. Capstone project examples include the development of a leadership seminar for middle school students, a cultural adaptation inventory designed to prepare students for travel abroad and a newly created internship program for pre-vet majors. This type of flexibility invites students, faculty and staff into the conversation of connecting well-being and learning in a way that is comfortable for them. This requires conversations, demystification and a low-stakes trial run. Faculty and staff need to be supported to engage in a pilot course or program to work out the kinks in implementation and to learn what they could not have known ahead of time. Campus leaders focused on building a culture of civic engagement and well-being on campus should focus on maximizing current efforts by focusing on what faculty and staff are already doing and then helping those efforts to be more transparent and intentional.

Fourth, explore strategies for integrating and reinforcing civic life throughout the fabric of campus. For example, engage students in the mid-term and national elections through voter registration drives. Web-based voter registration services such as TurboVote make it easy to both register and remind student voters of upcoming local, state and national elections. Collaborate with the campus debate team to engage students in difficult dialogue around complex issues. Incentivize civic action among individual students and/or student groups through competitive grant programs that provide financial support for projects that contribute to the common good. Partner with campus religious education workers to establish inter-faith dialogue. Anecdotal evidence suggests that students are anxious to discuss and understand the spiritual beliefs of others but report that conversations often turn into conflict or conversion. Facilitate opportunities for students to serve on local non-profit boards, government committees or municipal advisory boards. Work with the college or university alumni association or career services office to host events that feature civically engaged alumni. Provide the alumni with opportunities to discuss the personal and professional benefits of a rich civic life. Encourage groups such as learning communities, outdoor adventure enthusiasts, student organizations and Greek life to integrate a service component into existing activities. Develop and offer a workshop series for faculty members introducing them to service learning pedagogy and course construction and last, but not least, provide formal and informal opportunities for students to interact with someone different from them. Indeed, many more strategies, appropriate for and adapted for evolving institutional characteristics and needs, can be developed and enhanced over time.

Finally, campus leaders undertaking conversations about well-being should be mindful of how issues of equity affect these outcomes and for whom. The effort to take well-being seriously on a campus means recognizing that students are not a single, homogeneous group. Personal growth and well-being are likely to manifest themselves differently across diverse groups of students on the campus. Insights into how to improve well-being among students are dependent upon the sensitivity to recognize that not all students have the same support networks, access to resources or confidence to seek out mentors for guidance. As campuses engage in conversations about equity and student success, the degree to which all students are also truly flourishing is an important consideration. Attention to members of historically marginalized groups, as well as other areas of interest such as affiliation groups (i.e., student-athletes, fraternity/sorority members, international students), first-generation college students, veterans or other grouping, can help campus leaders learn ways in which desired results are achieved across campus. As needed, modifications and implementation enhancements can be made to assure desired equity and student success throughout campus.

Conclusion

The educational philosopher and champion of liberal education John Dewey once said, "To find out what one is fitted to do, and to secure the opportunity to do it, is the key to happiness" (Dewey, 1916). Colleges and universities, not only have the task of equipping students with the skills to succeed, but also have the opportunity to enable students to seek their happiness, fulfillment and purpose in applying those skills in ways that give meaning to their lives and careers. These are the kinds of testimonials campuses proudly post from their alums. Campus professionals should not wait until students graduate to understand how well-being connects with their learning and civic engagement. Students can be encouraged to recognize the importance of flourishing and community engagement from the moment they step onto campus.

> I think [college has] impacted everything from the way I vote to what I shop for to what I do with my garbage. . . . I'm more engaged in the community when it comes to different things that stand for something. I think that's what college should be about. I think it's impacted everything when it comes to my connection with the community and the world around me.
>
> (Student in Oregon)

References

American Presidency Project. (n.d.). Retrieved December 6, 2015, from http://www.presidency.ucsb.edu/data/turnout.php

Arends, K., Morfeld, A., Day, K., McEntarffer, R., Ernst, R., Shaddock, K., Yost, J., Pytilk Zillig, L., Herian, M., Major, L., Dierberger, J., Huffman, D., & Payne, H. (2015). *The Nebraska Civic Health Index*. Lincoln, NE: Nebraskans for Civic Reform.

Aristotle, Jowett, B., & Davis, H.W.C. (1920). *Aristotle's Politics*. Oxford: Clarendon Press.

Association of American Colleges and Universities Board of Directors (AAC&U). (1998). *Statement on Liberal Learning*. Washington, DC: Association of American Colleges and Universities.

Astin, A. W., Vogelgesang, L. J., Ikeda, E. K., & Yee, J. A. (2000). *How Service Learning Affects Students*. Los Angeles: University of California, Higher Education Research Institute.

Bergen-Cico, D., & Viscomi, J. (2008). Civic aspirations as a protective factor against college students' abuse of alcohol. *Journal of College and Character, X*, 1–14.

Dewey, J. (1916). *Democracy and Education: An Introduction to the Philosophy of Education*. New York: Macmillan.

Finley, A., & McNair, T. (2013). *Assessing Underserved Students Engagement in High-Impact Practices*. Washington, DC: Association of American Colleges and Universities.

Flanagan, C., & Bundick, M. (2011, Spring). Civic engagement and psychosocial well-being in college students. *Liberal Education, 97*(2), 20–27.

Friedli, L. (2009). *Mental Health, Resilience and Inequalities.* Copenhagen: World Health Organization.

Keyes, C.L.M. (2002). The mental health continuum: From languishing to flourishing in life. *Journal of Health and Social Behavior, 43*(2), 207–222.

Keyes, C.L.M. (2007). Promoting and protecting mental health as flourishing: A complementary strategy for improving national mental health. *American Psychologist, 62*(2), 95–108.

Mitchell, J. J., Reason, R. D., Hemer, K. M., & Finley, A. (2016). Perceptions of campus climates for civic learning as predictors of college students' mental health. *Journal of College and Character, 17*(1), 40–52.

National Leadership Council for Liberal Education and America's Promise. (2007). *College Learning for the New Global Century.* Washington, DC: Association of American Colleges and Universities. Retrieved from http://www.aacu.org/leap/documents/GlobalCentury_final.pdf

The National Task Force on Civic Learning and Democratic Engagement. (2012). *A Crucible Moment: College Learning and Democracy's Future.* Washington, DC: Association of American Colleges and Universities.

Putnam, R. D. (2000). *Bowling Alone: The Collapse and Revival of American Community.* New York: Simon & Schuster.

Reis, J., & Trockel, M. (2003). An empirical analysis of fraternity and sorority individual-environmental interactions with alcohol. *Journal of Applied Social Psychology, 33*(12), 2536–2552.

Ronan, B. (2011). *The Civic Spectrum.* Dayton, OH: Kettering Foundation.

Saltmarsh, J. A., & Zlotkowski, E. A. (2011). *Higher Education and Democracy: Essays on Service-Learning and Civic Engagement.* Philadelphia: Temple University Press.

Sander, T., & Putnam, R. (2010). Still bowling alone?: The post-9/11 split. *Journal of Democracy, 21*(1), 9–16.

Weitzman, E. R., & Chen, Y. (2005). Risk modifying effect of social capital on measures of heavy alcohol consumption, alcohol abuse, harms, and secondhand effects: National survey findings. *Journal Epedemial Community Health, 59*, 303–309.

Part VI
Campus Applications

12

Organizing Wellness Issues
Walking Together to Build Bridges for Campuses Today and Communities Tomorrow

TODD S. ROSE

If you want to walk fast, walk alone;
If you want to walk far, walk together.
—African Proverb

Introduction

The number of students attending college and the diversity of these students is increasing. According to the National Center for Educational Statistics (2015), between 2002 and 2012, enrollments in institutions that are deemed "degree granting" grew by nearly one-quarter to 20.6 million students. The number of full-time and part-time students is increasing, as is the number of students enrolled in non-degree-granting institutions such as those offering technical programs and programs that are less than two years in duration. A review of the demographics of students enrolled in college shows an increase in the number of historically underrepresented populations in colleges and universities. Between 1976 and 2012, the percentage of college students who identify as White declined from 80% to 60%. Thelin and Gasman (2011) describe this transformation of higher education from an activity once reserved for the elite and wealthy to one that is increasingly more accessible to a broader profile of individuals. Further, higher education may not only be more accessible, but this level of education may be more appropriate for a wide range of individuals in the nation's already well-educated populace.

Although colleges and universities once were able to predict student success using demographic and traditional academic variables, this method is no longer the exclusive angle by which institutions can understand the student quest to attain the goals in higher education. Attention to student wellness is increasingly important. Over a decade ago, Pritchard and Wilson (2003) noted the necessity of looking at issues of college student wellness issues as central to their success in college. At about the same time, a publication by NASPA (2004) indicates that students report health and wellness factors having a high effect on their academic performance.

In his introduction to the first book in this series on *Wellness Issues for Higher Education*, David Anderson (2016) paints the initiatives outlined in that volume (and obviously this volume) as a mandate for higher education, connecting the range of wellness issues addressed to missions as articulated by institutions. These connections reflect, not only a centrality of these issues to the lives of college students, but the responsibility of faculty and staff at all levels of the institutions to give both thoughtful consideration and energy into addressing these issues. Anderson and his chapter authors provide current information on issues that impact student success in college and beyond. The complexities of the challenge to address wellness on campus in meaningful ways outpace the understanding of the individual wellness issues. This is because students are often working to cope with more than one of these issues at a time and that there are impacts from one issue on another. For example, the sleepless nature of final exams is often coupled with poor nutrition and a diluted exercise regimen, resulting in poor academic performance, or a student with an unhealthy body image uses alcohol and tobacco to address the pain of not fitting the media-based image of attraction.

The breadth and the pervasiveness of issues of wellness on the college campus, as outlined in this volume and the preceding volume, leave us with this enduring question: Given the nature of our work and our organizations in higher education, how might we positively impact these issues going forward? In other words, what can and should we be doing differently so we can have a demonstrated impact on the lives of our students, both during their time in our institutions of higher education and subsequently as they enter the worlds of career, community, family, service, culture and health?

The intent of this chapter is twofold. The first aim is to provide two models of leadership that can contribute an enhanced commitment to addressing these wellness issues on the campus. The second aim is to provide six guiding principles that can undergird these campus efforts and to explore ways to overcome some of the obstacles that occur.

Leadership on Campus

Kotter's Steps to Leading Change

Retired Harvard Professor John Kotter, author of *Leading Change* (2012), called upon his years of consulting with clients and studying how changes succeed or fail in organizations to create an eight-step model to organizational transformation. The first steps lay the foundation for successful change. In these steps, the case is made for the critical need to change as well as organizing the right people to stimulate and manage the change. These steps are essential to the success of the organization and, as Kotter points out, should not be rushed through. Much like the foundation of the building, these steps provide the base and the support on which all the other steps in the change process reside. The second series of the steps are the planning for the change. These steps include creating the image of the new organization in the minds of those involved—an image of an organization that has embraced the changes and is enjoying the benefit of these changes. This image is to be shared consistently and liberally throughout the organization, reinforcing for all involved the commitment of the leadership to affecting these changes. The final series of steps in Kotter's model addresses the importance of enacting and embedding the changes in the organization. The necessity of recognizing the short-term successes, leveraging those successes further, as well as connecting the changes made with the new reality in the organization is critical for the organization to sustain these changes in the long term. This model is designed primarily for people in positions of formal authority in organizations.

A university focused on addressing the range of wellness issues may consider naming a high-profile leadership position, such as a vice president of wellness affairs; it may also consider memorializing the commitment to these issues in the public documents of the institution, whether that is the mission statement, strategic plan, proclamation or other well-regarded documents. For example, the portfolio of a senior administrator, whether the chief student affairs officer, an individual reporting to this administrator, or a new role, may be designed to provide intersection of the offices most directly working on issues of wellness (e.g., health, counseling, recreation, wellness/alcohol and other drug education); this may even include joint appointments of key teaching faculty in relevant areas of study. The importance of this role could be akin to that of the ombudsman, which, when initially designed, typically reported directly to the chief executive (e.g., president or chancellor) of the institution. This professional could use national and institutional data to educate the various campus and community constituencies on the urgency of various wellness issues and the necessity of addressing these issues through education, interventions and support as a means to further enhance the nature and quality of the college experience by students.

An advisory board of key stakeholders at the institution could provide inspiration, feedback and appropriate guidance to the efforts. Imagine parents of current students, once educated on the issues, helping to shape communication to other parents, giving suggested discussion topics for family conversations and offering tips on how to support their students during their college journey. Further, imagine the campus architect or interior designer on the advisory committee; upon better understanding the centrality of wellness to college student success, this individual can contribute valuable knowledge on how the design of the environment contributes to increased healthy socialization of individuals in an area. The two-way communication with this participant can have long-ranging ramifications for helping create the desired campus culture that best promotes wellness choices.

Codifying the commitment to these efforts is also important. Formally, the vision for these efforts should be documented in the strategic plan of the department, unit, division or institution. Further, this articulation of the important role of wellness efforts can be informative in both the searches for and the orientation of new employees. Imagine examining the knowledge and skills of the division of student affairs holistically to seize opportunities enhance the staff when the opportunities arise. The job description for a new member of the fraternity and sorority life staff including preferred experience in creating educational programming around body image and eating disorders may round out a superior team of subject matter experts in the division. Similarly, imagine how new faculty hired for the institution, whether in directly related fields of study such as health, social work, education or psychology or indirectly such as business, public affairs or computer science, can become advocates for and supporters of the campus effort for wellness issues.

Kezar and Grassroots Leadership

Not all change and impact on addressing the important wellness issues of students relies on formal leadership. A challenge in higher education is that often those working to address wellness issues in the institutions are not in positions that directly influence the formal prioritization and distribution of resources. Thus, a second model of leadership is introduced to help provide a framework for organizing leadership with wellness issues.

In the description of Kezar (2011), many of those currently working on issues are located, organizationally, on the fringes of the organization and lack formal authority or power. This is often true of those working on student wellness on the college campus. Kezar studied the work of several individuals and initiatives that grew on campuses through the work of leaders working at the grassroots level. Grassroots leadership efforts are those that promote campus reform and that are conducted by people without formal authority and power in the institution.

According to Kezar (2011), some characteristics of grassroots leadership include:

1. *Working in groups.* Grassroots leadership is primarily, but not exclusively, a group activity.
2. *Necessary for some changes to occur.* There are limits to the relying on the small number of people in the top-down model of leadership to create necessary change.
3. *Faced with long-term challenges to success.* Many grassroots efforts led by staff members are often derailed early in the process, are challenged with institutional power dynamics and involve individuals working on important issues without power who have even experienced workplace bullying by those unsupportive of their efforts.

An example of a grassroots leadership effort to address financial well-being in students may be a new assistant professor of law who has seen the challenges of law school continue as the students graduate with their law degree. These students have a passion using their legal talents to help low-income communities but are unable to take positions in public-interest law firms due to the high debt load of both personal and school loans. Over a period of years, this faculty member finds others at the institution equally alarmed by this issue. Through a successful series of educating peers on these issues and working with the development staff of the law school, a fund gets established to provide student loan relief to students who pursue careers in public sector or public-interest law.

Guiding Principles for Campus Efforts

Kotter's principles on leading change and Kezar's work to understand grassroots leadership provide sound advice. Informed by these two models, what follows are six principles for organizing wellness issues on the campus. An explanation of each principle and some suggested practices will follow each in order to invigorate some thinking that is both creative and strategic for the organization and anchoring work with these issues on campuses.

Principle 1: Start Where You Are

Whether you are the chief student affairs officer or a senior student affairs leader, working in a non-student affairs role at the institution, employed as a first-time professional in a student affairs division or have a position in an academic unit or as a tenured faculty member, you have the power to impact these issues on campus by starting where you are. In a formal leadership position, the task of prioritizing the resources, creating strategic plans and goal setting are among the many responsibilities. The ability to use these opportunities to address wellness issues on the campus is apparent. A starting point may be the collection of institutional data; this may be done by using or adapting a respected national survey (to provide a comparative set of data); it may be accomplished more expeditiously or in a less costly manner by engaging those with content expertise and needs assessment skills to prepare a locally appropriate instrument and protocols. The results could support the enhanced attention to the issues. What is important is that, if data is needed and timeliness is important, the process not drag on and unnecessarily delay planning and implementation efforts.

Similarly, a first-time student affairs educator, academic advisor or faculty member may have a different starting point, but the opportunity still exists. Reading any number of books on these topics can serve as valuable professional self-development. Perhaps carrying one of these books to meetings and appointments on campus will serve as a conversation starter and help to identify individuals who also have an interest in advancing these issues for students on campus. A reading group may develop, or the new professional may find that there is a current group of people who have already gathered around these issues. Whatever your position, there is always a sphere that you can influence.

Principle 2: Walk Together

Higher education is a place where new ideas are created, where discoveries are made and where deep passions exist, but often in isolation. Both Kotter (2012) and Kezar (2011) note the importance of working as a collective in advancing issues and change on the campus. Whether it be through a formal coalition or a loose network of colleagues, the importance of multiple parties working together to advance the understanding or wellness issues to the point of anchoring them into the fabric of the institution is paramount. This collective will serve to provide insight into the depths of the topics, the climate of the institution and even to strengthen the reach of the efforts. Kezar (2011) describes a network as a set of relationships among people that will help to accomplish goals now and in the future. An ideal network is one that is built over time and formed largely before the network is needed to address a particular issue. Networking can happen in the normal course of our daily work as our work intersects that of others. Broader networks can be created on campus by stepping outside the normal daily paths. A new professional might seek to formally meet several of the more seasoned leaders at the institution. Someone with more experience at the institution might reach out to a few new faculty or staff members by way of coffee or lunch to welcome them to the organization. Opportunities to serve on committees outside of a department or division at a school are often provided to individuals who are respected and express an interest in contributing beyond their assigned duties. This service provides individuals the chance to get to know people in other areas and create a broader reach of connections.

Principle 3: Play the Long Game

Advancing wellness issues within the organization means finding a place on the formal agenda and within the specified priorities of the institution. It also entails capturing some of the energy that is present among the people that make up the larger organization as a whole. The dynamic nature of colleges and universities necessitate that competing priorities will always be in play at the institution. In order to produce positive, recurring attention to these issues at institutions of higher education, the adoption of a long-term time horizon is necessary. Creating the vision for an environment where student wellness is attended to in and out of the class, and where strategies are identified to achieve this vision, is essential to transforming the environment. Kotter (2012) speaks to the need to plan and create short-term wins as important to keep in mind, as these wins create the foundation for the long term, enduring success of our work. In addition, these short-term milestones can create additional energy to the commitment toward long-term efforts and perseverance.

Principle 4: Create Relevance and Meaning

The beauty of a college environment is that it is a place where multiple generations, ethnicities, identities and demographics exist and flourish together. On any given day, the senior most faculty members, prospective new students and everyone in between may be in the same shared space—each with important tasks, goals and activities on which they place their focus. The pervasiveness of the need to address wellness issues on the campus, and the presence of wide variety of members of the educational community, challenge individuals' work on student wellness efforts to make these issues important to others. A succinct but well-researched article on the impact of sexual violence on student learning may be the correct strategy to make the issue relevant to faculty members, while a social media campaign about that same issue and its impact on the mental health and happiness might make the topic meaningful to students in their junior and senior years. Understanding the multiple audiences of an environment and providing the right information using the right mechanisms are important to advancing the understanding of the issue to elicit support.

Principle 5: Connect Efforts to the Existing Fabric of the Institution

Infusing important wellness issues into existing cultural, social and academic programming and offerings on campus provides an avenue to anchor the issues with existing audiences. A university with rich tradition of celebrating Hispanic heritage may be open to an additional program on the issues of career wellness and Hispanic students. A college that is grounded in a religious tradition may provide opportunities for the issue of student wellness to the existing tenets of the school. A small discussion group reading a book on dependence and recovery may be able to explore these in the context of spiritual wholeness. Creative ways to augment annual celebrations with wellness-oriented topics will take advantage of an already attentive audience and provide some legitimacy to the topic in the minds of those in the community. Academic coursework on wellness topics serve as a rich foundation for exploring ways of reaching a larger audience. Similarly, academic courses—whether on marketing and advertising, business practices and organizational health or on political systems, global economy or educational practices—can serve as a springboard for discussions and assignments on any of a range of wellness topics and how to infuse, more effectively, these issues within the lives of those served by the soon-to-graduate student applying his/her knowledge in the "real world."

Principle 6: Stay Fresh

Keeping knowledge of and energy toward these issues fresh is essential in advancing them on campus. Constantly updating a Blackboard site with relevant articles and reviews of books may provide a ready arsenal of information priming discussions across the campus. Inviting individuals who are interested in helping to an informal lunch with others concerned about the same topic can be invigorating and resourceful. This connection may provide a few ideas that inspire some new thinking in those concerned with the importance of these issues on the campus as well as in the surrounding community.

Once a formal guiding coalition is in place, providing the opportunity for members to rotate off the working group, while bringing on new ones may create a more sustainable, enduring presence on the campus. This effort provides those working with the efforts an opportunity to hear new thoughts and ideas or to take a break in their formal leadership role periodically.

Organizational Challenges, Obstacles and Opposition

Efforts to address student wellness issues on campus are often met with obstacles. The following are four common scenarios experienced by individuals involved in the efforts and some suggestions to how these might be addressed. While many more obstacles may be present, the important point here is to acknowledge that these challenges do exist and to prepare appropriate and effective strategies for overcoming them.

Scenario 1: Student Wellness Is Not Part of
the Strategic Plan of the Institution

If this is the case at your institution, this may be a great indicator of where to start efforts—either individual or collective efforts—to make the case for institutional attention to student wellness issues. The overall strategic plan of an organization is intended to focus the energy, efforts and resources of that organization to move forward. While student wellness may not be the language used in the strategic plan of the university, the chances are great that addressing issues of wellness are directly linked to the strategic plan. Student success, student retention, graduation rates or enrollment goals are often cited in the mission strategic plan of a college or university. Student wellness connects directly to those concepts.

If you are working with a group of colleagues or working alone, putting effort into collecting national or regional student data of the importance of student wellness to students' academic success and retention will be a good, early step to take. Resources such as the American College Health Association, NASPA: Student Affairs Professionals In Higher Education, NIRSA: Leaders in Collegiate Recreation, American College Personnel Association and others can be great resources of data. The ability to work to produce local data on your campus will also provide useful information. Areas that often have data and interest in student wellness issues and their impact on the student experience include student health services, counseling, housing and residence life, as well as sorority and fraternity life. Determining if these areas currently collect relevant information is generally simple. Areas that hold data are often willing to share the data if they are comfortable with how, when and with whom the data will be shared or used, that the integrity of the data will remain and that credit for developing the data will be properly noted. If there are no current data-gathering tools that ask questions that speak to the impact of student wellness and its importance to student success, looking for existing data collection efforts that may welcome a few appropriate, well-written questions is a good way to spend time. Perhaps student health is collecting data with students who use their services, or the recreation department is surveying students who use the facility; working with those areas to add a few questions into the current surveys at some future date that speak to student wellness may be the right strategy.

There are often multiple, competing areas that want survey questions asked, and those who implement surveys often want to hold the number of questions to a minimum to increase the likelihood that students will complete the surveys. As this is the case, it's important to not only be ready to provide succinct, beneficial questions to be added, but also to be patient in expecting questions to be added in future iterations of the survey. Using the interim time to help in the coordination/ implementation of the surveys and to continue to educate colleagues regarding the role of student wellness in student success would be time well spent.

Scenario 2: Budgets Are Being Cut, and We Have Been Told That
Spending Money on New Initiatives Is Not an Option Right Now

Colleges and universities often have more ideas and initiatives than they have resources. This presents a very real challenge for anyone on the campus who is looking to expand their efforts toward addressing student wellness issues. Assuming that no new institutional money is truly available, there are a few options available.

A first recommendation is to work within the confines of the current calendar, programming commitments or structure that exists on the campus. Can existing efforts be enhanced to add some value to efforts in addressing student wellness issues? Perhaps provide a small but special recognition to the resident assistants who do spring programming related to wellness issues. Offering to sponsor a "Wellness Warrior" award to the best RA program on the campus may raise the profile of the issues and reinforce individual desire for addressing wellness issues. If there is a major, annual, intra-campus athletic competition (e.g., Spring Relays), creating an avenue for teams to attend optional, additional programming might be a reasonable option. One example would be working with the campus recreation department to provide a 45-minute interactive program on sleep, nutrition or healthy competition. This program could be an enhancement to the athletic events and provide an opportunity for the "non-athletes" in the organization to contribute to the overall efforts of the team.

A second recommendation is to seek alternative resources to institutional funds. Is there a student organization that currently works on issues that are directly or indirectly related to any of the student wellness? A student organization might have funding options available that are outside the institutional resources (e.g., student fees). Are there local agencies or organizations that work on issues of wellness that are meaningful to students? Working in partnership with these organizations often creates additional support for the issues at low or no cost. Are there other colleges or universities in the area? Perhaps hosting a small conversation with local resources with the other institutions in the area to simply discuss the current efforts toward addressing student wellness issues, and to look at opportunities for collaboration in the future, are the best steps toward setting the stage for a more robust agenda of student wellness education.

Scenario 3: Earlier Coalitions of People Interested in
These Topics Have Been Short-Lived

Coalitions of people with similar interests and goals are important to the success of any effort. However, according to Kezar (2011), many efforts are derailed early. It's not simply that there is a coalition of people committed to the issues that is important, but having some key individuals as part of the effort is critical. Kezar points out that efforts are more successful when they include both faculty and staff. Faculty, particularly tenured, senior faculty, generally experience less severe pressure from institutional power dynamics. In addition, including students in the effort provides an energy and understanding, as well as the ownership, of a key population on the campus.

A strong coalition will consist of people committed to the issues, have some members with the wisdom and stature in the institution to navigate the political waters and have representation from key constituents on any campus—students and the faculty. It's also best to keep the core group as small as possible. Although the idea of keeping the core coalition large may seem logical as it can provide a greater voice and have representatives from populations across the campus, it may turn out to be ineffective. For example, the larger the group, the more complicated it is to find meeting times for the entire group to gather. As the passion and efforts for student wellness issues on campus grows, multiple opportunities for people to join in the efforts will surface. A well-organized central core of people is key to the long-term success of the efforts.

Beyond simply the composition of the coalition, the importance of recognizing the smaller successes is important to the long-term viability of the group. Kotter (2012) emphasizes the importance of planning for and creating short-term wins in a long-term change effort. Thus, identify some easily accomplished efforts that can provide an opportunity to gather data about positive impact as well as generate helpful publicity.

Scenario 4: The Coalition of People Concerned about Student Wellness Believes Senior Management Involvement in These Efforts Will Only Hamper the Efforts to Address Student Wellness Issues

This is a common, and very real, scenario that exists at some colleges and universities. Often, addressing student wellness issues runs contrary to an existing ethos at the institution. If the energy for enhancing student success through student wellness initiatives comes through grassroots efforts, those invested in these efforts often see the enlistment of executive-level support as resulting in yielding the control and prioritization of the efforts. If this is the case, efforts to institutionalize the commitment to student wellness issues may have to wait until the grassroots effort can provide evidence as to the importance and success of their priorities to their efforts. Time spent understanding the position of the executive management in addressing these issues is also well spent. Where does the senior student affairs officer land on these issues? Has it been mentioned as a priority in the divisional strategic efforts? What are the priorities of the faculty and student senate governing bodies? Who, at the executive level, would be most likely to support these efforts and in what format?

Finding the right entry point to institutionalize an effort is a good step. Is smoking on campus a major issue for the institution? Although this may not be the central student wellness issues in the estimation of people at the core of the effort, it may be considered the best avenue to illustrate expertise of the group in planning, educating and provoking change on the campus.

Conclusion

The importance of the student wellness on a college campus extends beyond the experience of that student. It has impact on the well-being of the university community, the family of the student, the persistence and graduation rates of the campus as well as the post-graduation success and satisfaction of students. Commitment to addressing these issues is connected to the purpose of each institution, as well as the purpose of higher education in general. Whether or not one is in a formal position of influence, or is simply keenly aware of the issues, avenues exist to advance the institutional efforts. The importance of building good relationships with individuals across the campus and keeping a long-term time horizon is the foundation to any successful effort.

References

Anderson, D. S. (2016). *Wellness Issues for Higher Education: A Guide for Student Affairs and Higher Education Professionals*. New York: Routledge.

Kezar, A. (2011). Grassroots leadership: Encounters with power dynamics and oppression. *International Journal of Qualitative Studies in Education, 24*(4), 471–500.

Kotter, J. P. (2012). *Leading Change*. Boston: Harvard Business School Press.

NASPA. (2004). *Leadership for a healthy campus: An ecological approach for student success*. Washington, DC: Author.

National Center for Educational Statistics. (2015). *Fast Facts*. Retrieved from https://nces.ed.gov/fastfacts/display.asp?id=98

Pritchard, M. E., & Wilson, G. S. (2003). Using emotional and social factors to predict student success. *Journal of College Student Development, 44*(1), 18–28.

Thelin, J. R., & Gasman, M. (2011). Historical overview of American higher education. In J. H. Schuh, S. R. Jones, S. R. Harper, & S. R Komives (Eds.), *Student Services: A Handbook for the Profession* (5th edition, pp. 3–23). San Francisco: Jossey-Bass.

Author Biographies

David S. Anderson, Ph.D., George Mason University

David Anderson is Professor Emeritus of Education and Human Development at George Mason University, where he worked for 28 years. He was Professor and Director, Center for the Advancement of Public Health. Early in his career, he served as a student affairs administrator at The Ohio State University, Radford University and Ohio University. He served as project director on over 180 projects at the national, state or local level. He taught graduate and undergraduate courses on drug and alcohol issues, community health and health communications. His strategic planning and program evaluation work emphasizes college students, youth, school and community leaders, program planners and policy makers. Specialty areas include wellness and health promotion, health and safety communication, drug/alcohol abuse prevention, strategic planning and needs assessment and evaluation. His research includes the College Alcohol Survey (1979–2015), Understanding Teen Drinking Cultures in America, COMPASS: A Roadmap to Healthy Living, Best of CHOICES, the IMPACT Evaluation Resource and the Wellness Assessment for Higher Education Professionals. In 2000, he was the first recipient of the Visionary Award sponsored by the Network of Colleges and Universities Committed to the Elimination of Drug and Alcohol Abuse.

Bryan Ashton, BSBA, The Ohio State University

Bryan Ashton serves as an assistant director within the Student Life Student Wellness Center, overseeing financial education and outreach, Scarlet & Gray Financial peer-to-peer financial coaching and holds a BSBA (with a specialization in Accounting) from the Fisher College of Business at The Ohio State University. He has been invited to speak at numerous national conferences on financial wellness, has authored numerous pieces on collegiate financial education and is the Co-Founder and Co-Chair of the National Summit on Collegiate Financial Wellness. Additionally, he most recently served on the research team for the National Student Financial Wellness Study administered through The Ohio State University.

M. Dolores Cimini, Ph.D., University at Albany, SUNY

Dr. M. Dolores Cimini has had leadership for campuswide alcohol and other drug prevention and treatment efforts at the University at Albany for over two decades. She has served as project director for numerous grant-funded projects

233

focused on the application of laboratory research to evidence-based prevention and intervention practice.

Beth DeRicco, Ph.D., Drexel University

Beth DeRicco is on the faculty at Drexel University and directs Higher Education Outreach for Caron Treatment Centers. She has worked at the campus, state and national levels to develop, evaluate and refine policies and programs that address alcohol and other drug use. Her work as Associate Center Director for the U.S. Department of Education's Higher Education Center focused on putting research into practice through the development of trainings, publications and workshops. She has been a principal or co-principal investigator on projects funded by local foundations and state and federal agencies, with a focus on applied research.

Ashley Finley, Ph.D., University of Iowa

Ashley Finley is the associate vice president of academic affairs and dean of the Dominican Experience at the Dominican University of California and the national evaluator for the Bringing Theory to Practice (BTtoP) Project.

Jan L. Gascoigne, Ph.D., MCHES Colorado School of Public Health

Jan Gascoigne is Associate Dean for Student Affairs and Assistant Professor in the Department of Community & Behavioral Health at the Colorado School of Public Health. Prior to joining the Colorado SPH, Dr. Gascoigne was the Director of Health Promotion for the BACCHUS Network for 11 years. In this role, she led the development of TobaccofreeU initiatives to address tobacco use in college and university students. She served on two CDC expert panels on collegiate tobacco control and led statewide collegiate tobacco control grants in Montana and Colorado.

Thomas Hall, Ph.D., University of Central Florida

Tom Hall is the director of the alcohol and other drug intervention and treatment program in Student Health Services at the University of Central Florida. He has over 20 years of experience providing substance abuse and mental health treatment. His research interests include developing brief intervention and treatment strategies as well as recovery services for college students. He has taught graduate-level social work and counselor education courses related to the treatment of substance use disorders, as well as group psychotherapy and family therapy. He is on the board of the Orange County Coalition for a Drug-Free Community and is active in local prevention and treatment efforts.

R. Britton Katz, Ph.D., Millsaps College

Brit Katz earned his B.A. and M.Ed. from Mississippi State University and the Ph.D. from the University of Mississippi. His college student development career began in 1982 at Mississippi State University, with subsequent student affairs appointments at the University of Southern Mississippi, the University of Louisiana-Monroe, Emory University and Millsaps College. He was named the Millsaps College Vice President for Student Life, Dean of Students and Assistant Professor of Education on August 1, 2003. His teaching interests include higher education law, student affairs administration and an anthropology-communications course on Walt Disney. He is the recipient of numerous professional recognitions.

Frances Lucas, Ph.D., Frances Lucas Consulting, LLC
Dr. Lucas got her B.A. in Communications at Mississippi State University and her M.A. and Ph.D. in Administration of Higher Education from the University of Alabama. Dr. Lucas is now an executive coach, works with organizations on how to reach their highest potential and keynotes conferences. Dr. Lucas is also a woman of firsts. Dr. Lucas was named President of Millsaps College, becoming the first female college president in Mississippi. Dr. Lucas served Emory University as Senior Vice-President for Campus Life and Vice-President at Baldwin-Wallace College in Ohio, where she was the first female vice president at both institutions.

Linda Major, MAM, University of Nebraska-Lincoln
Linda Major is Assistant Vice Chancellor for Student Affairs and the Director of the Center for Civic Engagement at the University of Nebraska-Lincoln. She is currently responsible for coordinating a comprehensive approach to address high-risk behaviors, facilitating division-wide assessment efforts and advancing civic-related programs on the campus and in the community.

Aaron Mauner, M.P.H., Colorado School of Public Health
Aaron graduated with honors from the University of Tennessee in 2011, with a Bachelor's of Science in Biology with a concentration in Biochemistry and Cellular and Molecular Biology and a Minor in Chemistry. In 2016, Aaron graduated from the Colorado School of Public Health with a Master's in Public Health with a concentration in Applied Biostatistics. In the fall of 2016, Aaron will be attending medical school at the University of Colorado. As a future physician, Aaron plans to use his knowledge of smoking habits and side effects to help his patients in the field of Oncology.

Michael P. McNeil, Ed.D., Columbia University
Michael is Executive Director of Alice! Health Promotion, Student Health Insurance, and Immunization Compliance and a member of the faculty in Sociomedical Sciences at the Mailman School of Public Health, both at Columbia University. He holds a doctorate in higher education leadership, a master's in health education, advanced training in public health, is a Certified Health Education Specialist (CHES) and a fellow of the American College Health Association (FACHA). Having spent more than 20 years in college health and student affairs, he focuses on evidence- and theory-informed administration and practice. His other interests include health communication, linking health with academic success, technology in health and student affairs and professional preparation. A widely respected colleague in student affairs and college health, he often presents at local, regional and national meetings on a host of topics and works to publish practice-oriented pieces that are dedicated to supporting curricular and co-curricular student success.

Nancy Mitchell, Ph.D., University of Nebraska-Lincoln
Nancy Mitchell is Director of Undergraduate Education Programs in Academic Affairs at the University of Nebraska-Lincoln. She helps facilitate student success, focusing on general education, assessment, curriculum, learning communities and transfer issues. She is also faculty member in the College of Journalism and Mass Communications at the University of Nebraska-Lincoln.

Karen S. Moses, Ed.D., Certified Health Education Specialist (CHES), Arizona State University
Dr. Moses is Director of ASU Wellness and has provided leadership in ASU wellness initiatives, programs and services for over 27 years. Under her direction, ASU Wellness incorporates theory-based and evidence-informed strategies to help students adopt and maintain a healthy lifestyle and create a university environment that supports student well-being. She is an active leader in developing, implementing and evaluating sexual violence prevention efforts at ASU. She serves as the Principal Investigator and Project Director for a Sexual Violence Prevention and Education Grant through the Arizona Department of Health Services that has been funded from 2003 to 2017. She served as Title IX Deputy Coordinator for Students at ASU from 2012 to 2014. Karen completed her bachelor's and master's degrees in Nutrition and Dietetics and her doctorate in Higher Education Leadership at Arizona State University.

Mimi Nichter, Ph.D., University of Arizona
Mimi Nichter is Professor in the School of Anthropology, and she holds joint appointments in the Norton School of Family and Consumer Sciences and the College of Public Health. She is the author of *Fat Talk: What Girls and Their Parents Say about Dieting* and *Lighting Up: The Rise of Social Smoking on College Campuses.* She has long-standing interests in health and development in the United States and in South and Southeast Asia. She also has an extensive background working in maternal and child health and women's reproductive health.

Bridget Guernsey Riordan, Ph.D., Emory University
Bridget Guernsey Riordan is Assistant Vice President for Alumni Relations, Parent and Family Programs in the Division of Campus Life at Emory University. Prior to this position, she served Emory as Dean of Students, Assistant to the Vice President and Director of Student Activities. She received her bachelor's degree from Ball State University. Upon graduation, she worked for Alpha Chi Omega Fraternity as a traveling consultant. She then worked in student affairs at the University of Cincinnati, where she received her master's degree, and the University of Pittsburgh, where she received her doctoral degree. She served as an adjunct faculty member at Georgia State University and received a certificate in higher-education law from the Stetson School of Law. She has served as President of the Association of Fraternity Advisors and has done research on fraternal organizations, alcohol policy development and risk management issues.

Todd S. Rose, Ph.D., George Mason University
Todd Rose is Executive Director of INTO Mason and is a member of the faculty in the Higher Education program at George Mason University. He has over 25 years of experience in higher education at four different institutions. Prior to his career in higher education, he was a commercial lending officer in Nashville, TN. He holds a BBA in Finance (with a minor in Economics) from Southern Methodist University (TX) an M.B.A. from Baldwin-Wallace University (OH) and a Ph.D. in Educational Leadership and Research, focusing on Higher Education from the University of Southern Mississippi (MS).

Nicole Taylor, Ph.D., Texas State University
Nicole Taylor is Associate Professor in the Department of Anthropology. Prior to this position, she served as Director of Scholar Programs at the School for Advanced Research. She also has experience conducting research and evaluation in the areas of substance abuse, education and poverty, childhood obesity and school climate. Her current research explores contemporary social issues related to education and health, including teasing and bullying in schools, childhood obesity and body image concerns among youth. She is the author of *Schooled on Fat: What Teens Tell Us about Gender, Body Image, and Obesity*.

Index

CPSIA information can be obtained
at www.ICGtesting.com
Printed in the USA
FFOW03n1312281117
43824114-42754FF